SINGLE AFTER FIFTY
how to have the time of your life

Single After Fifty

how to have the time of your life

Adeline McConnell
&
Beverly Anderson

MCGRAW-HILL BOOK COMPANY
NEW YORK   ST. LOUIS   SAN FRANCISCO
DÜSSELDORF   MEXICO

234567890 BPBP 78321098

Library of Congress Cataloging in Publication Data

McConnell, Adeline.
  Single after fifty.
  1. Single people. 2. Middle age. I. Nemiro, Beverly Anderson, joint
author. II. Title.
HQ800.M355   301.4   78-17232
ISBN 0-07-044873-6

To all the singles we interviewed, with affection and gratitude.

Contents

Contents

Preface

This is a book for and about people over fifty who are single.

Our purpose is to show, by real-life examples, how the enormous population of men and women at midage and older can and do lead happier, more self-styled, meaningful, and productive lives by overcoming problems special to their age and circumstance.

It is dedicated with affection to all who have been left single by death or divorce (or both), by abandonment or withdrawal of a love, and for those who choose to be single. These people are often referred to as "over the hill," yet many of them don't feel they have passed that over-the-hill mark. Insurance companies estimate that a woman at the age of fifty can expect to live for another twenty-five years; a man, twenty-three; so they do, indeed, have more years left than ever before. Figures also reveal that three out of four women find themselves suddenly, often shockingly, alone in America. There is a growing group of single older men as well.

We are not pretending to be authorities. Our authorities are hundreds of single men and women, midage and older, who have shared their life stories and lifestyles. These people represent a generation that has lived through more changes than any other generation in history. Their experiences and their wit and wisdom provide inspiration to all who find confusion, perplexity, and ambivalence clouding their outlook.

They have found a rhythm to existence. They feel comfortable with themselves and their life situations. They are realizing the full potential of their freedom with its attendant assets and liabilities. They have turned tragedy, disillusionment, or disappointment—what seemed a dead end—into a new beginning.

Our thought originally was to relate primarily to women, but as Beverly conducted divorce seminars at the University of Colorado and the University of California and attended therapy groups, and as Adeline led rap sessions for Parents without Partners, we became aware that the subculture of older singles with problems is not a "sorority." Intensely personal contacts with men provided glimpses into the instabilities they feel and the problems they face after the loss of a spouse, whether by choice or not. This then, we concluded, should be a book for and about both sexes.

Male and female emotions presented here provide a means of identification for the reader to see himself or herself again and again. Our interviewees talk about their feelings, good and bad; about love and loyalty, bitterness and betrayal, heartbreak and heartmend. They show not only "I can do it" but also "How I can do it." It is like one friend saying to another, "Here's what worked for me."

They speak out about their methods of handling shock and grief when the continuity of their lives is broken, of structuring independent personalities from the wreckage of despair. They show how they learned to live effectively and happily as singles, describing how they develop a new support system of friends, handle single-parent problems with older children still at home, keep their coupled friends, get along with their "ex" in cases of divorce; and deal with lawyers, doctors, and other service people. They make suggestions for managing money; finding, keeping, changing jobs; looking better; meeting and attracting the opposite sex; handling sexual relationships, including the part money plays in them. They advise about choosing and decorating new homes, cultivating habits of personal safety, even dealing with such pesky problems as entertaining alone and marketing and cooking for one.

Preface

We have gathered these ideas over a three-year period from more than 500 divorced or widowed (or both) persons, and from those who have never been married. Over a hundred of these people, carefully selected because they were leading happy and fulfilled lives, responded to a twenty-six-page questionnaire with such sensitivity and insight that we frequently quote their answers verbatim. Those who presented the most practical and imaginative solutions to the problems they faced we interviewed personally in greater depth. To protect their identities, we have given them fictitious names and altered details that might make them recognizable.

This book is a rich source of information for all who desire and are willing to improve the quality of their lives. It is about all older singles who are faced with new situations and the vast possibilities available to them. It is the stuff life is made of, as old-fashioned as it is up-to-the-minute. It reveals the kind of reality that can be interpreted in terms of one's own experience.

It shows how to live life with luster when you are fifty, or older, and single.

Acknowledgments

Because we have promised them anonymity, we cannot list by name the hundreds of people we interviewed, a hundred of whom spent many hours filling out a twenty-six-page questionnaire with great insight and depth of feeling. It is from their wisdom and candor that this book was created, and we wish to express our deep gratitude to them here. We wish to acknowledge our debt to *Modern Maturity* magazine, in which we found some striking examples of the rich lives led by singles over fifty. We also wish to thank particularly Frederic W. Hills, Editor-in-Chief of the General Book Division at McGraw-Hill, and Peggy Tsukahira, Associate Editor, for their outstanding patience, sensitivity, and inspiration as they worked with us, as well as the following people, who went out of their way to assist us: Martin Alexander, M.D., Anna Mae Anderson, Martin Anderson, Richard H. Anderson, Ph.D., Donald E. Bower, Gerald P. Cavanaugh, Ted Cobb, Nora Denny, Helen Dollaghan, Rev. Robert M. Eddy, Frederick Epstein, Barbara Griess, Jean Herron, William Hines, M.D., Eva Hodges, David Hopkins, J. F. Images, Morris Jones, Diana Koin, M.D., Charles J. Little, Paul Loof, M.S.W., Bill Maki, Julie MacKay, R.N.; Gladys McConnell, Rob McConnell, Ross McConnell, Jarrell McCracken, Joan McCracken, Dee Martin Nemiro, Guy Nemiro, Lee Anna Nemiro, Lavelle Olexa, Frances Pace, Jean Pascoe, Clarisse Pinkola-Estes, Paul Polak, M.D., James E. Pope, Peggy Pope, Miles Rader, Francis Ranney, Homer Reed, Roselyn Riek, R.N., Robert Rollick, Sheri Safran, Lee San Miguel, Detective A. J. Sandoval, Richard O. Shaver, D.M.D.; Edith Sherman, Ph.D., Jean Sherrod, J. K. Smith, Dorothea Spellman, Professor Emeritus, Richard Vanden-

Acknowledgments

Bergh, M.D., Vera Webster, Dawn Shaw Wilson, Robert Winkel, Rita Winkel, Henry Worosello, Rev. W. Spencer Wren, Jean Yancey.

We also owe a special debt of gratitude to Jacqueline M. Gilbert, assistant to the executive director of Parents Without Partners, who helped in the distribution of our questionnaires and the arrangement of interviews across the country. Thanks go as well to the National Writers Club and to the University of Colorado and the University of California, for their encouragement, support, and help.

.. The last of life, for which the first was made. . . .

—Robert Browning

CHAPTER 1

Singles Country

From the standpoint of preparation for single living, we both started at point zero.

ADELINE'S STORY

I was known laughingly by my family and close friends as Queenie because of the way my sensitive, well-loved, school-teacher husband Bob pampered and cared for me. One beautiful morning in May, Bob pumped up my bicycle tires, mounted our bikes on the rear of our power wagon, and waited patiently for me to put on my lipstick before we set out to join a biking party in the Rocky Mountains outside of Boulder, Colorado. On the return ride, coasting headily down a foothills canyon, he collided head-on with a car, ending in a split second our twenty-five years of outstandingly good marriage.

The coroner and the mortician advised against my viewing his body. We honored Bob's strongly expressed feelings about conventional funerals. We never had a ceremony of any kind to mark his passing. It was almost as if he had simply disappeared.

The man in the family, the strength, the confidant, the companion, the lover, the balancer of the checkbook, caretaker of the income tax, total financial mentor, house custodian, son-advisor, escort, unfailing ego support, chief

1

wage earner, tender of the automobiles, doer of the laundry: the quintessence of a husband, my total friend and support, had just vanished.

Someone has described grief as a slide into a bowl, a slide that levels out at the bottom before the climb back out can begin. It's hard to say when the leveling-out took place for me. Somewhere back down there I had a traumatic mastectomy (three months after Bob's death), which left me feeling not only bereft, but old and disfigured as well. The view from the bottom of the bowl offered little to inspire the long climb out.

BEVERLY'S STORY

I was married in the fifties, a time when tea dancing, convertibles, and romantic fiction novels prevailed. I was the girl who held a glamour job in fashion and modeling for a short time before marriage, and when married, did everything my husband, Dr. Spock, and the women's magazines told me to do, and did it well.

My husband worked twenty years to become president of his company. With this position came a new Cadillac sedan, invitations to all the openings, a generous expense account, and unchallenged authority at work. And at home.

In public we were the Ideal Couple. Since fashion was part of my husband's business, I worked at staying slim and dressed with studied care for every occasion. I gave dinner parties for associates, worked on charity benefits, and diligently kept up the house and relationships with our teenage children. I fitted my hobbies of writing and part-time teaching into my husband's schedule. When we were at home together, however, I felt an agonizing sense of isolation. My husband ignored me and when I tried to discuss my feelings he refused to respond. His trips around the country and abroad became more and more frequent and his interest in me became less and less. When it became clear he wanted his freedom, I was forced to accept the crushing reality. I had reached the watershed of middle age and my husband no longer wanted me.

The long and painful divorce threw me into a state of depression such as I had never known. The morning I was notified by mail that my husband had hired a third lawyer to work on his case, hopelessness overwhelmed me. I went to the bathroom, took all the sleeping capsules I could collect —at least a hundred—lay down, and felt a sense of peace for the first time in years. My taking those pills, I thought as I put my head on the pillow, had nothing whatsoever to do with my husband. It did have everything to do with me, what a failure I was as a woman and how old and unappealing I had become. What was I going to do with the rest of my life, alone and unprepared?

Glaring lights overhead scorched my eyes as they opened reluctantly. I was in a white cubiclelike room, strapped down, a male nurse standing over me. Sad and furious at finding my suicide unsuccessful, I felt the ultimate failure. In one year's space I had lost my husband, my free-lance job on a magazine, my home, and even my role as mother as my daughters had left for college. As a loser, I now felt complete.

For about two years after each of us became single, we struggled alone searching for guideposts to our futures. We attended seminars for divorced people, workshops on grief, therapy and encounter groups, grasping and striving for ways to adapt to our new lives.

In addition, we scoured magazine racks and book-shelves, and found there was help aplenty for singles— singles in their twenties, thirties, and maybe as late as their forties, but only bits and pieces for people like us. Everyone seemed to be saying by omission that by the age of fifty you should know how to adapt to any circumstance and solve any problem. Yet to be suddenly single at fifty was to wake up in a foreign world after years of marital slumber, a world of outlooks and mores and responsibilities different from that of our single youth.

When we renewed a long-standing friendship at a Christmas party in 1976 (and only those who have been through one of those Christmases alone can appreciate its bleakness), we had arrived at the same point. We had coped with our grief, despair, and fear. Middle-aged and single though we were, we were beginning to feel a renewed appetite for the years ahead of us. We felt a desire to share our experiences and to help others who might be facing the ordeal we had survived and who wanted to build the same satisfying future we sensed we could have.

That is how this book began.

CHAPTER 2

Welcome To The Group
from wreckage to renewal

"I still remember sobbing, 'I don't believe it! I don't believe it!'" said one of the many newly singled people we interviewed. "It was as if I were listening to myself and watching the whole scene—making it up, as if it were a dream."

Whether the separation from their spouses was abrupt or gradual, after years of secure, predictable living in the married world, people re-enter the single one with all the shock and disorientation of a crash landing on the moon.

"Even in the next couple of weeks, I couldn't seem to get a handle on my situation," the woman continued. "I went around with a guarded feeling as if something were going to sneak up and surprise me. I wanted to know what to expect, what course these feelings were going to take; but when I asked others who had been through the same experience, I got answers like: 'You never really get over it.' It made me wonder if I were going to carry that terrible leaden feeling around inside me for the rest of my life."

The force of their re-entry into the singles world made such confusion common among many newly widowed and divorced people, especially if they suffered a feeling of abandonment as did Stella, Sally, and Steve.

STELLA

It was a glittering morning in Aspen, Colorado. Stella and Herb had made it out onto the ski slopes early, even after dawdling over the last cup of coffee at breakfast. It was a joke among all their friends, the "one more cup of coffee" Stella and Herb always had, which gave them an excuse to visit a little longer. They had not, after twenty-seven years of marriage, run out of things to talk about.

Now, with the children grown, Stella was thinking as she stood in the lift line, they would have all the time in the world for coffee. There would be lots of vacations together like this one, the first real trip they'd had in a long time. She was looking affectionately at Herb's bulky parka and the ridiculous red cap that didn't match, which he always insisted on wearing, when the parka suddenly hunched over and the figure inside crumpled to the ground. By the time the ski patrol had gotten Herb to the first aid hut, his heart attack was over and Stella was single.

SALLY

To onlookers, Sally and Jim were the perfect couple: socially and financially successful, with a beautiful home, membership in the best country club in their Long Island community, two handsome sons at Harvard. But somewhere in the latter part of their twenty-four years of marriage, a feeling of "Is-this-all-there-is?" set in. Then Jim began to object to playing golf with some of their longtime golfing friends on Sunday afternoons.

"It's Marge and Helen," he finally confessed. "They're old women."

With a sudden chill, Sally realized he was talking about women who were younger than she. One day Jim had unexpectedly come upon her doing facial exercises before the mirror.

"It's like a facelift without surgery," she explained laughingly, and he had replied:

"Don't you think it's too late?"

6

Sally had not responded, too stunned to think of anything to say, but she had infuriated him later by letting his supply of clean shirts run out. Now, she thought, it all seemed like a set-up: his deliberate insults, the senseless quarrels, the escalating hostility, until one day she had burst out impulsively:

"All right! If it's all that bad, why don't you just get out!" She hadn't really meant it, but he did.

STEVE

It came as no shock to Steve M. in California when his wife asked for a divorce. Emily had been depressed for about three years. Steve had gotten her to see a psychiatrist, but after a few sessions she had stopped. There had been the quarrels—about a fishing trip he had taken fourteen years before, about a rental property he had bought without consulting her two years later. Finally Steve had accepted a job in another part of the state, thinking time and distance might lend perspective to the problem, but his daily phone conversations with Emily went from impersonal to remote in tone, and he lost the courage to mention her joining him, knowing how evasive her answers always were. One evening, she said she wanted a divorce, and that's when he flew home.

Around the dining-room table that Sunday afternoon, Steve and his children, who had flown home from college, fought to keep the family identity, fought and talked so long and hard that Emily finally consented to stay married—under certain conditions. Steve must give up his sailing, his deep-sea fishing, and his photography, a combination of loves that formed the cornerstone of his budding career as an outdoor photographer, a career that might make early retirement from his Veterans Administration job possible.

"She knew I couldn't accept those terms," he said

7

later. "I had to recognize that she just didn't want, after twenty-six years and three kids, to be married to me any more."

In company with many other single men and women we interviewed, Stella, Sally, and Steve found themselves alone and bewildered, unprepared and unskilled to cope with their new lives as older singles.

Many of the single men and women we talked to agreed that it helps to know, at such a time, about grief: how it works for others, what complicates and prolongs it; what, if anything, can alleviate it.

Although some psychologists believe that the analogy between death and divorce is overstated, there is growing belief in the social, psychological, and medical fields that any loss that disrupts your understanding of who and what you are can precipitate the grief process. Although personalities differ in their abilities to cope, the greater the change in your life caused by the loss, and the more dependent you were on your spouse, the more your sense of identity will be upset and the greater will be your grief.

Without understanding this principle, it might be hard for some people to sympathize strongly with someone like Toni S.

Toni at fifty-two is beautiful, rich, talented, with a host of good friends, male admirers by the dozen, and a good relationship with her three grown children. Even after her divorce from one of the community's leading businessmen and her consequent loss of social prestige, her picture still appears frequently on the social page of the newspaper in her midwestern city, where she is top glamour. Yet today, two years after the end of her marriage, despite a busy and productive life as an interior decorator, she still considers suicide. She grieves—not for the husband of twenty-five years, who left her for a younger woman, but for the life she led as his wife.

"I was shot down!" she cried out in anguish. "If you've never had that kind of life, you don't miss it. But I *hate* not being invited to the gorgeous parties I used to go to. It was marvelous to sit next to the chancellor of a university at dinner or to have a party in honor of the art museum director on opening night of a new exhibit. I loved going to New York, staying at the best hotels, having huge bouquets from leading businesses delivered to my room, eating at the finest restaurants, driven there by liveried chauffeurs. Everyone catered to me. I was really somebody. And now I'm a nobody."

Now Toni sometimes finds herself in whole groups of nobodies, where nobody even recognizes that her blouse is a Dior original. At the occasional social gatherings of former friends in which she is included, she looks around the room and realizes that her three-hundred-dollar evening gown does not quite measure up. After one such evening, she returned home to pace the floor in anguish until 4 A.M., when she sat down to review her will. Her problems may sound absurd to a displaced homemaker who is struggling to stay alive. But the mental anguish she suffers is just as real as, and possibly more acute than, that of others who have been bereft.

In contrast to Toni is Maria G., sixty-five, a widow who lives in a small home on a minuscule retirement income. Maria moved to the United States from Mexico after her husband underwent an operation that resulted in the amputation of his leg below the knee.

"I had read about the help that was being given in the States to handicapped war veterans. I also wanted to get Carlos away from the people who had known him as a successful banker, from the word *pobrecito* [poor thing]."

9

Maria, who had been born in the States, stayed with family friends in Texas, found a job, and sent for her husband. She was able to get him the artificial limb and therapy he needed and a job in the same small factory in which she was working. At lunch one day in the plant cafeteria, the director called Maria aside and asked her why she never sat down to eat. When Maria explained that all the chairs were usually taken, the director said:

"My dear, you have come into a different world. You will have to learn to push and shove with the rest of us."

In the years that followed, Maria learned to push and shove, not just for herself but also for her Hispanic people, taking an active role in community groups and eventually finding a job in the federal government's War on Poverty program in the sixties. She assessed the needs of the Hispanic community, drew up proposals, and delivered speeches so compelling that her audiences were left totally silent when she finished. A photograph in her living room still commemorates the day she was hostess to Lady Bird Johnson during the first lady's visit to her city.

Maria's personal life, on the other hand, was a litany of misfortune. A car running a red light made a broadside hit on the car in which her husband was riding and severed his spinal cord, paralyzing his legs. Later, while nursing him through terminal cancer, she herself had a heart attack.

When her husband died, Maria grieved.

"We had been through so much together. We had been so close," she said. "But I felt I had given him the very best I had, and as I looked over at him, after he closed his eyes, I had a feeling of relief that his suffering was over."

Unlike Toni, Maria suffers no sense of failure, no loss of self-esteem. She has never even lost sight of her goal in life: to help as many people as she can. To this end, she feels she has a personal relationship with God, with whom she has made many "deals."

"I wanted the free health clinic, and we got it. I wanted a day-care center, and we got that, too," she said, smiling. Her present "deal" is a course she is planning to teach to minority children to give them a background in their culture. The first lesson will be "Who Am I?"

"People make much better human beings," she said, "if they know who they are."

In so saying, Maria summed up the difference between herself and other women, like Toni, whose identity is tied to being someone's wife, and whose sense of personal disorganization in losing their husbands is often compounded by the loss of their role as a mother as well. As Toni explained it:

"It seemed as if all my roots came up at once. The last of my children left for college and I had to move out of my home the same year that I got my divorce."

GRIEF WORK

Even the men and women who did not suffer such drastic changes in their lifestyle as Toni did had to do their "grief work," a term coined by Sigmund Freud for the process of disengagement from the lost person that bereaved people must go through if they are to make a healthy recovery. The first stage in this process, as experienced by those we interviewed, was shock that stunned them into numbness. Even people who had preparation for the end of their marriages were not spared. A woman whose husband had been ill for twenty-two of the twenty-three years of their life together, who had been told many, many times that he would not live, was so dazed when the time of death arrived that she has no memory whatever of the days that followed.

"I must have made all the necessary arrangements," she recalls, five years later, "but I don't remember how." At this stage, shock is often accompanied by denial. A number of widows and widowers had a strong sense of a husband's or wife's presence after death. One woman had a vision of her husband sitting beside her in bed the night after he died.

"He put his arm around my shoulders and said, 'Don't worry. Everything will be all right.' It was very comforting."

Another widow pretended her husband was on a trip and could thus forget her pain for a while, even laugh and joke with others.

"I used to wonder if they thought I was crazy to be laughing and joking like that," she said. "But it really helped. Even though I knew I was just pretending, it gave me a rest from grieving."

A man had a vivid dream one night of his late wife chatting with him in the backyard as she watered the vegetable garden. He realized it was a dream, even while it was going on, and knew in his dream that she was dead. But he made up his mind to enjoy the moments they were sharing together.

For the divorced, denial took a more active form. Said one man:

"During the three-month waiting period I tried to take my wife to supper and talk things out. These sessions always ended up in her becoming upset over the most simple things. It left me frustrated, but wanting to try again. I tried driving by her apartment to get a glimpse of her, yet every time she would see me she seemed beside herself with fury. Eventually I found myself tooting my horn at her just to make her mad."

A woman reported that "for the first two years, when I was only legally separated, I lived with the hope of a reconciliation. Then he asked for the divorce and on the day of the final hearing, he was on his way to get married."

Still another woman remembers the chill of suspicion, a numbness that started at the tip of her toes and spread right up to her neck when she learned while waiting for her own divorce to become final that her best woman friend had also filed for divorce. The real reason her husband had left her suddenly became clear, and her hope for a resolution of their problems vanished.

Denial, numbness, the sense of unreality that dominate the early days of grief serve a purpose. They allow the mind to absorb the terrible reality of loss a little at a time as it progresses toward the second stage of grief: realization.

Along with the pangs of intense longing and anguish that are part of this stage of grieving go a preoccupation with thoughts of the person you have lost, a repetitious recalling of the events that led up to the death or the divorce and the circumstances surrounding it, and attempts to make sense out of the whole event.

A man, looking back at the age of seventy-one to the time when he became single in Japan at forty-eight, remembers suddenly being on a plane to America, leaving his wife and two small children behind him.

"She just didn't want to come with me," he said. "I sat on the plane thinking, 'It's all over. I have no reason to make a home, because there's no one to put in it.'"

"Our home in the mountains seemed like an empty tomb," another man said.

Frustrated as well as puzzled were the men whose wives left them for no other reason than to establish an identity of their own. One successful surgeon was torn between understanding his wife's need to live her own life and feeling too stunned really to understand.

"All the uprooting, when there really was no reason for it, in a family that had never had any divorces," he said.

The anguished feelings of yearning and sorrow come in intermittent pangs and waves beginning within hours or days after a loss, increasing to full force within five to fourteen days, and becoming less frequent as time passes. They may never cease entirely.

"Even today," a sixty-year-old woman who had been widowed in her early thirties attested, "I occasionally have a welling up of feeling when I come across an old picture or visit a spot where Stan and I spent time together."

For widows and widowers, funeral services were a mixed blessing, even though some psychiatrists believe they help finalize a death. Some people derived comfort from them, others found them agonizing; most were still too numb to respond more than automatically.

For both the widowed and the divorced, too, anger was part of this stage of realization. Bitterness and humiliation combined to heighten the divorced person's rage to a point where he or she took, or wanted to take, a fierce revenge on anyone of the opposite sex.

One man said, "I just wanted to screw up every woman I met, and I did, too. I really messed some of them up, and it made me feel good to do it."

Another, more responsible, said that he simply didn't date for many months after his divorce because he knew the lust for revenge would be there.

With the widowed, the bitterness and hostility toward the opposite sex seemed lacking, but the anger was certainly present—anger at the dead person for dying and leaving the survivor to handle the hurt and the problems, anger at those who were still alive, anger turned in upon themselves as guilt, and anger directed at the world in general, at the very friends who came to help through those first days of suffering.

"I wanted the person driving the car that killed my wife to have been careless and drunk and so in the wrong that I could have him in court and take away every penny he had," one widower recalled. "I wanted the county to be in the wrong for not having the road adequately posted. I wanted to *blame* somebody. I wanted revenge!"

Because there was no clear fault on anyone's part, this

man found no revenge. But for months his relationships with others suffered as he took offense, found fault, and lashed out in his everyday dealings with people.

"One good thing about being older is that you've got the independence to do what feels right for you," one woman said. "We gave vent to much of our anger by insisting upon the cheapest possible burial—by cremation, which is the way my husband would have wanted it. The mortician, who must have sensed that he had better not argue, went along with our wishes without a word. The cost was $250 and Social Security paid it. It gave me satisfaction to think that Sam and I had scored a small final victory over the establishment.

"While the funeral parlor took care of the cremation, we had our own service. We packed a picnic lunch, picked up my mother-in-law, who was totally in accord with our feelings, and went out to a wooded park where we had spent many happy family holidays. It was a beautiful spring day. We didn't talk about anything in particular. When someone felt like crying, he cried. It was comforting just to be together, away from everyone. For our family, a funeral would have been a mockery. Church was not a part of our life, and to have a minister, who didn't even know my husband, discuss his virtues would have infuriated us all. We never even considered whether people would be critical. If they really meant it when they said, 'If there's anything we can do to help—,' they were glad to know we were doing what helped us the most."

THE SECOND STAGE

Guilt is still another facet of the grieving process which, along with anger, is strongest at the second stage of grief. Divorced people are sometimes tormented by what they might or might not have done to destroy their marriages. Sometimes they ask themselves:

15

"What is wrong with me to have gotten into this defective marriage in the first place and then to have stayed in it for so long?"

The widowed blamed themselves as well.

"I wasn't at the hospital when she died. I felt as if I'd let her down."

"All I could remember were the times I'd been irritable when I'd been caring for him."

One woman even blamed herself for thinking that the only way her chain-smoking husband would avoid terminal cancer would be to die an accidental death. When he did, she felt responsible, feeling she had had a kind of death wish.

Most of the people we talked to found their anguish, guilt, and anger lessening during the first few weeks after death or divorce but for those whose feelings toward their spouses had been ambivalent, swinging back and forth between love and hostility, between wanting and not wanting to be married, recovery was difficult.

"I had very mixed feelings about my wife," one widower said. "She was a good person, but very domineering. It got worse as she grew older, and I was actually beginning to think about a divorce, although I hadn't said anything and perhaps I'd never have gotten up the nerve—I really depended on her. But I was beginning to notice other women more. I still remember one Christmas party talking to a very attractive—and very young—woman and thinking, 'Gee! I'm really turning her on.' "

At the peak of this man's ambivalence, his wife ran a red light, her car was broadsided, and she was dead on arrival at the hospital.

"It's been over a year now, and I can't shake the guilt. I tell myself it's ridiculous, but I find myself wondering if she didn't sense my restlessness, if she weren't unhappy enough to become careless of living."

Denial and numbness; anguish, anxiety, anger, and guilt—these are the emotions that take turns dominating many new singles as they move back and forth between the first grief stage of disbelief and shock and the second stage of realization. In the same seesaw manner, as the first year goes by, these emotions that are so pronounced in the first two stages give way to a third, depressive, state that will be discussed in the next chapter.

Not all the abandoned men and women, however, regard their loss as a disaster. One man, after recovering from his perplexity at being moved out of his own house, found himself thinking:

"At last! Finally the whole web of pain, frustration, anxiety is over. Relief. Since my marriage had not been a happy one, I had more grief in it than out of it."

A sixty-five-year-old woman who had five years in which to contemplate a crumbling union realized that "I was relieved that the battle to preserve my marriage was over. Now all the uncertainty of wondering 'What next?' was ended."

Many men and women who wanted their freedom, however, felt the same trauma, bitterness, sense of failure, even feelings of rejection experienced by those who had been abandoned. They worried about children still at home. They felt pity and concern over alcoholic or otherwise inadequate spouses. They suffered guilt because they had left wives or husbands of many years for another, more desirable partner.

A woman who felt she and her husband had outgrown each other in many ways experienced a happy elation immediately after leaving home. But the elation was short-lived. "When I chose to become single, I did not anticipate anything except success in every move," she said. "I found out, very much to my surprise, that I was grieving as reminders of what I'd 'lost' or 'given up' came to me. Ours was the death

17

of a marriage, not just a divorce, and even now, when things are not going well, the misery of grief still comes up from the subconscious to haunt me."

After moving out of his marriage, one man said, "I felt a tremendous longing for my wife and family unit approximately three months later, even though I did not want to resume life with the same woman."

Another woman: "I grieved for my children, for the loss of my marriage, for the loss of time invested in the marriage, for the uneasiness of not belonging to someone. I felt like a part of me was gone. My grieving lasted sporadically for at least two years. I had feelings of guilt and failure for not having a successful marriage and for disappointing my children. They seemed to blame me for the marriage falling apart."

In some cases, the loss was mitigated by experience. Many of those who had been through all this once or twice before found the whole scenario had lost its poignancy and gone somewhat flat.

When Stuart P.'s wife Joan decided she had had all she could take of small-town living in Texas and told him she was leaving for California to find a job that would challenge her ability, he made no protest. Joan had given up her job as a buyer in a department store to follow him into retirement in another town, and had been restless and unhappy without an outlet for her abundant energy.

It was okay, he said. Yes, they could meet from time to time for visits. And as she eased her sports car out of the driveway and drove off down the street, not without a few tears, he gently closed the door behind her and poured himself a drink. After three marriages, it was kind of a relief, really. He turned his thoughts to the tomatoes he'd planted that spring and worried a little about the cutworms. Then he looked around the living room. Now, he thought, with sudden, expectant pleasure, he could redecorate the house.

But those, like Stuart, who escaped the jolts of separation and an uprooted lifestyle, were a small minority. Most of the new singles—widowed, divorced, or separated—had to cope with their agony, deliberately or instinctively, reviewing the circumstances of their bereavement over and over, making sense out of it, and finally integrating it into a new view of the world. Adjusting to the new life they were to build for themselves, they would gain new insights, new strengths, new emotional maturity, until they became, like a healed fracture, stronger than they were before.

CHAPTER 3

Remodeling The Interior
prescriptions for healing

Knowing what to expect of grief, coming to a full understanding that life will be forever different from what it was before, can be helpful to the healing process. But what can you, the new single, do to help yourself regain an identity as a human being with a proper niche, as a person who is productive, at peace, and even—possibly—happy?

First, know that it will happen for you as it has for all the others who have been willing to try. The most comforting message a widow in our survey received was a penned note on a sympathy card that said:

"Joy will return, for it is in you."

Joy is in everybody, but sometimes it needs help surfacing, and even in the early stages of single living you can start preparing the ground.

You should avoid change when possible. According to the Social Readjustment Rating Scale worked out by Dr. Thomas H. Holmes of the University of Washington Medical School and Dr. Richard H. Rahe, a neuropsychiatric researcher with the U.S. Navy in a landmark study based on thousands of medical histories and tested on more thousands of people, change can affect your health. The higher your life-change score within a two-year period, the more likely you are to get sick; and the greater the amount of change, the more serious your illness is likely to be. With 450 life-change units, your chances of getting sick are 90 percent; with 300 units, 66 percent; with 150 units, 33 percent.

At the top of the list of changes detrimental to your health is death of a spouse, with 100 units, and divorce, with 73. Other changes to which newly single people are prone include marriage, 50; getting fired, 47; marital reconciliation, 45; sex difficulties, 39; change in financial state for better or worse, 38; change to a different line of work, 36; son or daughter leaving home, 29; revision of personal habits such as dress and associations, 24; moving, 20; change in recreation, 19; change in social activities, 18; change in sleeping habits, 16; change in eating habits, 15; minor violations of the law such as getting a traffic ticket for jaywalking, 11.

Perhaps through instinctive response to the threat of too much change, many new singles spent a lot of time at home in familiar surroundings, finding security in their accustomed routines. One woman spent all her spare time in bed, answering notes, doing her bookwork, reading a long, absorbing novel. Some people thought it felt good to eat soft, soothing foods, take warm baths and hot showers.

It helps to vent your feelings, so go ahead and cry. Scream if you want to. One divorcée would get into the shower, turn the water on full blast, and let loose. Another yelled his rage and frustration in his car, driving along with the windows rolled up. Still another took refuge in his "private moping place," an oversized bedroom closet where the clothes soaked up the sound of his sobs.

Talk—to old friends who have remained true and who have the patience to listen; to other singles at rap sessions, where you may get ideas from those farther along in the healing process; perhaps even to strangers. One divorcée bought a bus ticket to a town seventy miles away so that she could tell her tale once more to a seatmate she would never see again.

Your children can be fiercely supportive, incredibly wise, intuitively consoling. Let them be.

"My son never demonstrated his affection for me until his father left," one woman said. "When I told him that his dad wanted a divorce, he put his arm around my shoulders and squeezed me hard and said simply, 'Oh, Mom, I love you.'"

"Every time I tried to stifle my tears," a widow remembered, "my daughters would put their arms around me and say, 'Go ahead and cry, Mom. Don't hold it back.' And I would let myself cry."

"I don't know what I would have done without my children," said a man who lived alone in an apartment after his wife divorced him. "They called me every day and came to see me on the weekends."

You may, like Sybil K., have to learn to be comforted. Sybil was struck by the words of the policeman who broke the news of her husband's death. "And now," he said, "you must help me to help you."

"It had never been easy for me to receive," she remembered. "I made myself ask for help, and friends came out of the woodwork to respond. I don't think I cooked a meal for three weeks. They also offered what I needed most—hugs and human warmth, and even tears. Thirty-one years of marriage develops some staunch friends, and the most comforting experience came from the realization of how good, how supportive, they really were."

DEPRESSION

But at last, after the shock of your loss has been absorbed, after the numbness has worn off and reality sets in, after all the comforters have returned to their absorbing lives, comes the final stage of grief: depression. Some psychologists believe it must run its course, like the common cold.

You know you're suffering from depression when you don't feel like doing anything, when the past and future appear totally dreary, when you're certain nothing is going to work out right, when you lose interest in people, food, and sex.

Some singles, recognizing their depression for what it was, comforted themselves with such thoughts as "It only hurts for a little while," "Wait it out," and "Tomorrow morning the sun will rise again." From a holding pattern of getting through each day, however, they eventually began to reframe their thoughts.

"I was sound enough to know," a widower said, "that if I didn't find some plan of living which would drive this depressive state away, real trouble would visit me."

This man was fortunate. Many people do not recognize their depression and "real trouble" does occur. The accompanying anxiety, tension, and withdrawal can alienate family and friends. Their inability to concentrate, their difficulty in making decisions, their tendency to procrastinate can lead to loss of jobs, which increases their lack of self-esteem. The ultimate response to depression is suicide.

For most of the singles we interviewed, however, depression wore itself out with some homespun self-help.

Making themselves look back at their marriages they realized, like one woman, that "being completely happy is not a condition of life. Few of us had married bliss 365 days a year."

A widower, who sensed he was beginning to idealize his wife to a point that no other woman could measure up to her, tried this exercise:

"I made myself sit down one day and think of all the things Irma used to do that drove me up the wall. She was a wonderful woman, and I loved her; but she never had dinner on time, and it used to make me squirm at parties when she told a story and didn't get her facts straight."

GENERATING ENERGY

Depression ends when you start to think of yourself as an effective human being, so that is what you must learn to do—no small assignment when you feel rejected, unloved, hostile, bitter, insecure, a failure, and alone. But start you must, and the first task is to build up your energy. You may, like one widow, feel so physically exhausted that you find yourself saying, "It's first my right foot, then my left." Nevertheless, put one in front of the other and walk—out of doors—even if it's only around the block. Like all the single people we talked to, *make* yourself do it, and do it again tomorrow and tomorrow and tomorrow at a regular, planned time. Or work out indoors. Whatever you do, it should be easy, at first, and pleasant. Exercise to music, to records, or while watching TV. But do it every day, increasing the amount.

INSOMNIA

The exercise will improve your sleep. Insomnia typically accompanies the death or divorce of a spouse, and the first remedies many people seek are tranquilizers and sleeping pills, which can create a drug dependency and worsen their sleep problem. There are many better ways to deal with it.

1. Make your bed a pleasant place, with a soft cheerful comforter and well-plumped pillows, a good reading light, a good book, and a radio close at hand. That way, you can read at night until you drowse. For company one widow tuned in on talk shows when she woke up at night and became so engrossed in everyone's problems that she forgot her own. A divorcée, unable to concentrate enough to read, checked out a beautifully illustrated book on painting from the library and submerged herself in the pictures.

2. Be sure your mattress is firm and comfortable.

25

3. Avoid a stuffy room.
4. Eat a light, early dinner.
5. Avoid spices.
6. Don't have a "nightcap"—at least no more than one. Alcohol may relax you initially, but too much tends to wake you up in the middle of the night.
7. If you do wake up in the middle of the night, don't toss and turn. Get up and use the time to accomplish some specific job. Then back to bed with the "did-it" feeling that can put you right to sleep.
8. Learn to relax. Think pleasant thoughts, picture places you love to visit. On a cold winter night, take an old-fashioned hot water bottle to bed, lie on your back, and let it warm and support your neck muscles. Try one of the relaxation techniques that go: "My right foot is asleep. My right ankle is asleep." And on and on until you've put your whole self to sleep.
9. Have a regular bedtime and wakeup time.
10. Follow a familiar bedtime routine. One man likes to take a warm bath, then turn his clock radio to soothing FM music, light a candle, prepare a cup of hot malted milk, sip the hot malted milk, and—he never finishes the cup.

Besides exercising, you can build energy by monitoring your diet, cutting down on alcohol, coffee, cigarettes, and other stimulants and replacing them with high-protein snacks and vitamin supplements. Eating at frequent, regularly spaced intervals does more to maintain your energy level than eating the same amount of food all at once.

THE DECISION

The next step toward increasing your energy is the hardest: you must make a decision. Many newly single people feel paralyzed. They can't decide which tie to put on, which dress to wear, and as a result they fiddle with small matters, evading big ones. To get over this block, pick out a small, simple task like cleaning out a drawer, getting the car fixed, scrubbing the floor—*anything* that needs to be done. To get yourself started, you may have to say, like one man, "Go, baby! Get off it, asshole!" or use a lead-in technique like that of the widow who copied a paragraph from the newspaper on her typewriter to start her on her thank-you notes to friends. While you're doing the job, give it your total here-and-now attention, then after completing it, sit back for a moment and feel good that it's finished. The next task will be easier.

Finally, you can raise your energy by organizing and planning your time. Make a "to-do" list, starting at first with easy jobs, building your momentum. Later, put the tough jobs first and reward yourself with the easier, pleasanter ones. As you finish each, you can draw a big, thick, satisfying line through that item on your list.

Make a schedule, first for your days, then for your weeks as well. Get in the habit, a never-married single advised, of setting deadlines and working backward from them. If you're going out for dinner at six, plan to stop and get ready at five-fifteen.

By planning, you will find that your time expands. A busy schoolteacher who does her own house and yard work, schedules a little of it each day so that her weekends are free. By staying ahead, you will be able to do things at *your* convenience instead of being dominated by a deadline.

When you feel you've gotten your life under sufficient control, you should sit down some quiet evening, decide what you want from your future, and write it down, the way a small-businessman in his middle sixties did.

"One day when I felt I was beating my brains out," he said, "I pushed aside my papers and made a list of what I wanted: a new car, even the model; an apartment; the dollars I wanted in my checking account and the amount I wanted

27

in my savings. I then arranged them in priority order. Five years later, I ran upon that list and found I had gotten almost everything I had put down."

Some singles who employ this technique like to set a target date for getting what they want, along with dates for completing everything they have to do to get it.

Others believe in evoking a vivid mental picture.

"Once a day, I sit down with myself and visualize in specific detail what I want," an Oregon painter said. "Next year at this time, I want to have my own house. I picture the neighborhood, the people I will be entertaining in it, even the flowers I'll have on the dining-room table. I know I'll have it, because that's the way it always turns out."

One businessman even overcame stage fright by seeing himself, Walter Mitty-style, rising easily to his feet behind the banquet table, listening to the appreciative laughter that greeted his opening joke, progressing coolly, smoothly, confidently through his talk, and sitting down to rousing applause.

Your goals can be set for one day, one week, six months, a year, five years. Beyond that, many people think they become too subject to change. Some cautioned, also, against getting locked into a set of goals or plans so that there is no room for the unscheduled and unexpected.

"Schedules are fine for the everyday meat and potatoes of living," a woman said, "but it's the unusual and unplanned event that adds the spice."

Having vented your feelings, reconstructed your thinking, and raised your energy level, you're ready for the next step in overcoming your depression: stop talking about it. By now, your good friends and true deserve a break. So, before calling someone on the phone or going to visit, do a little homework. Memorize, if necessary, some interesting, positive topics of conversation, a good joke or a funny story, and surprise everybody by substituting it for the broken record they have all been listening to so patiently.

TAKING CHARGE

The seeds of final recovery are often encapsulated in new responsibilities, overwhelming though they may seem at first.

"I was bitter and angry," a divorcée recalled, "because I had tried so hard to be a good wife. Life was shattered for me. However, I noticed as I started to receive my very own bills, as I started balancing my very own checkbook, that I felt proud that I could handle things myself and that my husband wasn't running my life for me any more."

"I felt so good the first time I changed a washer on a leaky faucet," said a woman who had learned how to do it from a home-repair book. "All those years, I thought it was something only a husband or a plumber could do."

"Every time I took the car for repairs, I could hear them tuning up the cash register as they saw me drive in," another related. "So I signed up for a fix-your-car class and, while I don't try to repair everything myself, I can now discuss carburetors with the best of them. I also know what to do for my car on a regular schedule, so not so many things go wrong."

No less proud were the men who learned to cook and iron, to manage their homes and their children. The owner of a record shop whose young wife had left him for the women's movement said:

"She wanted to explore lesbianism and I, left with our two small children, explored my gin bottle. I got bombed every night, felt rotten the next day. One morning I woke up to a house that looked like hell, kids running screaming through the mess, and decided it was time to do something. I got busy and learned how to raise children and run a household."

Another, who looks back with satisfaction years after his divorce, remarked:

"We made it! I ran that house like a top sergeant, but we went camping in the mountains on weekends. The kids are gone now, but they still check up on me and nobody, but nobody, had better say anything derogatory to any of them about their old man."

None of the singles we talked to found his or her self-restoration easy or spontaneous. Over and over, people said: "I forced myself to do it." "I made up my mind." But as the resolution took place, action followed, and the singles began to move. They read, they walked, they went out with other singles, they learned to play bridge, they golfed, they bowled, they took up crocheting and needlework, they joined travel groups, they went to plays, concerts, movies, art galleries, poetry readings, church; they did volunteer work and got jobs, they called friends and visited with them on the phone, they joined groups, they accepted every invitation and invited everybody back. They got involved in things they'd never done or dreamed of doing.

"I could have sat back in my dowdiness and lived on my alimony," said a real estate agent. "Some women do, because their alimony would stop if they got a job. But when I found I had something of value to offer people, it meant more than anything money could buy."

A widowed housewife went to school and learned Spanish; she learned to speak it so well, in fact, that she is now leading private tours to Mexico.

An accountant made himself an authority on roses and their culture; now he is in demand as a speaker.

A businessman estimates he has had more than a hundred "adopted nephews," disadvantaged kids he's taken on trips to the zoo, for bike rides, swimming, and picnics.

"Helping others is a real morale booster," he said. "My new life began at fifty-three."

A librarian loves to "invent things to do" in her home—build a table, make a new bedspread, panel a wall with mirrors.

Gaining assurance, the singles began to reach and stretch.

"I challenged myself," said a financial consultant who was starting his own business. "I approached a total stranger on a business deal. I'd prepared myself carefully, so I got a positive response from him, and I was able to use that contact to reach a higher one. I kept going up, gaining confidence as I went, and now I deal directly with the president of the company."

Simon J. found the road back to effectiveness and self-confidence particularly steep, because he had lost so much. The same year his wife of nineteen years left him, believing she was not accomplishing anything with her life, he watched his flourishing business go into bankruptcy. Fleeing the scene, he took his daughter and visited his family in Virginia, stopping in the Everglades along the way, seeing the lake where he had water-skied as a boy. The trip strengthened his sense of identity and the ties between him and his daughter, but when they got back, Simon was almost broke.

Scanning the want ads, his eye riveted on one that said: "Earn $150 a day." In 1960 that was a fortune, but it meant traveling, selling paint franchises up and down the coast of Florida, and he would need a flashy new car. He spent two hours haggling with the salesman at a used-car lot, persuading him to accept a ridiculously low down payment. Then, feeling old, bald, and washed up, he went out and bought a toupee.

Driving his new car, wearing his toupee, Simon started out—and made $300 his first day on the road.

"That job got me out of my home state, out of the setting of my divorce. I found myself a part of the traveling-salesman group, a network of men from all walks of life, and I belonged. They showed me how to get along on the road, how to have a good time again, how to meet women."

Simon had been a faithful husband; preparing for his first night out, he looked anxiously in his mirror, adjusting his toupee.

Later, at the bar, he hesitated to approach the attractive brunette who had caught his eye until one of his salesman friends leaned over and prodded, "Okay, now *do* it!" The brunette was receptive and Simon woke up the next morning for the first time in months in bed with a woman.

"That job in Florida did as much for me as a trip around the world," he said. "I began to make money, attract women, regain my self-confidence. And I finally threw away my toupee."

TAKING CARE

Along with becoming effective again, a lot of people must learn to be good to themselves—sometimes for the first time in many years.

A mother who had raised five children realized one day after her divorce that she had never, in twenty-seven years of marriage, had a bath. Hurried showers, yes, when no one else needed the bathroom, but never a leisurely tub.

"I'd been reading a women's magazine—another luxury I'd never had time for—and decided to try their superbath. I filled the tub with warm water, added three-fourths cup of milk, a tablespoon of salad oil, turned on the stereo, took the phone off the hook, put a lighted candle in the bathroom, and turned off all the lights. With a rolled-up towel under my neck, I soaked my cares away for over an hour, thinking about all the good things I'd done in my life—all the great things I was going to do,"

"After my divorce, I took myself out to dinner at the

very best spot in town," another woman said, "and ordered exactly what I wanted, reading the menu, for a change, from left to right. I relished the total relaxation and sense of leisure, not having to make bright conversation to entertain someone who would only be irritated by what I said. The best part was my after-dinner coffee. For twenty-three years, I had had to gulp it down, my husband standing over me with our coats. This time, I sat and sipped and savored every drop."

A man whose family finances had always weighed so heavily that he'd never allowed himself anything better than Gallo wine went out and bought himself a carton of champagne, packaged in splits.

"I could never read in bed, because my wife always grumbled about the light," he reported. "But now I read and sip my champagne, and feel like a king."

"One of the nicest things I've done," a woman public relations director offered, "was to organize a new me. After that first long, depressing summer, a friend who is a buyer for a large department store came for a visit. We went around to all the stores and she told me what would be good to wear, how I could change my makeup and hair, what kind of new clothes to buy. I felt like a different person, putting on clothes I never would have picked out if left to my own devices. It changed my mood. I think doing something to change yourself is a great upper."

LONELINESS

In the process of becoming busy and productive, of learning to think of yourself as a worthwhile person, you are also overcoming one of the greatest problems many single people face: loneliness. "No one to say, 'Hello, darling' to me when I walk in the door." "No one to snuggle up to at night." "No one on earth to share my problems." "No one who really cares what happens to me." These were the first agonized reactions to single living for many people.

But just as they grew in self-esteem and happiness, they evaluated their outlook on being alone.

"Loneliness is a problem you have, not one the world is imposing on you."

"Loneliness is egocentric. There is so much available to do that loneliness in the old-fashioned sense is gone."

Still, the problem of loneliness persists for some. Coming home alone in the early evening or at night, seeing the beautiful countryside around her house bathed in moonlight or covered with snow brings it flooding over one woman, even though her days are filled with activity. Another feels overpowered each time her son visits and she returns, after taking him to the airport, to her empty house. Both busy themselves with household chores, singing or humming as they do so, and the feeling dissipates.

Anticipating the times you might be lonely and planning for them, particularly for the devastating Sunday afternoons and holidays, is one way of meeting the problem. There are many activities that can turn disaster to delight in any urban area. Tramping through the snowy woods one Sunday after a Hallowe'en tour of Colorado ghost towns, a widower commented: "Thank God for the Mountain Club."

Alone does not have to mean lonely. Loneliness includes depression, and by banishing depression many singles came to value their solitude.

"I *must* have long periods of being alone in order to keep sane," a sales agent said. "It is during those times that I re-establish priorities, get creative ideas, rest, do what I want to do (always many more projects around than I have time for)."

Plan to do something that will make you feel good when you're alone, and avoid thinking of anything else while you're doing it. Cook a really good meal for yourself, perhaps invite a neighbor in. Hot baths with bubbles, fresh fruit with cheese, a good stereo, a good book, a warm, mellow relationship with the opposite sex, and good, positive thinking were antidotes to loneliness other singles offered.

DEALING WITH NEGATIVE FEELINGS

Besides loneliness, there are other negative feelings and thoughts that can loom large to defeat you: worry, anger, frustration, sluggishness, irritability, and other demons. Here's what has worked for many in dealing with all of them:

1. Think about what causes the feeling, then if possible avoid the people or situations that bring it on.

2. Share the problem so you can look at it logically.

3. Do something physical: take a walk, a shower, a shopping trip.

4. If it's available, have some sex.

5. Enjoy a good companion.

6. Change your scene, your task.

7. Eliminate trivia, and with it pressure, from your schedule. Learn to say no.

8. Drop out for a while. Take the phone off the hook. Take a trip for the weekend.

9. Learn never to put yourself down. You don't have to brag, but it's okay to put in a good word for Number One occasionally.

10. Accept the fact that a certain amount of bad feeling is legitimate.

11. Accept what you can't control, but at the same time, see if there's something in the situation you might reverse. The woman who offered this comment looked forward all week to the singles dances she attended. When she slipped on a curbing and twisted her knee, she kept right

on going to the party. "I couldn't dance," she said, "but I challenged myself to see how many people I could attract to my table to chat."

12. Read inspirational books.

13. Don't talk about the depressing aspects of life. You drive away your friends and drag your own spirits down.

14. Relax. Breathe as deeply as you can, hold it, yawn if possible, then exhale slowly and totally.

15. Wash your brain into positive thinking. Say things like: "I will be successful." "I will be confident." A man who made such affirmations during his daily swimming workout each time he completed a lap said, "The more you groove them, the more you believe them, and the more you will keep your mind turned to the positive and the constructive."

16. Remember your successes, past crises you have overcome.

17. The moment negative feelings begin, deliberately change your thoughts. Don't allow them to take hold and grow.

18. Worry, if you must, constructively, with the idea of improving the situation. Otherwise, as one man said, "Why go through the same thing twice?"

19. If you have faith in God, let Him do the worrying. Numbers of single men and women are finding this approach useful. Said a woman, "I'm just giving the Guy upstairs my problem. He said He could handle it better than I, so I decided, 'Why not?'"

20. Choose to be happy. Set the stage for happiness in the morning. Suggested one woman:

"First of all, I open up my bedroom drapes, get a good look at the mountain view, weather, and Mother Nature in general—then try to carry on in the same spirit all day.

Said a man: "I have breakfast on a silver tray,

complete with doily and napkin, on my patio. I bask in the sun and feed the squirrel that comes to visit me. It only takes twenty minutes, but it establishes my mood for the day."

THERAPISTS AND COUNSELORS

While most of the singles in our survey were their own psychotherapists, a number went out into the crowded marketplace to look for help. Psychiatrists, psychologists, psychotherapists, family doctors, college-sponsored seminars, singles rap sessions, and the many popular psychology get-better groups, such as Transcendental Meditation, yoga, est, ministered to them with varying degrees of success.

The most available and cheapest source of support is that offered by such singles groups as Parents Without Partners and some churches, in which members get together to vent their feelings, talk over problems, and offer each other ideas. Making use of such a sounding board for bottled-up emotions in a safe, caring atmosphere, knowing that others share your problems and feelings, that you are not unique or alone, is one kind of therapy.

"I thought I was a freak," one man said, "because I was so angry at my wife for dying and leaving me with all those chores, until others in my group confessed they felt the same way. It really made me feel I was one of the human race, that I was acceptable."

Sometimes participants in these groups become very close, such as those in the one Emma P. belonged to at her church.

"It was nothing professional; anyone could form one like it," she explained. "There were fifteen people, each of us with his own special problem. One woman, for example, had lost a leg to cancer. We met once a week for discussion, fellowship, and prayers."

Drawing upon the warmth and acceptance of the

37

other members of her group, Emma began to feel better and decided to make a trip to Santa Fe with her grown daughter for the opera, which they both loved. When they returned to their hotel room after the first night's performance, the phone rang. It was her group. Everyone had gotten together to call her and wish her a happy holiday.

Your family minister, however, might not be your best source of counsel and guidance. Help for singles, one churchman thought, is one of the great gaps in a family-oriented institution.

"It always bothers me when Ann Landers advises someone to go and see their priest or rabbi or minister," he said. "I know there are those who are extremely adept at counseling, but there are others who don't know what in the dickens to do."

Sometimes, however, self-help books and popular psychology classes are not enough. If you are seized by recurring panic, if you don't seem able to feel or show your grief when it is the appropriate reaction, if your guilt or anger becomes exaggerated or obsessive, if you continue to have physical symptoms (nausea, headache, loss of appetite), or if your grief and depression persist beyond a reasonable length of time—six months, a year—then you may need professional therapy. How do you find it?

A variety of licensed professionals, not just psychiatrists, can be qualified psychotherapists, and one may be found through the recommendation of a family doctor or through a state-approved Mental Health Center. Ask the following questions when looking for the man or woman who will best meet your needs and with whom you will feel comfortable:

1. Does he give feedback? Unless you are interested only in a listening post (which is free), you should expect some guidance, some opinions, some discussion with your

therapist. The traditional psychoanalytic approach, in which the professional stays quiet, can often make you feel worse than ever.

2. What kinds of patients has he dealt with most successfully in the past? A therapist who deals extremely well with teenagers may not be what you're looking for.

3. How many patients does he have? If the number is too high, he won't have time to give you the thought and help you may need.

4. How much does he charge, and how does he present his bills—monthly or as a big balloon at the end of treatment?

5. Does he charge for phone conversations?

6. When and how often does he take vacations? Will he be there when you need him?

COMING OUT OF GRIEF

Almost all the single men and women in our survey believe they are over their grief. They knew they were healed, they said:

"When I made decisions on my own."

"When all of a sudden I felt free."

"When I began to realize that I no longer felt like crying as I drove home from work."

"When I started helping others who had been through the same experience."

"When I started calling myself single instead of a widow."

Not only have they coped, but overwhelmingly they feel that becoming single has opened avenues to a richer and more interesting life. They have become more confident, more alert, more positive, more outgoing, more tolerant, more flexible, more open, more content. In their own words, here is their evaluation:

"I never realized until I became single how stagnant I had become. Most of my associations and activities were ritualized and I was never exposed to real stimulation."

"I don't feel as if something were pushing me down."

"It has forced me to get out of my house and back into the world."

"I am looking for a new career in other fields, a move which would have affected my wife's need for security."

"I found out the talents I possessed that had either been hidden or I had been too lazy or too busy doing something else to discover."

"Being single has helped me be aware of the power I have. It has helped me realize I am responsible for my life."

"My life is definitely fuller, as I am doing things I thought impossible before."

"I have been able to realize capabilities that were unknown to me during my marriage."

"I attract others to me because I feel that I finally have my head together, know who I am and what I want out of life."

"I can do what I want, when I want, and go where I wish with whom I wish. I have discovered an awareness of me."

"I'm free to plan my own schedule, eat when I want, work on projects I feel like doing when I want to, meet and surround myself with creative people whom I enjoy, originate my own entertainment and professional work."

"I made up my mind I would never be bored again, and I never have."

As time went on, the rewards and compensations of single living accumulated for these people, as they can for you, if you are willing to make the effort to re-establish joy in your life. You can do it, as we have shown, by

- exploring your feelings
- exercising
- monitoring your diet
- developing your ability to make decisions
- organizing your time
- establishing your goals
- building your self-esteem by gaining competence in your daily living
- learning to control your feelings by substituting positive thoughts for negative ones
- seeking help if you need it.

In so doing, you will set the stage for a new life, not an interim between marriages, in which you will explore new friendships, new vistas, new experiences, no longer dependent on some "other half," but as a new whole person.

CHAPTER 4

Other VIPs
culling and cultivating relationships

The end of marriage often has a domino effect on a single's entire support system, bringing a collapse of friendships that have taken years to nurture and build, an alienation of children and in-laws, bringing changes, even, in the casual relationships of life—the doctors, lawyers, and other mechanical props of living. As a former California socialite, still reeling in amazement, said:

"I thought I was a darling woman and everybody loved me. Suddenly I find I'm not a darling woman at all and *nobody* seems to love me."

After the debris from your blasted life has settled, the first thing you notice on looking around are the friends you have left. Your couple friends, and that's most of them, will tend to drift away, and the ones who stay do so by an altered set of rules.

MARRIED FRIENDS

"When Walt was alive," a widow said, "we had such marvelous parties with Henry and Dee. It was nothing for me to plop down in Henry's lap—no one thought anything of it. The first time I did that after becoming single, I could feel the electric sparks snap in the air."

A divorced man remembers wistfully: "I used to stop in at friends' houses after work for a drink and visit. I

43

wouldn't think of doing that now, for fear the husband might not be home and I'd be there, a single man, alone with his wife."

Those who have kept their married friends, however, prize them highly.

"They're a lovely buffer," a woman noted.

"One of the really good, positive things I had going for me was my friendship with a couple who made me feel totally welcome in their home," a salesman said. "I could stop in any time. We'd have drinks, dinner. After dinner, Sam and I would play pinochle and when Ellen got tired, she'd just go on up to bed."

Such relationships, however, are points of contact in parallel but generally unconnected worlds—the oil and water of single and coupled living; and those who make them work follow careful guidelines:

1. Never flirt, make or accept a pass from "the opposite." Some men become expert at not recognizing overtures from wives. One, who even has wives of friends drop in at his house, simply pours them a drink, keeps them in the living room, and never says anything he wouldn't say in front of their husbands.

Women sometimes feel outrage or hurt when husbands of old friends start out by saying "If there's anything I can do to help" and end by suggesting a weekend à deux in a neighboring town.

One woman told of her family doctor who called, sometimes as late as ten o'clock on a warm summer night, to suggest that she leave her back door unlatched.

"Leave the lights off," he cautioned. "I can find my way upstairs to your bedroom."

"At that time, it was so early in the game I didn't know how to handle it," she said. "I would make up excuses. Now, when such things happen, I simply say, 'I don't care to have that kind of relationship with a married man.' Then, instead of being upset, I simply dismiss the incident."

2. Never threaten a couple's relationship by glamorizing single living. One woman, who tries to play down the dates and good times that seem so sparkling to her married women friends, tells them:

"You've got the stability and warmth of a family unit, the sense of security and the good warm feeling that goes with it. If you've got a good marriage that's working, hang in there."

3. Pay back invitations. Even single men believe in reciprocating with dinner at home, having a party with both singles and couples, or a dinner out.

4. Instead of playing the fifth wheel, get yourself a partner—one not too good-looking, who might threaten the hostess, if you're a male—and make it an even number.

5. Be nice to the children. Remember their names, at least, their interests and accomplishments. Do them a favor if possible; they can be interesting friends.

6. Be a friend to both husband and wife. Give equal time and have something to offer each. One of the worst faux pas a man can make is to take a husband out for a night on the town.

7. Be careful of becoming involved in marital disagreements. Don't offer advice unless asked, and then try to be scrupulously objective.

8. Recognize the difference in your situations and don't intrude. Don't stay too long or have your feelings hurt if they don't include you in their parties.

9. Keep in touch and let them know you care about them.

"I treasure every couple friend I've got," a woman said. "I don't see them often, but I know they're there, that I can call on them for help if I need it. And that is enormously comforting to me."

NEW LIFE, NEW FRIENDS

Almost all of the singles, however, think it's a grave mistake to cling to the married world, and many abandon it entirely, finding that their interests soon diverge from those of their married friends.

Unhampered now by the likes and dislikes, the social skills (or lack of them) of a mate, they set about making friends more aggressively and usually more productively than when they were married.

Marcia L., for instance, had always lived in the shadow of her gregarious and charming husband. At parties she clung to his side, feeling uncomfortable and out of place, with nothing of interest to talk about after a day of washing dishes, scrubbing floors, caring for children. When he told her to "go mingle" she felt cast adrift and hurt, watching from the sidelines as women hugged and kissed him.

"We didn't do that much hugging at home," she remembered.

After her divorce, she realized that no one was going to invite her anywhere because of her husband and that she would have to project her own personality. She got herself together, found a job, then started going to church and other group meetings. Now, a part of the business world, meeting people every day, she finds she is contributing as much to conversations and discussions as anyone.

"I also try to do nice things for people. The woman down the street is single and never went anywhere, so I took her along to some of the groups I had joined, and we got to be good friends. There's always something nice you can do for somebody if you're looking."

Finding other singles equally interested in forming friendships, the widowed and divorced gained confidence and refined their social skills:

"Making friends is much easier now because I'm

willing to take more risks and people are more responsive to me. It's a beautiful development in my life."

"I am generally the first one to open a conversation with someone new. With a cheerful countenance, most anyone can make new friends."

"I call other women up just to say hello and chat and make lunch or movie dates, and I keep calling until they take me up. If they don't I just move on to someone else and don't take it personally."

"Stay active and in circulation. Never turn down an invitation."

"Mix with people of all ages, show an interest in their lives, be a good listener, and usually you will be included with a group of friends."

With a strong sense of their limited time, singles over fifty choose their friends with care, and most are rewarded with warmer, deeper, more accepting friendships than they had as marrieds. While they value the older friends for the continuity they give to their lives and the depth of feeling that years of association and loyalty can bring, few are willing to tolerate an emotional expense. Having traded off unsatisfactory marriages for a new and better lifestyle, some are questioning values they had always held regarding friendship itself.

"People who say there are no friends like old friends have become socially lazy," a man maintained. "I hang onto the best of the old, those with whom there is a common thread, but I no longer hesitate to let those who have outlived their usefulness fade away."

"Maybe friends, like marriages, aren't meant to be forever," said a woman. "People change in different directions. I don't think it's a bad idea to take inventory once in a while and ask yourself if your friendships are rewarding or just a habit. Sometimes you don't even realize you're not enjoying people very much until you stop seeing them."

What, then, makes a good friend in the single world? One man summed it up very well:

"If I feel good about me when I am with that person, if he and I have mutual interest, if there's rapport with trust, if my energy and joy are greater after being with him, then I know it's a relationship worth cultivating."

Despite their willingness to let unrewarding friendships die, most singles go to considerable lengths to maintain the ones they keep, to create out of them a rich and glowing warmth. Sometimes the creation involves clash and strife, as with the solid relationship that emerged between Olga K. and Marty R., who confronted each other bitterly in group therapy.

One of the men in the group invited Olga out on a date and told about the good time they had at the next meeting. Marty became furious.

"What's so great about Olga?" she demanded. "Why didn't you invite me?"

"Well!" Olga flared, "What's *your* problem, Marty?"

Before the dust settled, Marty realized that she did indeed have a problem, and that it had nothing to do with Olga. It involved her own insecurity with men.

Olga, for her part, felt her friendship with Marty was worth the battle.

"Anyone who's in group therapy is here to improve himself, and his perspective on life, and those are the kinds of friends I want to have."

"Some of my best friends are ones I've had the most ferocious fights with," one of them said. "You don't fight with people you don't care anything about."

Talking out misunderstanding, being open, sincere, trustworthy, and interested are ways in which singles maintain their friends. They show they care by writing notes, sending cards, making phone calls, offering invitations, initiating activities. They are positive. "Never make your aches, pains, incapacities the highlight of your conversation," one warns.

And most important of all, they listen. "It's much like a marriage partner," one observed. "The mutual respect and caring for each other has to grow."

CHILDREN

Singles who still have children at home often find that, freed of marital tension and divisiveness, they are closer to them than they were during their marriage. Sometimes, however, initial ill feeling has to be overcome.

"My teenagers at first blamed me for leaving, particularly when we had financial struggles," a woman said. "Now that they can see that we are 'making it' and that I am successfully managing my life and raising them too, they seem to understand that it might have been for the best."

A father who picked up his nine-year-old son shortly after his separation was rudely startled as they drove along in his car to have his son blurt out:

"Why did you run off and leave Mama and me?"

"I pulled over to the side and we talked about it right then," he said. "I told him honestly that it was his mother who had asked for the divorce, but that I would have if she hadn't, because we just couldn't get along. I told him, as objectively as I could, exactly what the problem had been: money. He listened very intently—and accepted, and we have been on good terms ever since."

Another mother, whose son elected to live with his father and share his anger at her leaving him, made it clear that she wanted him to come and see her whenever he wished but never pushed him. There were many weeks between visits, but she accepted the intervals without protest, remaining warm and welcoming when he did come, open about the problems she and his father had had. Eventually they were not only reconciled, but he chose, during teenage clashes with his father, to move in with her.

In one instance, learning that their father had feet of clay actually broke down the barriers between a man and his older sons. Stanley J. had been converted to Catholicism when he married and, unable to accept the tenets of the church wholeheartedly, overcompensated for his lack of conviction:

"I became an uptight, strict Catholic, bearing my own cross, suffering, feeling guilty. I was an authoritarian parent, not one the kids could confide in because of all the absolutes I laid on them."

Stanley left the church and his rigid, unhappy marriage at the same time, uprooted from both by a love affair with another woman.

"I decided I never really had believed all that stuff," he said, "so I pulled my old self back from the shelf where I'd laid it twenty years before, got involved with singles groups, attended raps and seminars, read the popular psychology books, and began to revamp my image so that I had some self-esteem. Two of my older boys have come to live with me, and friends marvel at the openness between us, the banter that goes back and forth."

It seems only human that fathers and mothers should state their case to their children on the subject of their divorce, but having done so, the wisest course seems to be to refrain from criticizing an ex-spouse. If the parents themselves don't recognize that fact, their children are quick to point it out.

"They made me realize I was beating a dead horse," a mother said. "They were quite aware of their father's good and bad points. They had them summed up better than I, and they didn't want to hear them over and over. They made me aware that I mustn't keep boring other people with my hurts."

Eventually, most recognized that, for the sake of the children themselves, you should encourage them to think well of the other parent. As one mother told her children, who were fiercely protective and angered by their father's desertion:

"You've got to make peace with your dad, or you'll never have peace with yourself."

A father said, "She is the mother of my child, and I love her for that."

Struggling singlehandedly with teenage problems, the mothers and fathers worked them out, sometimes by trial and error, sometimes with help.

"At first I got a lot of 'You're too strict and inhibiting,' but I tried to think each problem through and asked for help from child psychiatrists when I needed it," a mother said.

"I've tried to be open, honest, and caring."

"Being a male when females are needed for my daughters has been a problem. Their frankness helps me to help them, and if knowledge is needed, we look it up together."

The most successful parents eschew rigid, authoritarian roles, recognizing that their children have personalities of their own, each one different, and allowing them to make their own decisions.

"It's harder being brought up that way," a seventeen-year-old daughter of a single mother attested. "You can't blame anybody but yourself when things don't work out. But the feeling of self-dependence I have now is worth it."

Christie J., a widowed schoolteacher, tried to adopt her late husband's authoritarianism as she watched her son's grades slide from A's to C's in high school.

"When he brought home a D in math his senior year, I panicked. I thought the end had come. I had counseled, nagged, checked on his papers, curtailed privileges, and finally even suspended his use of the car. Nothing seemed to work.

"That Christmas, when his two older brothers came home from college, we held a family conference. The consensus was that he should take the responsibility for his grades himself. We told him we'd support him in whatever path he decided to take, hoped he would not close the doors that would lead to future options, and restored all the privileges. He was on his own.

"It was terribly hard for me to keep my peace, but I did. I also lavished praise and support for every success that was important to *him*—a new trick in gymnastics, a ribbon in swimming. I took time to talk, not about school and grades, but about girls and friends and his philosophy of life. I let him know I was really proud of the many good qualities he had. The best result was the close warm feeling we developed for each other. But there were peripheral benefits, too.

"Yesterday, he came beaming into the house and said he had something to show me. With a flourish, he took two tests out of his notebook and laid them on the kitchen table.

"'Take a look at these from your cool son,' he said. They were both A's."

Allowing young people to make their own decisions, however, does not mean there should be no rules. There should. Clearly spelled out, with expectations of having them followed.

Said a mother: "When my seventeen-year-old son came to live with me, I sat down before I even fixed dinner and told him we had to work out some guidelines. He would have to go back to school, if he were going to stay with me, and start saving some money. We talked about what time at night the stereo should be off or turned low enough so I could sleep, about entertaining and drinking in moderation.

There were not many regulations, but I made it clear I expected them to be followed."

In three cases, parents were faced with children who seemed determined not to follow the rules. In one, a father who as a result of his divorce had moved from the spacious home of which he had been so proud into a far more modest condominium felt further demeaned when his eighteen-year-old son left dirty dishes in the sink and his room in a mess.

"I'm proud of my home, son," he reasoned. "The way we keep it speaks for both of us." But the disorder continued.

Two other fathers had problems with curfews. One of them, whose seventeen-year-old daughter persistently stayed out until early morning hours visiting an older boyfriend in his apartment, lost so much sleep that his performance on his job suffered.

All three of the fathers finally resolved the conflicts with speedy simplicity. They gave the young people an option: if they couldn't follow the rules, they should think about living someplace else.

"You really get their attention," one of the fathers said, "when you offer the alternative with no bitterness, with assurances of love and a desire for a continued warm relationship, but with the resolve of meaning what you say."

In all three cases, the young people decided to cooperate.

Besides establishing open communication and closeness with their children, successful parents gave them a large measure of support even when it meant putting their own needs and desires in the background. One father canceled his New Year's Eve plans to chaperone a party his daughter wanted to have. Another took his daughter, instead of a woman friend, on a hiking vacation in Hawaii. Still another kept open house for his children's friends on weekends and never in seven years missed a week seeing them. Still another made the time to listen whenever his son called. Late one Sunday afternoon, his ten-year-old phoned to tell him he needed pine cones for a school project. They had been together the entire previous day, and the father was about to leave to pick up a new and intriguing dinner date.

"I called and told her I'd be late, and we drove out to the park to pick up the cones," he said. "Kids *need* your attention and time. You're saying, 'I think enough of you to want to help you.'"

One of the biggest hassles parents face when teenage sons and daughters live at home is the restriction it imposes upon their sex lives. You might introduce a new friend gradually, dating away from home until the relationship has a chance to develop. Most of the singles in our survey follow the rule one man sets for himself: "It's either her place or not at all."

They are, however, open about their sexual relationships. "There's no sense in playing games with teenagers," a mother said. "They certainly know what's going on, and I don't want them to think of sex as anything but a normal, healthy pleasure shared by two adults who think a lot of each other."

"I used to think that my sex experience was something utterly intimate and private and never discussed it with anyone," said another. "Now I talk very openly, although not explicitly, with my children. My happiness has been contagious, and my girls who are in college feel free to discuss their questions and problems with me."

Even these mothers, though, do not bring male friends home to spend the night when their children are there.

"It's not so much what the children would think," one

said. "I doubt if they'd think anything of it. But I wouldn't feel comfortable."

A father who shares his apartment with his sixteen- and eighteen-year-old sons, on the other hand, has made his lifestyle clear to them from the outset—"if not what it is, what I would like it to be"—and has no hesitation about announcing that a woman friend will be coming for dinner and will probably spend the night.

Parents should distinguish between self-restraint in what they consider to be the best interests of their children and denying their own legitimate needs. Many tend to overcompensate to their children for the lack of a mother or father, and sometimes the children capitalize on their concern.

A mother who recognized that her children had become experts at laying guilt trips on her learned to absolve herself. Now when they say, "You mean you're taking that big luscious cake to the potluck and we don't even get a piece?" she points to the cake mix in the cupboard and gives them permission to whip one up for themselves.

Occasionally, children don't want a parent to date at all.

"We talked it out," said Dora L., the mother of one of these, "and I had to make Gary realize that it is pretty lonely without a companion."

After Dora was widowed her son resented every man she went out with. He didn't deliver phone messages and when she went out on dates she returned to a sink full of dirty dishes. The climax occurred one night when she came home to find a wild party raging in the living room.

"Why is it that every time I go out with Dick, things go wrong at home?" she asked later.

Gary looked abashed, then blurted out, "You're always going out with Dick."

"Hey, wait a second," Dora said. "I only go out with

him once a week. You go over to see Susan every night. While you're gone, I sometimes get pretty lonely. And when you leave for college next year, it's going to be really lonely with no one here at all."

"For the first time, I think he thought of me as a human being instead of just a mother," she said later. "Then he put his arm around my shoulder and gave me a squeeze. The next time I went out for the evening, I came home to an immaculate kitchen."

In some respects, a one-parent family can work to the advantage of children. The self-dependence fostered by a working parent, the necessity to help with household chores and even family finances can contribute to a young person's development.

A mother whose teenagers pay for their own clothes, buy and maintain their own cars, and contribute a modest rate of room and board besides, voluntarily offering more when it is needed, said:

"It makes me mad when I hear people make pitying remarks about kids from broken homes. I'm proud of my kids, the help they've given me, and the straight A's they make in school. Especially when I look around and see some of the young people from *un*broken homes who are not doing nearly so well."

To those parents who have been open, loving, and supportive toward their children, the benefits in love and loyalty and candor are returned in generous portion:

"My daughter became the best friend I had in the world. She could say, 'You're wrong,' and I would accept it."

"I've learned as much from my son as he has learned from me."

The happiest of the parents are those who cut the strings and let their children go, making minimal demands on them afterward.

"The most fulfilling thing I've ever done has been to raise my children. At takeoff time, I felt no need to cling, because I had developed my own career, my own interests, my own friends. When they come back to visit, it's a joyous reunion. When they leave again, it's kind of nice, too, because I can go back to all the things I've been doing.

"I am careful to let them live their own lives. I also do not ask my son to do all sorts of odd jobs for his 'poor helpless mother.' I hire them done, if possible, so our meetings are happy, leisurely events."

THE "EX"

Besides your friends and your children, a very important person in your life, if you're divorced, is your ex-husband or ex-wife. Widowhood, some divorcées believe, is easier than losing a mate by divorce since there is no ghost that keeps returning, no wounds that keep reopening. For closing the wounds and putting the ghosts to rest, they have these suggestions:

When you're angry, keep quiet.

Don't argue. You couldn't win when you were married, so don't try now.

Don't criticize.

Don't lay guilt.

Don't discuss the past.

Don't pry or interfere with each other's lives.

If you're attacked, don't retaliate.

Keep your financial dealings scrupulously fair.

Go 60 percent of the way. Give help when it's needed.

Keep your contacts short and friendly, limiting conversation to impersonal, positive subjects and business matters or to problems relating to your children.

Be clear. Make up your mind that it's over.

By following these rules, Marilyn J. overcame one of the most difficult problems of anyone in our survey.

When she became convinced that her marriage had no future, Marilyn returned to the States from the South American oil camp where the family had been living. Her children at first elected to stay with their father, but when he returned to the States too, they decided to move in with her. To be near them, Marilyn's "ex" found an apartment down the street. When he was lonely, which was almost every night, he would call the children on the phone, and when he wanted to see them, he would simply walk into the house unannounced.

"It was infuriating," Marilyn said. "But I tried to remember that he was going through the same trauma I had gone through the year before when I thought I had lost my children. I knew it hurt him to come into his own house where he'd rocked them as babies, and I tried to be patient, believing things would work out without a confrontation, which they did. One night he walked in when I was entertaining a date, and I think he was as embarrassed as I was. After that, he always called before he came over."

With her husband living nearby, contacts were frequent.

"I'd always had a feeling of inferiority around him, one of the reasons I got divorced. He was expert at making biting, sarcastic, put-down remarks—I'd almost rather he hit me than to be at the receiving end of one of them. But I learned to get up and walk away instead of responding and getting into one of those battles no one wins; and gradually he stopped making his jibes, because he got no reaction. Meantime I was reconstructing my life, having some successes, beginning to feel good about myself and to get over my bitterness toward him.

"I also learned not to say anything negative about him in front of the children, knowing it would be repeated to him and belittle me in their eyes, besides hurting their image of their father. They knew his weaknesses as well as I did."

Two years after her divorce, Marilyn knew she had gotten over her bitterness when her husband drove up one day and they chatted pleasantly at the curbside. He had met another woman with whom he hoped to begin a new life.

"I was able to mirror his good feelings because I was getting my life together, too. We'd both come a long way, standing there visiting together like neighbors, and I was glad to find I could say 'That's great, Art. I'm happy for you' and mean it."

The divorcées are the first to admit that the rules they lay down are hard to follow, but the alternative is worse, as Marilyn decided after attending a seminar for newly divorced persons.

"I looked around that room, saw the bitterness in their eyes and on their faces, and decided right then that life was too short to allow such feelings to dominate it."

DOCTORS, LAWYERS, AND OTHER SERVICES

Nowhere do singles need the help and support of their VIPs more than in dealing with the peripheral people in their lives: the doctors, lawyers, housepainters, car mechanics, and others who should be a part of every single's security system but who are sometimes more exploitive than helpful, especially toward women.

A set of guidelines thought through before your hour of need can avert real problems. The following list has evolved from tear-soaked experiences.

1. No matter who you are dealing with—doctor, lawyer, banker, broker, mechanic—reverence is inappropriate and can work to your disadvantage. Remember *you* are paying *them,* and unlike God, they expect to collect.
2. Shop around. Just as you would get three estimates if you're having your house painted, you should in-

terview three lawyers before getting a contested divorce and get three opinions before having an operation.

When Hannah G. was faced with a mastectomy, her family doctor sent her to a general surgeon, who told her nothing of the options open to her: a lumpectomy, which removes the malignant area from the breast; a modified mastectomy, which removes the breast alone; and the far more disfiguring radical surgery, which would remove not only the breast but the underlying muscle and lymph nodes. When she mentioned that she would like to get another opinion, her family doctor reminded her irritably that he had spent a good deal of time going over her X-rays and discussing her case.

On her own, Hannah persevered. She visited the cancer clinic of the state hospital, with the names of two doctors to see there. The two, it turned out, had opposing opinions, one believing in radical surgery in all cases, the other in the modified operation.

"When one of them came in to see me, he positioned his chair in front of the door so the other one couldn't get in. I felt I'd walked into the middle of a political in-fight and it increased my indecision—and my terror. I fled from them both."

Hannah then turned to her network of friends and located doctors they had used and liked. She asked these doctors to recommend specialists.

"It was like getting a fix," she said. "I went to see the specialists who got the most recommendations, and even though some turned cold when I told them I was getting other opinions, I thought my life and health were too important to me to be bothered by their reaction. I finally found a cancer surgeon I liked, who recommended a modified operation. Instead of taking six weeks to recover, I was back on the job in three."

3. Ask what the final charge will be and get the es-

60

timate in writing, a minimum and maximum amount to allow for flexibility if that seems fair.

4. Some lawyers will not give a firm estimate of their final fee. If you have one of these, ask what his hourly charges are and *insist* on having a monthly itemized statement.

5. Don't hesitate to bargain. Grace L. asked her divorce lawyer repeatedly how much his charges would be, but he only told her not to worry. When she got the final shattering bill, she showed it to a lawyer friend. Acting on his advice, she went to see the divorce attorney, checkbook in hand.

"I will pay you this moment if we can arrive at a figure I think is satisfactory, which is twenty percent less than your bill," she said.

After he had recovered from his astonishment, he burst out laughing and accepted, an agreement Grace thinks he would not have made had he believed he was entitled to every cent.

6. Search out as much information as you can. If you're getting a divorce, join singles groups and attend divorce seminars to better understand the legalities involved and to get the benefit of other singles' experience. If you are widowed, don't be pressured into hasty decisions. You have months to make them. Use that time to find out all you can about state laws governing inheritances.

When her children were small, Anne L. had agreed with her husband that his estate should be left in trust, with a bank and her mother-in-law named as co-trustees and co-executors. After his death, Anne, along with her son, now twenty-one, and her mother-in-law sat down at a table in the conference room of the law firm that was to settle the estate. Across from them sat the bank's representative, the junior partner assigned to her case by the law firm, the head of the firm's estate department, and a secretary.

"If I'd been all by myself, it could have been pretty intimidating," she said. "As matters developed, however, I just got mad. If my husband could have seen that arrogant lawyer and the bank's representative deciding on the disposition of our money almost as if we weren't there, he would have been furious. The senior lawyer would not even give us an estimate of his charges, and the bank's representative tried to shame us by implying that we were suspicious—and cheap, too."

Anne, however, was familiar with the inheritance laws of her state and knew that she could claim half of everything, trust or no trust.

"When I told them I thought I might elect against the will, the whole atmosphere of the meeting changed. When we left, the bank's representative even offered to underwrite our parking ticket."

In the week that followed, with the considerable help of her son and the cooperation of her mother-in-law, Anne persuaded both the bank and the law firm to withdraw, leaving her mother-in-law as sole executrix and trustee, thereby saving, she estimates, about $12,000.

7. These final words are reserved for dealings with divorce lawyers. Never view them as the father figures they sometimes appear. One man suggests that no lawyer should be asked or allowed to give advice on the equity of a settlement. "He'll always say it's not enough, if only to prolong the proceedings and make more money. His role should be that of a technician to advise his client of legalities," he said.

Another divorcée had an amicable settlement worked out with his wife until her lawyer said, "Well, Mrs. B., how do you know your husband is telling the truth?"

"He tried to make her think I was hiding my assets when I'd been out of a job for three months and was borrowing money to live on."

Still another man felt his troubled marriage would

have been saved had not his wife called their lawyer, a family friend, for advice.

"Just leave it to me," the attorney had told her, and started divorce proceedings.

For a male, service people present less of a problem. But for Harry, the people who come to clean his condominium are a constant aggravation. "They put wrong things in the dishwasher, mix my dark wool socks with white sheets when they do the washing, and turn the heat way down when they leave, even if a blizzard is raging outside. Sometimes they turn the air conditioning *and* the heat on when they leave. I switched from that cleaning service to a woman who'd been recommended. She was prompt and efficient for a while. I came home from work last Friday early and saw a stranger in my home. It was her daughter; she had the key to my unit and was watching television while ironing and there was a bottle of opened beer on the counter. The biggest problem for men like me is that I am not there during the day. If I need a plumber or repair person I have to have them on Saturday mornings."

However you choose them, keep them, or edit them out of your life, your friends and relations are perhaps the most important facet of living as a single. Unlike your children, they will not grow up and leave home. Unlike a spouse, there are enough of them that no one is critical to your happiness. In all their rich variety, friends enhance and delight the many facets of your personality as no one person, however close, could possibly do.

"You are what your environment is," one man said, "and your environment includes the people around you. When you're over fifty and single, you had better surround yourself with all the warm, kindly, down-to-earth people you can find."

CHAPTER 5

Broke But Not Poor
what to do about money

Money, like health, is often unappreciated until it's not there. For many single men and women, the end of their marriage is a double-barreled loss, bringing with it a sharply reduced income. Economizing at this age is sharply different from the economies of their younger years when they were moving up, not down, and when saving money was a challenge, even fun. Men who drove Mercedes had to trade them in for Chevvies and women with Baker furniture were cramming it into small apartments.

"When I was married in 1951, I was so proud of covering orange crates for nightstands with marbleized wallpaper," said one woman. "The thought of having to do that again now is demeaning. I also think it's demeaning to have to go out and find a job. It's one thing to open up a boutique as a fun pastime when your husband can carry you through the lean months and quite another to *have* to go out and seriously battle the competition from younger women in the job market."

One man in his fifties recalled taking his high school dates out in his dad's convertible for a hamburger and root-beer float at a drive-in and feeling very stud about it.

"Now just asking a woman out to dinner shoots my entertainment budget for the week," he said.

At this age, there are fewer years left in which to

recoup losses. Retirement looms alarmingly near, and the future for some people is terrifying. Money becomes a very important material and psychological factor.

Women whose husbands have always handled major financial matters often feel battered by unaccustomed bills and incomprehensible forms.

"I hated to open the mail," a widow said. "I never knew what sledge-hammer payment was coming due next."

Men, for their part, are sometimes alimony- and settlement-poor.

"My greatest fear in life is being poor again," said a man whose third wife had demolished his bank account. "I grew up in the Depression when my dad bought rubber insoles at Woolworth's to cover the holes in my shoes. I thought I'd made it big and now here I am again, economizing."

One of the major problems is the adjustment itself to less money, even if the situation is temporary.

A land developer whose income was in six figures suffered a two-year period after his divorce when his income fell to zero and he had to dip into his capital to subsist. He sold some of his furniture and his museum-quality chess set, and unabashedly told his dates that his income was depressed at the moment when he invited them to a home-cooked dinner or to attend the free lectures and events the community offered.

A woman spent her thousand-dollar savings on a new wardrobe to wear job-hunting. At her interviews she looked prosperous, which was her intention, but at home she was more than frugal. After she found a job, she sold her car and joined an office car pool. She dropped her country club membership, her season symphony tickets, and cut out all luxury purchases such as convenience foods at the grocery store, selecting instead fresh produce. She used the mail instead of the phone to communicate with her sons in college, took her lunch to work, and said no to some of the after-work bar stops with her co-workers.

It doesn't take long, other singles discovered, to learn new habits of budgeting when it's necessary. You can eliminate magazine subscriptions, set priorities on contributions to causes, eat out less, spend less on clothes, take a list to the grocery store and rigidly adhere to it, shut down charge accounts, and patronize "nearly new" shops.

"I was amazed," one said, "at how much money I used to fritter away. It doesn't *have* to cost that much to live."

One woman sat down with a calendar, circled the dates her major bills came due, and put aside money every month toward paying them. Another, buried in a blizzard of forms, bought a set of manila file folders and organized her finances.

Sometimes, in spite of all the economy measures, the gap between income and necessary spending widens at an alarming rate and a job becomes imperative for a single woman. After twenty-five or more years of bending to the irregularities of family living, she must suddenly develop habits of punctuality and grooming, planning and routine.

"The thought was terrifying," said a woman who hadn't worked in twenty-two years. "I'd read with mild curiosity about displaced homemakers. Now suddenly it was me. At the age of fifty-six with a long history of PTA to put into my résumé, where could I possibly get a job?"

Another resolutely squared her shoulders and concluded:

"I had to discipline myself to have faith in me and project it to a job out there. You can't cut yourself off at the pass before you start up."

Those women who were happiest stopped living in the past, when they were supported by their husbands, and attacked their new project—job-hunting—with vigor and enthusiasm, learning new ways to express themselves effectively in interviews, new skills that would make them of value in the job world. They got help from other women who were already employed, from books on speech and job-hunting, and from talking to husbands of women friends.

"My best friend's husband employs several dozen women in his business, so I queried him about the qualities an older woman should emphasize in an interview," recounted one. "I'd worked to raise money for the art museum, so I asked the chairman of the board if I could use him as a reference. I exploited every friendship, every contact. No one was safe."

Telling themselves that they were wiser, more stable, more experienced in dealing with people than were their younger competitors, the women went back to school to brush up on old skills or learn new ones. They took classes in accounting, real estate, secretarial skills, food, and fashion photography. Some worked as temporary office help to get the feel of the business world again before going after a job. One woman went out on as many interviews as she could, just to gain confidence.

"Your last interview may be for the job you really want, and you'll be ready," she said. "In the meantime, you'll see what women in the offices are wearing, so you can look the part. I found out, too, that companies are looking for good workers even if they are older.

Some used their age as a selling point.

"I just told the personnel director that I *had* to work. I had children to support and no husband. I was stable and I would stay, not be quitting when the drapes were paid for or to have a baby," said a computer programmer.

Others were told their age was okay.

"You're just right," the head of a real estate agency said to a fifty-year-old housewife. "You've raised a family and you know houses. You can talk to the woman, and it's the woman who buys the home."

They became aware of the image they were projecting and tried to appear confident, calm, a winner. A secretary said she made herself relax by pushing her thumb against her index finger, which kept her from thinking about herself.

"Don't overreact. Don't overplay," advised another.

Women are not the only ones who are out beating the bushes for work. A good number of the men we talked to lost their jobs about the same time they lost their wives. One of these, who honed the skill of job-hunting to its sharpest edge, was James B., who was divorced twice within six months. That same year, he looked up from his desk fifteen minutes before quitting time one afternoon to see the president of the company accompanied by the chairman of the board and the company attorney troop into his office. They presented him with a lengthy letter of explanation and told him that he was fired as vice-president.

"When I get emotional, my voice cracks, and it didn't," he said in retrospect. "I was so proud of me."

For the next three weeks, James rose early and went to his new "office," the public library, where he studied the books that dealt with the psychology of finding a job. Using the help of the librarian and the many references and periodicals, he made a list of all the companies that might be right for him, and wrote 150 individual letters of inquiry to the presidents or vice-presidents of each. He also wrote a personal profile of himself, putting down everything he had ever done in his life, not to send to prospective employers, but to build his own morale.

"If I'd gone right out to see people, my confidence would have been low, I would not have done my thinking and planning, and I would have squandered my best contacts," he said.

By the end of three weeks, he had psyched himself up

69

for his first interview. The employer told him that he was much more positive than the average applicant, but the job went to someone else.

Every day James set himself goals: so many phone calls in priority order, so many letters, so much reading, so many interviews. Before each interview he committed to memory the critical statistics about a company and the names of company officers. Sometimes he found himself sitting in the personnel office next to truck drivers and high school graduates, waiting to be interviewed by a young man or woman half his age.

He went to see every contact he had. If his contact knew of no opening, perhaps he knew someone who might know of one, and could James use his name when he called? At the end of nearly three months and fifty interviews there were still no offers, and he was beginning to feel disheartened. As a last-ditch try, he went back over the interviews he had had, called the people who had been the most responsive, and found the opening he had been looking for. The personnel director had forgotten all about him, but James refreshed his memory and was hired.

As a financial controller in a medium-sized business, he makes less than he did before, but the future in advancement and salary looks better.

"I held out for what I really wanted," he said with satisfaction, "and I got it."

Others, too, found what they wanted, and most had several offers.

"Impossible to find work after fifty? Bullshit!" said a Philadelphia accountant who decided at fifty-one that he wanted a change of scenery. He had a friend send him a yellow-pages phone book from San Francisco, sent out 500 résumés to businesses there, received ten positive replies, packed up his bags, and went West.

One woman found a position as a steel salesperson that provided on-the-job training. Age was no barrier, since the employer's mother was doing outstandingly well in the same position. Another went to work for a small company, believing it would offer a variety of experience, which it did.

"I learned to do everything: display ads, makeup, meeting customers," she said. "When I'm ready, I'll move on to something better."

Another changed from her first job with a small business to that of communications specialist in a bank, which offered more money and benefits. Still another found work as an executive secretary with an oil company, where she was trained in oil and land leasing and acquisitions.

What they all did—men and women—was summed up by a diminutive but determined secretary:

"I just kept looking until I found the job I wanted, the salary I wanted, and a boss who felt I was competent, even though I was older."

Once employed, the older singles discovered that they could not only hold their own, but they could get more done than many younger employees. Unencumbered with young children or spouses, they channeled their energies, enthusiasm, dedication into their work. They were flexible, free to travel or take an assignment on a moment's notice. They were more relaxed, without the pressure of domestic problems. Their very age bespoke experience, judgment, responsibility, credibility.

"I find it easier to enforce library policies. My decisions are almost always accepted, and I know I'm a more effective supervisor."

"I know about not getting discouraged. The job isn't nearly the drain on me."

"I'm not afraid of making mistakes. I know I'm going

to make them, along with many wise decisions. I don't expect perfection of myself so I'm willing to take risks."

"With maturity, you learn to let everyone do his own thing and to become uncritical, analytical but not censoring."

No effort is too great for some, particularly those like Beulah B., who works in a competitive field. A real estate salesperson, Beulah finds babysitters, cleaning women, and yard boys for her clients. She has vacuumed, dusted, washed windows herself—anything to make a house more presentable.

Once she helped a husband decorate a house, sending samples of material to his wife in another town. When the woman arrived, she was able to walk into a home, sight unseen, that was completely decorated and ready to live in.

Nancy C., who holds a job in Salt Lake City with an affiliate of one of the largest advertising companies in the country, started out by writing releases for food editors. As new accounts came in, she asked if she could handle them; and the boss, discovering her capabilities, let her. Once, when a young account executive who had been sent out from New York couldn't cope with the rural backgrounds of the clients and refused to do the job, Nancy volunteered and got it. Today, having weathered a cutback period in which fifty-five of the seventy-three people in the agency lost their jobs, she holds the position of account executive, one of nine people in the company to make all major decisions.

"At fifty-five, I'm the oldest lady at the agency," she said, "and still going strong."

Some singles supplement their income with business ventures, beginning modestly and expanding. One such is Julie B., whose only financial asset after her husband's estate was settled was her house in Boston, which she sold, getting enough for the equity to buy a duplex. By renting one side,

she was able to deduct half of all depreciation and maintenance costs from her income tax and to live rent-free as she
built up her equity to a point where she could sell the duplex
and buy a five-unit property. Meanwhile, she set about
learning to become a landlord, taking classes in real estate,
reading books.

"Knowing the ropes is the name of the game for anyone who is in business for himself. I also have a job, since
most rental properties generate no income for three to four
years."

She has learned to show apartments to advantage,
screen tenants, write rental agreements, collect and bank the
rents, and make minor repairs herself.

"There are marvelous how-to-do-it books," she says.
"If a man can read a book and do it, so can I."

Charles B., who at seventy-two has operated his own
appliance-repair service since he was in his late forties, says:

"The most important thing in starting your own business is to find something you like to do, then keep plugging
and watch it grow." Even though he restricts his service to
one make of machine in one area in town, his biggest
problem is keeping his business small enough to maintain his
leisurely living pace.

A woman in her middle sixties carved out her own job,
teaching survival-skill classes to retirees in Michigan, showing them how to deal with Social Security, crime, inheritance
laws, money, nutrition, and death. Another, tired of
teaching exercise classes at the Y for a pittance, canvassed
high-rent apartments and now takes exercise to the tenants
at a high hourly rate. Still another woman brushed up her
typing skills, advertised in newspapers and college bulletins,
and soon had more work than she could handle—term
papers from students, local authors' manuscripts, legal
work—enough to support herself and two teenagers very adequately. And if you like adventure, you might want to

follow the course of the lady who kicked over the traces, sold her belongings, and went mountain climbing in the Himalayas and the Andes, exploring in Ethiopia and the Sahara with expeditions. To finance her trips, she works at temporary jobs on the docks in California or as caretaker for a ski lodge in Vermont.

As a result of their freedom and newfound abilities to make and manage money, the attitudes of many singles toward it have changed. Some said they felt less anxiety about money, freer to take risks, more at liberty to spend even with a lessened income.

"My lifestyle is less expensive, and I can probably do without many expensive habits I thought were necessary to my identity before."

"Possessions can become a drag... my values have changed."

"I find other ways besides spending to make me feel good about myself."

"I can now gamble on a business venture or an idea without an 'I told you so' if it doesn't work out."

"I like the security of knowing what my financial status is even if it's stringent and quite inflexible. I was in the dark about it for twenty-seven years."

"I have been delighted to find I'm a good money manager. I allow myself more material things in life because I know that I have paid my bills and can afford them. I've even been able to assist my children in college."

Part of being a good money manager is a long-range money plan such as that started by a retired government worker at the age of fifty—which, she says, is not soon enough. She started a savings plan, bought a small home, a new car, and had them paid for by the time she was ready to retire at sixty-two. During that period, she bought everything with the idea that it would be for her comfort when she was older. Now, at sixty-seven, she pays cash for everything to avoid interest charges and keeps very little money on hand.

"I found out a long time ago that if I have cash in my purse, I will buy things I don't need," she said.

Another retiree who had planned just as carefully invested her modest savings in certificates of deposit at 8.5 percent. She converted her basement into an apartment furnished with castoff but good-looking furniture and now gets monthly rent from that, along with the security of a man in the house.

Today she has put it all together with her pension, Social Security, and insurance and is *"Glad, glad, glad"* not to have to get up every morning and go to work.

"I've done a good life's work," she smiled, "and now I'm enjoying the fruits of my labors."

CHAPTER 6

The Look
how to create your own image

When Mike P., who operates a crane, goes skiing and someone asks him what he does for a living, he loves to look the questioner straight in the eye and say he's president of a bank. Nobody dreams of doubting him. That's because Mike, at fifty-two, in excellent shape, with commanding posture and well-tailored ski clothes, looks the part.

Today any man or woman can look the part of a bank president or whatever he or she pleases. It may take some thought and effort and a little bit of time, but all the fixings are available to make you, over fifty though you may be, look better than you've ever looked in your life: more vital, more successful, even handsomer or more beautiful.

Many singles came upon the scene in flabby, overweight condition brought on by nervous, unhappy nibbling or long-established habits of self-neglect. With regular programs of diet and exercise, they improved not only their figures and muscle tone but also their zest for living and their self-image. You can too.

EXERCISE

When you get older, your measurements may be the same, but they are lower. It all hangs down: breasts, stomachs, fanny, upper arms, and chin. So exercise should be tailored to defy the pull of gravity on these areas. Bicycling uphill does it for everything. So does cross-country skiing, swimming, tennis, racquetball, squash. Whatever you do, you should do it regularly and vigorously or supplement with indoor exercises like these:

The Chin and Neck Lift. Lie on bed or table, hands grasping the sides, head hanging over the edge. Slowly inhale while raising your head up and forward until your chin touches your collarbone, then slowly exhale as you let your head return to its original position. Do this three times the first day, increasing two times each day, until you can do it nine times.

The Thrust (for tuning up abdomen, fanny, and sex life). Stand in front of a mirror with feet about eighteen inches apart, hands on your waist with elbows bent. Bend knees a bit. Grip anus tight and thrust pelvis forward. Release. Start with eight thrusts the first day. Add a few each day until you're thrusting thirty times.

The Cross-Country Ski Swing (for firming upper arms, legs, waist, and midtorso). Stand in front of a mirror with right foot about eighteen inches in front of left foot, weight of the body centered over feet. Reach forward with left hand, as if holding a ski pole, while reaching back with right hand, as if holding ski pole. Now reverse the hands and feet, jumping while you do it. Jump four times while you inhale, four times while you exhale. Repeat the series of four six times the first day. Add a few each day until you're jumping eighty times, resting as needed.

Bicycle-on-the-Floor (for firming upper thighs and stomach). Lie on your back with arms alongside body. Take a deep breath. Raise both legs slightly off the floor. With left leg in this position, bend right leg toward chest, then reverse the position, bending left leg toward chest. Legs should never touch the floor. Bend each leg twenty times to start, working up to sixty.

The Plough (to keep spine limber and flexible, tone legs, and improve circulation). Lie on the floor with arms alongside your body, palms down. Raise your legs and swing them over your head, keeping your knees straight, until your toes touch the floor as nearly as possible. Hold this position while you count to ten, then slowly lower hips and legs back to beginning position. Do this two times the first day, increasing one time each day until you can do it six times.

DIET

Regular, vigorous exercise—and we're talking about breathing hard and sweating—pays a second dividend: it decreases your appetite. If, after following your regimen, you still have a problem with overeating, try these suggestions from singles who have shaped up:

1. Clear your house, office, car, of every irresistible morsel: salty snacks, cookies—all the "grabbables." Like Emma J., the home-based typist, who followed this course to a svelte size 10, you may be surprised at how many snack breaks you take. On the first day of her program, Emma reached more than a dozen times for a cracker or a potato chip that wasn't there. By midafternoon, she was rummaging in the back corners of cupboards for overlooked goodies. But by the third day, her compulsion had vanished.

2. Make each meal a ceremony. Take your diet dinner to the table, sit down, and make it last. Have with you a good book, and if you're still hungry when you've finished, don't leave your seat, but read until your food has begun to digest and satisfied your appetite.

3. Take small bites, and while you're chewing them—slowly—put your fork down on your plate instead of reloading it.

4. Try chopsticks.

5. Enjoy the sensation of eating. You may not have

really tasted a bite of food since before the days of the car pool. Roll your food over your tongue, listen to it crunch, feel it slide down your throat. Savor it.

6. If you think you don't snack, but you're still overweight, put an equal quantity of everything you nibble into a container and check the collection at the end of the day.

Dieting is done in your head. If you can adopt the attitude toward mealtime that one determined single did, you will have the problem licked. She looks on meals as her next opportunity to take off a few more ounces—as a time not to eat less but to lose more.

START AT THE TOP

Exercise and diet are an excellent defense against wrinkles, because they improve the tone of your skin. So are moisturizers and lotions. Besides dryness and poor skin tone, however, there are other, less obvious wrinkle-makers—like pillows. The next time you snuggle into your pillow, notice what it's doing to your face: pushing your cheek up under your eye, stretching the skin away from the side of your nose. One of the most wrinkle-free fifty-five-year-old women in our survey has not slept on a pillow since she was twenty. Are you a face feeler? Do you lean your face on your hand, with your elbow on the table? Ask your children or grandchildren, who will *love* to do it, to imitate your facial mannerisms over a ten-minute period to see which ones might be prime line-producers.

Besides its carcinogenic dangers, consider what smoking does to promote wrinkles around your mouth when you purse your lips to take a puff and again to blow it out.

Almost everyone over the age of fifty has considered at one time or another, even if only in the dark back corners

80

The Look

of his or her mind, the possibility of a facelift. Brenda K. was one who had never quite gotten up the nerve. Brenda's pretty, heart-shaped face was marred by dark, baggy circles under her eyes that had built up during the sleepless nights before her divorce. They were so bad that she hated to get up in the morning and face her mirror.

"I felt so tortured, so ugly, so unwanted," she said.

When a friend suggested an eyelift and a doctor to do it, she took a week off from work and had the operation. Five days later the stitches came out and, the following night at a party with old friends who knew nothing of the surgery, everyone marveled at how wonderfully rested Brenda looked.

Maxine J., on the other hand, went all the way and had a complete lift. Five months later she still had to turn her whole torso in order to turn her head. Three months after that her neck was still stiff, and an antibiotic cream she had been using around her eyes had caused a rash. The doctor never indicated to Maxine the degree of discomfort she would experience, nor the length of time it would take her to recover. Even so, she would do it again, and will in another eight to ten years when it becomes necessary, so happy is she now to be able to pass a mirror and feel good about it.

Others in our survey, who have not taken the step, find comfort in knowing that if things get too bad and they want a surgical tuck here and there, the ultimate remedy is there for the buying.

The nicest present Marcia S. ever received was the return of her smile. Struggling to make ends meet in raising her three teenagers, Marcia had thought she could get by without replacing a missing molar if she just didn't smile too much or too broadly.

Last Christmas, Marcia's dearest friend said he wanted to give her something special, something that would improve her self-confidence, perhaps even help her get the job she was after. It was, of course, a bridge, which did all the things for Marcia that her friend predicted.

If *you* need a bridge, make the sacrifice and enjoy the same benefits. It will also support and prolong the life of your remaining teeth.

And if you have no remaining teeth, or anticipate having none, there is no need to feel self-conscious about it today. Great improvements have been made in dentures. They don't have to click, a nervous habit that can be overcome. While exactly perfect teeth would be a dead giveaway for dentures, there is no reason why your new teeth, made to your order, should not be better-looking than your old ones, especially if the old ones were discolored or unsightly. In fact, why not take two pairs, an extra one for trips in case something happens to the one you're wearing, like losing it in the surf.

If you *do* have remaining teeth, take care of them, because the cost of preventing deterioration is one-seventh the cost of repairing the damage. It's worth five minutes of your time each day to floss and brush, following the instructions your dentist will give you at your six-month checkup. Until you learn to clean them properly, some dentists recommend a disclosing agent, a tablet that dissolves in your mouth and coats the plaque you missed, so it will show up under a bright light.

Glasses today are something you put on, not take off, because they can be a real cosmetic device. Do you have a long, narrow face? Try large, round frames to shorten it. A square jaw? An aviator shape may be for you. With a galaxy of colors to choose from, use them to complement your own hair and skin tones or to create an illusion: thick black rims for a scholarly look, tinted lenses for a slight air of mystery or to camouflage crow's feet.

GROOMING

Both men and women in our survey stressed grooming as one of the most important features they look for in those of the opposite sex. For a totally immaculate image that tells the world you think well of you, develop some habits that are as much a part of your everyday living as brushing your teeth.

Brush your clothes, particularly if they've been hanging in the closet collecting dust on the shoulders.

Check for spots in a good light with your glasses on.

Permanent press does not mean never press. A touchup on collar, cuffs, and shirtfronts turns passable into impeccable.

Wash, not just behind your ears but inside the wells.

Check for greaselines at the collar of your shirt and grayness at the cuffs.

When you take your clothes off, inspect for rips and loose buttons. Don't *ever* think a small rip in an inconspicuous seam is not going to show.

Keep the creases in your pants razor-edge-sharp.

Take off your jacket and fold it neatly on the seat of the car while you're driving.

Make a fold in your skirt or pants at the lap line while you're driving, to avoid a mass of wrinkles when you arrive.

Keep your car immaculate. It speaks for you.

Polish your shoes. Keep the heels straight and in repair.

Use plenty of moisturizer on hands and feet, and keep the nails on both clean and well trimmed.

ACCESSORIES

Back in the forties, fashion models followed the Rule of Ten. Standing before a mirror, fully dressed, they counted each accessory: hat or veil, gloves, corsage, long-stemmed umbrella, giving each a value of one. For the tastefully dressed, the total score should never be greater than ten.

Today the accessories have changed—gone are the hats, the flowers, and usually the gloves. But the Rule of Ten, after falling into obscurity for a long while, is coming back. It's a good rule to follow for men as well as for women.

THE RULE OF TEN FOR WOMEN

Shoes, one color	1
More than one color, add	1
Decorated with bow or ornament, add	1
Stockings, textured or colored	1
Ensemble, one color	1
More than one color, add	1
For each decoration (gold belt) or contrast (ruffled collar), add	1
Accessories	
Earrings	1
Bracelet	1
Brooch	1
Necklace or neck ornament	1
Colored hair ornament	1
Scarf or shawl	1
Hat	1
With ornament or decoration, add	1
Handbag, one color	1
More than one color, add	1
Other, for each item add	1
Gloves, one color	1
More than one color, add	1

THE RULE OF TEN FOR MEN

Shoes, one color	1
More than one color, add	1
Socks, patterned or any color except black or dark gray	1
Suit, two- or three-piece	1
More than one color, except chalk or pin stripe, add	1
Sport coat	1
Pants	1
Belt	1
Shirt, solid color	1
Striped, add	1
Patterned or printed, add	1
Tie, ascot, or kerchief	1
Jewelry	
Studs	1
Cufflinks	1
Necklace	1
Bracelet	1
Other	1
Hat	1
Gloves	1

THE RULE OF TEN FOR MEN AND WOMEN

No points for wristwatch, tassels of same color or small buckles on shoes. If the total points add up to 10 or under, you can be confident you haven't overdone it. If over 10, subtract something. *If in doubt, leave it off.*

FOR WOMEN ONLY

If you've been a trendy dresser all through your marriage, use Laszlo products, and have updated your hair style within the last year, this section may not be for you. But if, in the course of raising a family and running to the grocery store, you have lost touch with the world of fashion and fragile, pampered beauty, read on. Other single women who have rediscovered or never lost track of it would love to help put together a new you.

One of them is Toni S., a former socialite. After her divorce Toni had to scale down her wardrobe budget from $12,000 a year to $1000, but she still looks like a million dollars, because she knows the tricks.

Toni thinks you should start with your hair. There's no such thing any more, she says, as hair you can't do a thing with. And that's lucky, because your hair is the most important thing about the way you look. If you don't believe it, says Toni, picture a woman in a $21,000 Russian sable coat with her hair wet. There are conditioners to give your hair body, protein packs for damaged or weakened hair. You can even use stale champagne, if you have some around the house, as a super-setting lotion. No longer need you sleep on a headful of rollers or bobby pins; you can blow your hair dry or roll it up on modern-day electric curling irons at the last minute.

Before doing any of these things, however, Toni thinks you should find a good hairdresser, because a good cut is basic to everything else. Leaf through newspapers and magazines (*not* the fashion magazines) for pictures of real live people who look the way you would like to look. Clip the pictures and take them along, or take one of yourself wearing a haircut you really liked.

Don't let your hairdresser bully you. Finding she

could no longer afford her French stylist, Toni went shopping for someone new. Her first try turned out to be an authoritative artiste, whose very manner discouraged participation. Hardly had she begun to tell him that she didn't want the haircut of the month that was pictured on the wall, than he began snipping.

"That's just what I'm giving you," he said cheerfully. "You'll love it!"

In a voice that was firm and calm and over fifty, Toni said clearly:

"Stop. I don't think we're understanding each other."

The stylist stopped in midsnip, listened as she explained what she wanted, and did as she asked. Once they understood each other, she stayed with him because he knew what to do with her fine, silky blond hair, which so many hairdressers in her past had complained about.

Toni thinks you should take a good look at your hair style. Have you changed it in the past five years? Should you? Some women, like Princess Grace of Monaco, wear the same classic style through the years, a little tighter or fuller, longer or shorter to make it contemporary. You might, like her, have the style that is just right for you. But if you're still wearing the high, teased-and-lacquered, back-combed coiffure every well-heeled matron used to wear, or an Italian-boy cut that looks as if you were on your way to the grocery store, then think about adopting simpler, less contrived lines that have fullness and movement. Try growing it to chin length and having it cut bluntly so that it swings when you walk and the breeze can move it.

When Toni takes a trip, she questions her hairdresser relentlessly beforehand about how to set her hair. She finds out what size rollers to use and exactly where to put them—in her case, on the diagonal because it makes a prettier, less boxy line—how much tension to put on her hair as it's being rolled up (wet hair stretches, so it should not be pulled too tight or there will be breakage). She carries her own conditioner and her own tint with her.

When she gets to Europe, or Buenos Aires, or Hong Kong, she looks at the local hairdresser with her misty blue eyes and says:

"You're going to hate me because I want you to do so many special things. But I've lived with me for so long that I know exactly what it takes to look the way I want."

Then she gives very specific instructions.

"You can't expect a man or woman who's never laid eyes on you before to know you the way your hairdresser in Omaha does," she said.

Toni believes a woman's best friends, in maintaining her cut and hair set, are still old-fashioned bobby pins. Electric curlers are a boon for last-minute emergencies, but they can be drying if used regularly, and those that have spiky rollers can split hairs. Approach blow-drying cautiously, because it doesn't produce as strong and lasting a set. The mother of the bride at a wedding we went to recently looked adorable in her Prince Valiant hairdo (which must be blown dry) when the reception began, but three hours later her coiffure had drooped and she had aged. On a younger woman, limp hair can look romantic; when you're older, a hairdo that stays perky is more becoming.

If you think growing old gracefully means letting your hair grow gray, we think you're wrong. There are women with beautiful, sparkling gray hair, but we have found men over fifty to prefer sparkling other colors, and there are so many to choose from. A good start is to visit your local wig salon and try them all, the way Katy T., a Boston schoolteacher, did. Katy always thought she'd have more fun as a blonde, but quickly changed her mind when she put on ten years with the Jean Harlow hair of her girlhood dreams.

What she settled for, and happily, was a brightened-up version of her own hair, in a lighter shade.

Lighter is better when coloring your hair. Dark hair casts down-dragging shadows, while a lighter color gives your face a lift.

But whatever the color, whatever the cut, the most important thing about your hair is to keep it shiny-clean. Wash the day *before* it becomes necessary.

MAKEUP

After fifty, you should be doing more with your hair but less with your makeup. When Midge B. was married to her city's foremost trial lawyer, she thought nothing of spending $150 for an expensive line of "treatment" that pampered her delicate porcelain skin. Now she follows the same procedure outlined by manufacturers of "the treatment" but with supermarket ingredients and dime-store cosmetics—and her skin is still delicate, still porcelain. Here's what she does.

Donning a shower cap to protect her hair, she spreads baby oil all over her face and neck. She fills the washbasin with water, dips in a bar of mild soap, then rubs it gently across her face and neck. With soapy, wet hands, she slides very lightly *over* the surface of her skin, rinsing by splashing water sixty times on her face and neck without touching it, and patting it dry with a towel. The point, of course, is to avoid moving the skin or muscles since such movement encourages wrinkles and breaks down tissues. This splashdown happens twice a day.

Afterward Midge applies moisturizer with her fingers—and who's to say, besides the manufacturers, that sky-high-priced brands are any better than Pond's from Woolworth's? Certainly not Midge. She blots off the excess moisturizer with a linen blotter, which can be bought by the pad at the drugstore and is less abrasive than Kleenex. She uses these same blotters during the day to blot her face, since her skin is oily, making it unnecessary to redo her makeup.

Midge puts her foundation on with a cotton ball, feathering it into her neck so there is no sharp line at the jaw. At fifty-seven, she thinks it should be sheer in texture, a beige rather than peach or pink, which with the rouge an older woman usually needs would give too much color. She applies her rouge in tiny, multiple dots, blending them with her third finger, the weakest, to insure a light touch. Powder goes on in the conventional T—across the forehead and down the nose and chin, with a clean cotton ball used to dust off the excess.

And there, for a fraction of any manufacturer's cost, you have, if not "the" treatment, a pretty good substitute.

After fifty, we think women should avoid false eyelashes and the Minnie Mouse look. It's all right—good, in fact—to put on lots of mascara, so long as your lashes don't become beaded or clumped together, a hazard that can be avoided by buying a tiny eyelash comb and brush at the dime store. Watch out for mascara packaged in cylindrical containers, which in your warm bathroom forms a culture for bacteria that can be harmful to your eyes. Cake mascara, though a little harder to find, is still preferred by the pros because the consistency can be controlled and it can create the illusion of thicker eyelashes. Apply coats of it, if you want to, letting one eye dry while you do the other.

Be careful of eyeshadow. Forget the ice blues and Mediterranean greens of yesteryear, and go after softer, paler tones. Avoid, at all costs, frosted shadow, which catches and cakes and glistens within the lines, and if your lids are wrinkled, don't use eyeshadow at all. You *should* use a soft taupe shade lightly beneath your eyebrows if the pads of your eyes are beginning to droop. It will make them less obtrusive. If you use eyeliner at all (and we are not enthusiastic about it), it should be a very narrow line, delicately done. Finally, brush your brows with powdered color, stand back and see that your eyes still have it.

Light and bright is the rule for lipstick, and it should be applied with a brush. You may have to shop for one that does not "cry"—seep into the vertical grooves of the skin above and below your mouth. Try half a dozen if you must; this action varies with the individual.

Finally, if you can't help it, hide it. Use cover cream for brown spots or a mixture of lemon juice and sea salt to bleach them; cover cream, too, for tennis or swimming if you have spidery viens on your legs; long sleeves if you don't like your arms; pants suits if you don't like your legs; high collars, a pretty scarf, or three or four strands or pearls if you've got a crepey neck, colorless nail polish if you don't want to draw attention to your hands.

If you are newly single, you may have to begin building a wardrobe from scratch, depending upon your lifestyle during your marriage. A closetful of cocktail dresses and tennis shorts is not going to make it in the business world. But just because you've got less money to spend doesn't mean you can't still shop in the designer salons, even if you don't buy there. They are great places in which to saturate yourself with what's new, drench yourself in taste and style so you will make a better choice in the budget shop if you have to go there to spend your money.

A good designer ensemble, however, the cost of which can be prorated over endless years, with alterations to make it contemporary, is a good investment—particularly if it has four or five pieces made of the same fabric. For good fabric, fit, design, and workmanship, along with a perky, youthful look, try Geoffrey Beene's "Beene Bag" line, Bill Blass's "Blassport", Ralph Lauren, Calvin Klein, Bill Haire for Friedricks, Anne Klein, Nipon, and Kasper for J.L. Sport. If their styles are not classic, they are forerunners enough that you will get several years of wear for your money.

Or you might do what Ginnie L. did. She found a super seamstress, who copied an old Anne Klein skirt she'd bought a few years back and stitched up a Valentino-styled scarf in the same fabric. That's what she was wearing when she later ran into an old friend, an editor for *Vogue,* who commented, "Oh, Ginnie, you always look so smart!"

With an ensemble and a dress, you will have a foundation wardrobe on which to build, one you can expand with separates. Separates are youthful, casual, versatile, and if you hit a season when the styles don't look good on *you,* they will help you bridge the year.

Buying a chic outfit, however, is not enough. Becky C., one of the best-dressed women in our survey, believes in fit—totally perfect fit. With a relative pittance to spend after her divorce, she wondered how she would ever make the scene at the first major ball she was invited to attend after becoming single. She dreaded meeting her husband there with his new and younger girlfriend, seeing their old friends, knowing they were thinking "Poor thing." So she searched the city with determination to find a gown that outclassed her budget. Finally, in the bridal salon of a department store, for a bargain price, she discovered a dress that could have passed for a designer original—but two sizes too big. Becky bought it, and spent the money to have it altered—almost a third the cost of the dress—so that the fit was impeccable. The day after the dance, on the social page of the newspaper, in full view of the world and her ex-husband, it was cited as *the* dress of the evening.

Becky warns that if you're planning to lose five pounds, lose first and then go shopping. Even though some department stores are removing their three-way mirrors to conserve space, insist on finding one somewhere in the store and looking long and hard at the back view. If you're making a major purchase, ask to have the alterations lady come in and look at you to make sure there is nothing that needs improvement. Don't be satisfied to have only one sleeve or pantleg pinned up, because your arms and legs are seldom identical.

The women we talked to who looked smashing had made a study of color. One of them even bought seven inexpensive dresses in seven different colors, listened carefully for comments when she wore them, and noted the effect of each on her hair and skin at different times of day in different lights. The same kind of experimentation can be done with scarves, which can add vitality and youth to your neutral important suit. When you buy a new outfit, buy a scarf at the same time. Build a wardrobe of scarves and learn to tie them—the scarf department may even have a free, giveaway booklet, or you can check the public library. A well-draped scarf is the older woman's best friend.

If you can have only two pairs of shoes, have a beautiful pair of loafers and a beautiful pair of pumps. Look at any of the super-classic designers: the image they project includes a shoe that's a pump. It elongates the line of the leg and foot. It's uncluttered, simple, classic. Stay with medium heels, unless you're going to be sitting down a lot. They allow a youthful, swingy walk.

Economize on your pantyhose; the best of them can give you runs for your money. Some of the best-dressed women we talked to wore dime-store pantyhose. Just be sure you buy a brand that fits the crotch so there is less strain on the nylon. No need for panties. They only make an ugly dent in your leg and spoil the line of your slacks.

But do wear other kinds of underwear—it can be a big morale booster. One woman thought it was kind of fun to be known for a color and wore pale blue underwear underneath everything. A lot of younger women today are not wearing underwear at all. They take off their clothes and there they are. At our age, we think it's a lot sexier if you take off your clothes and there is a beautiful slip.

For precision grooming, "keepers," the little bands that hold shoulder straps in place, add little to the cost of a garment and insure feminine neatness.

On the outside, we would like to think of every single woman over fifty wearing a fur coat in the winter, but if you can't afford a good one—and we don't think you should settle for anything skimpier than stroller length—at least get a coat with a fur collar, which has a very softening effect against the face. We think men react to fur the way they do to beautiful underwear and beautiful jewelry. For a one-and-only coat, buy a plain, one-color or camel's hair with a raglan sleeve, or one cut large enough for you to wear over a suit. You need gloves only in cold weather, and they could be pigskin, silk-lined if you like the luxury.

That leaves your handbag, which doesn't have to match anything any more. In fact, it's smarter if it doesn't. So buy a good one, sleek and expensive, and wear it with everything. Avoid the old-lady look the oversized organizer gives. One lady lost a pair of gloves in hers and couldn't find them for over a week, even though she knew they were in there somewhere.

THE SEXY EXTRAS

These, we believe, can create an image of fastidious femininity that will make men want to treat a woman accordingly. Here they are:

1. Lacy lingerie under a high-necked, but semi-sheer blouse.

2. Cashmere sweaters, especially white, that look innocent but cast interesting shadows.

3. Silk shirts that button (or unbutton) down the front.

94

4. Floor-length nightgowns.
5. Short fingernails.
6. Trench coats.
7. A clean, uncluttered handbag.
8. Real or real-looking jewelry, especially pearls.
9. Sunglasses.
10. Soft, well-groomed feet.
11. A clean and healthy look.
12. Neck openings that allow you to slip in and out of your clothes gracefully without mussing your hair.
13. Waistlines.
14. A clean, casual, sportive look.

FOR MEN ONLY

With the decline of macho prejudice it's no longer a reflection on your male image to take an interest in your appearance, even to having your hair styled, curled, and dyed in a salon that once catered only to women. Now it's possible to buy the same youth preservatives women have always used in wrappings that are designed for men.

Stock up on moisturizer, since older skin is usually drier and more prone to wrinkles. You can buy lotion and lubricants at any drug store, in musky herbal or various woodsy scents.

Fragrance, a male tradition that reaches back into history, is making a comeback in after-shave lotions and balms as well as in cologned splash or friction lotion that is sprayed or rubbed all over the body after showering. But be careful. One of the most objectionable mistakes a man can make, according to the women we interviewed, is too much scent. A retired Marine officer in our survey decided to find out about fragrance from the horse's mouth while stationed in France and went to visit perfume factories there. The same odor that is subtle on one person, he learned, can explode into suffocating sweetness on another, so when he tries a new scent, he applies it sparingly and checks it out with his girlfriend, who has a sharper sense of smell.

But no fragrance can substitute for cleanliness. Men usually have oilier skin than women and perspire more, so they need to take more baths and showers. *No* man can afford not to use a deodorant.

Even cosmetics are creeping into men's medicine cabinets. Try a bronzer for a slightly tanned and healthy look. If you have a blemish, use a cover-up cream. Clean, well-groomed nails are as important for a man as for a woman. Why not get a manicure while you're having a haircut—with buffed, not polished nails? Better still, get your girlfriend to give you a manicure—it's soothing, sensual, sexy. Perhaps, in exchange, you could give her a rubdown with warmed oil.

More hair grows in noses and ears as you get older. The most immaculate man in our survey carries a small pair of scissors in his pocket, and when he finds a mirror in a good light, clips them out, along with the stray and wiry hairs that grow from his eyebrows.

Other facial hair, however, can be an effective cosmetic device. A beard will cover up a receding chin, a mustache lessen the impact of an overly large nose, sideburns add width to a narrow face.

If you've got a fine, thick, Kennedy-style shock of gray hair, take it to the best barber you can find (he will usually be in a women's beauty salon) and tip him well. After you leave, give it a little push in front with your fingers for a more casual look.

If you have almost no hair at all, don't comb a few strands over the top; just wear it as it is. Not one woman we talked to said she minded a bald head, and some even liked it. Thanks to Telly Savalas and Yul Brynner, it's got a good image.

The Look

One of the best-dressed men-about-town we talked to looks not for a clerk but for a clothier when he goes shopping. The clothier is the one who knows his business, who can look you over appraisingly and come up with the right color and style. When you've found one, stick with him. He will save you time and money and make you look your best.

Such a clothier is Clark H., fifty-four, who runs "the" clothing store for men in a midwestern city of two million people. Clark claims he can make *any* man over the age of fifty look like the chairman of the board. Here's the basic wardrobe if money is limited. It starts with a conservative, soft-shouldered suit in Oxford gray or navy. A chalk stripe, which can be worn for business or evening, projects the very most successful image; your second suit should be a solid color. In addition, a navy-blue sport coat and a second one, if you can afford it, in tweed, both worn with gray flannel slacks, will provide all the versatility you need. Your belt, in either brown or black, should match your shoes.

Don't wear polyester leisure suits. Clark emphasizes dark colors because they are slenderizing and don't show spots as readily as lighter colors, nor do they show wrinkles as much.

The most masculine shirts a man can own are white, blue, or yellow cotton Oxford cloth with a long sleeve. They can be worn anytime, anywhere. For a planned careless look, leave the top button or two open—never more—tie a silk square around your neck, and catch it with a metal ring. You'll have a mannish, neat, sportive look, far more virile than a print or patterned sport shirt could ever give you. Unless you're very slender, don't wear knits, and leave European-cut shirts to the very young.

Wearing conservative, solid-color clothes, you can express your individuality with your necktie, but not with a tie clip or tac.

For shoes, buy a plain-toe or wingtip and a loafer in either black or brown. Your socks should all be knee-length black, not sagging at the ankle and not showing skin.

Instead of an overcoat, wear a handsome raglan-sleeve beige raincoat. If you live in a cold climate and really need an overcoat, get a basic herringbone or classic polo coat, either single or double-breasted camel's hair. If you wear a hat, it should be a soft, crushable, tweedy type, not felt. Gloves should be simple gray, brown, or black calf.

Stay away from jewelry except for cufflinks or perhaps one simple, understated, meaningful piece, such as a family ring, a small St. Christopher's medal or gold coin around the neck.

For extra sex appeal, we offer the following:

1. Sweaters over open-neck Oxford-cloth shirts.
2. Shirtcuffs that show below the coat sleeves.
3. Jockey shorts.
4. Pants that fit.
5. Clean fingernails.
6. Smooth, unscaly feet.
7. Trimmed toenails.
8. Sunglasses.
9. A barely visible pendant, worn under the shirt, or thin gold link bracelet.
10. Crossed legs, the ankle of one leg resting on the knee of the other.
11. Clean, ungreasy, touchable hair.
12. Antique studs and cufflinks.
13. Handsome leather slip-on shoes.
14. Pressed pajamas.
15. Tweeds.

By the time you have put the final touches to your appearance, you will be well into the great adventure of single living. Just *learning* to look good is an exercise in fulfillment that can be as exciting as the final reward, a reward that is far more than an attractive exterior. Exercise, diet, the development of new habits of grooming, and new approaches to dress are a part of the growth process that can make you stronger, more confident of yourself, more assured than ever that the new you is worthy of all your efforts.

CHAPTER 7

You've Got More Opportunities Than You Think
how and where to meet the opposite sex

Forty years ago in a New Jersey suburb, an unmarried Latin teacher in her early fifties on her way to work each morning would pass a silver-haired single doctor. So regularly did their paths cross that she always knew whether she was a little early or a little late, according to the spot at which she met him. Even though the years went by, they never spoke, since nice women did not speak or establish eye contact on the street with men to whom they had not been introduced.

One day in nearby Manhattan, where she had gone on a shopping trip, the teacher came up out of the subway and there at the top of the steps stood the doctor. In their astonishment at the unexpected encounter, they greeted each other with warm delight. That was on Saturday.

The following Monday, on her way to work, the little Latin teacher found her pulse pounding as she approached the spot where she would meet the doctor. Should she speak? Smile, perhaps? Or just look? But as he approached, drew abreast, and passed, she did none of these things; the crisis over, the two resumed their walks to work and passed each other on the street—as distant, respectable, and isolated as they were before.

Some of the best opportunities for meeting people turn up, as this one did, in everyday routines. By clinging to a convention made meaningless by the circumstances, the teacher—and the doctor—ruled out these opportunities and denied themselves the human contacts and relationships they craved.

Today the lack of a proper introduction is no longer a barrier to friendship between the sexes. The men and women we surveyed have long since shed their inhibitions, even though many of them were brought up in the era of the Latin teacher and the doctor she might have met.

"Where do you meet men?" a fifty-five-year-old woman responded laughingly. "You meet them *everywhere!*"

And the other singles who are looking for and finding special partners to share their lives for a little while or longer are saying the same thing.

Swimming in a pool, playing on a tennis court, hiking with a mountain club, shopping in the grocery store, having coffee, at the bank, selling real estate, paying the rent, admiring a painting in an art museum, jogging in the park, sitting in an airplane, serving on a grand jury, riding in an elevator, having lunch in a restaurant, changing money in a foreign country, working in a dry-cleaning establishment, riding a ski lift, sharing a taxi with a stranger during the rush hour, backpacking in the mountains, confronting in an encounter group—these are some of the avenues that led them, if not to a meaningful and enduring relationship, at least to a pleasant lunch.

"For years our mothers told us not to talk to strange men," an attractive, dark-eyed woman of forty-nine said, "and when I was young and single, I never did. Instead, I picked my husband from a limited selection, and now I'm divorced. Today, I take time to be friendly. It brightens up my whole trip to the grocery store to chat with someone new.

"More than that. I met a very attractive man in the

fruits and vegetables who asked me if I knew how to prepare artichokes. He told me his wife had died, and he didn't manage too well in the kitchen. We kept meeting each other on our trips to the supermarket, and we ended up learning what to do with artichokes together."

"I think cafeterias are much better than bars for meeting men," remarked a gently curved, petite woman who described herself as an "M & M girl—between menopause and Medicare." Become a regular customer at the same cafeteria, she recommends. Then select the man you would like to meet and establish eye contact. Later, add a small smile. Finally, since cafeterias are crowded at lunchtime, you might ask to share his table (or he might ask to share yours).

"It's basically like children saying, 'Come over and play in my yard.' But sometimes, after all this time, you forget how to do it."

A retired city official formed his own group at the cafeteria where he regularly ate his evening meal. Tired of solitary dining, he looked around the room and invited other singles to join him. Soon he had a company of twelve, ten men and two women. When the M & M lady, who ate at this cafeteria in the evening, established eye contact, he invited her to join them.

"I dropped out of the group," he said later, "after I married her."

Some men believe in offering a helping hand to damsels who have locked their keys in the car, dropped their groceries, or are otherwise distressed. Results may not always bear fruit, but they are usually interesting.

"I offered to help a woman with a stalled car on a downtown street once," a good-natured, fifty-one-year-old widower said. "I don't know much about stalled cars, but she knew less. It turned out she was out of gas, late to an appointment, and very upset. While she went on to her appointment, I got gas for her car and later drove it over to pick her up. Things were progressing nicely until I found out she was a hooker. We both had a good laugh about it and, no, I didn't follow up."

Although social barriers to such casual encounters have disappeared, it cost many of our singles considerable courage and effort to break down the barriers inside their heads.

The experience of their single youth, light years ago, had not prepared them for today's social scene, and few looked forward to a second adolescence in the latter half of their lives. There were no guideposts, no role models in magazines or on television and movie screens in a world where it seemed as if the only ones entitled to love were the young. No wonder that the mere act of getting to the party was sometimes insurmountable—that one woman felt chained to the house, immobilized; that another would get all dressed up, even drive partway there, and never reach the front door; that a tall and handsome surgeon could not bring himself to pick up the phone and call a woman for a date.

It was through a painful process of understanding that only they could help themselves that they finally began to move out.

"I soon realized that no one was particularly interested in organizing my social activities and that it was up to me to do so," said the surgeon.

"I bought an inexpensive car, got dressed up pretty, opened the door and walked out *by myself* to discussion group meetings and to potluck suppers," said the immobilized woman.

The woman who could not get all the way to the party alone found a friend to go with her.

Some were driven out of their homes by feelings they could no longer endure.

"My children were grown and gone. No matter how many lights were on, no matter how high up I turned the stereo, the house became cavernous at night," a woman said. "I was literally propelled out of it by the terrible loneliness."

At the end of a particularly bad weekend, a wisp of an Englishwoman, sixty-two, grabbed the telephone book, leafed through it for the addresses of singles groups, and found one ten blocks from her home. Putting on her most becoming dress, she walked to the dance that was being held that very evening.

"I didn't meet anyone special, although I did later; but it was such a lift just to get out and chat with people," she said.

Even after arriving on the scene, coming face to face with others as lonely as they, the biggest problem our single men and women had to overcome was their own shyness.

"I never seemed to know what to say," moaned a retired Air Force colonel, fifty-four, six-foot-three, outstandingly handsome, the owner of his own business.

"I have a terrible inferiority complex," confessed a successful investment manager, fifty-eight.

"I talk too much or not at all. I say the wrong thing," complained a salesman, fifty-three.

"Self-consciousness is my biggest hurdle," said a taxi driver, fifty.

And the women:

"I am almost as shy as I was years ago at a sorority tea dance," confessed an ebullient, outdoorsy socialite, fifty-one.

"Having been married for thirty-two years, I'd forgotten how to flirt," remembered an attractive widow, sixty.

"I still haven't overcome my feelings of shyness and inferiority," reflected a strikingly good-looking and successful singer, forty-eight.

All of these people, and many more who shared their feelings, made themselves do what they found most difficult. They started conversations and bluffed their way through. They forced smiles until they felt like smiling. They made

105

themselves relax by becoming aware of their tension. They looked at themselves as if they were someone else and laughed. And they kept on going out until it seemed like the natural thing to do.

Perhaps the most effective remedy for shyness was found by Jeff K., who had the worst case of it. An attractive, boyish-looking fifty-two-year-old cartographer, Jeff was nearly fifty years old before he could strike up a conversation with a woman and carry it through adequately.

"It was just terrible," he said. "I used to cross the street rather than meet someone I knew. Then, after I became single, I made up my mind that I wasn't going to miss out on the good conversations, the good times, and the good friends any more. I joined a singles group and became involved in the rap sessions that took place in the homes of members. In the course of the discussions, I began to see that the women were shy, too; that it was very difficult for them to come in cold for the first time to a group that was already formed unless someone opened up and started talking to them. As I became an old-timer, it gave me a good feeling to make them feel wanted, to make them want to come back. Now I realize I have something to offer, and I really like women. I think they're the nicest people!"

"Shy is selfish. You have to make the moves of friendship," said an attractive blonde. A teacher of classes for divorced women, she advises them to take the responsibility, to force themselves if necessary. "Look around and find someone who is just as lonely as you are. They're the ones at a party who are looking over the books. Introduce yourself. Say you don't know anyone."

What is there to lose?

A college professor estimates that out of ten chances he might get one rebuff in introducing himself to women under many varied circumstances, including jogging in the park.

"It's really amazing how people respond to genuine warmth and interest," he said.

But there is always that one rebuff. A tall, aristocratic research scientist, for instance, was intrigued by a striking-looking woman as she got into her car in a parking lot. Summoning his courage, he walked over and told her he would like to know her. Icily, she replied:

"Do you do this kind of thing all the time?"

"I wanted to say no, and that it had taken quite a bit of courage to do it this time, but she was already gone," he said. "We would all like to be introduced, of course, but it's just not always possible. You have to be ready for a turndown and not view it as the ultimate tragedy. Don't think of it as something that's wrong with you. It's the problem of the person who refuses friendship. Now that I think about it, that poor woman never got to know me."

Many men wished that women would assume some of the burden of risking.

"Some women think we're on the make when we approach them, and become offended," one said. "If a woman takes the initiative, on the other hand, she suffers far less likelihood of being rejected."

Not one man said he would mind having a woman call him on the phone and most were delighted at the thought.

"I have two daughters, twenty-two and twenty-six years old," said a gynecologist. "I tell them if they meet a gentleman they really like, they should make a move, invite him to dinner or to a play."

The women in our survey who have taken the initiative have been pleased with the results. At fifty-seven, Mollie G. was walking her bicycle with a flat tire to a filling station, thinking as she did so that she had not met anyone new in quite a while. At that moment, her eye was caught by an interesting-looking man studying a road map in a car bearing a license plate, from Wyoming, her home state. She went over, tapped on the window, and asked him if he had a pump in his car for her flat tire. He did not have a pump, but he did end in renting an apartment two blocks from Mollie's and they developed a lasting friendship.

In her involvement with the activities of a political organization, Sandra P. was much attracted to a good-natured, easygoing engineer.

"We had a marvelous time together, but it never went beyond the meetings. One night, I did what all the speakers at my singles group had been urging us to do. I took a deep breath, called him up, and invited him to go to the movies. He was really pleased. I picked him up in my car and paid for the tickets when we got there. Then, during intermission, while he was standing in the lobby eating a huge bag of popcorn I'd gotten for him, he looked down at me with a big grin and said:

"I suppose you'll be wanting something for all this at the end of the evening."

Sandra gave a little gasp before his humor sank in.

"I didn't realize how tense I was about the whole situation. But then we both burst out laughing, and today, he's one of my best friends."

In the minds of many of the men we interviewed, there is a distinction between taking the initiative and being jarringly aggressive.

John D., an outgoing, fifty-four-year-old manufacturer, met his fiancée, Sheri, at a business cocktail party to which he had been invited by friends to meet another woman. Sheri noted his broad shoulders and handsome shock of gray hair from across the room, asked who he was, and went over and introduced herself.

"Normally, I might be scared away by a woman taking the initiative that plainly, but that's before I met Sheri," he said. "It was the way she did it. She doesn't know a stranger,

108

and there was no sexual connotation in anything she said. Instead of turning me off, I wanted to know her better. We spent most of the evening talking, except for the times my friends dragged me away to talk to the other woman."

Even after that evening, John didn't follow up until Sheri phoned to ask him to do some volunteer work in the community. That's when he invited her to lunch.

In contrast to Sheri's friendly approach was that of a young woman at John's place of work who asked him frequently for a date. John evaded, until one day he simply said:

"Look. You're young enough to be my daughter. I'd feel foolish going out with you."

She looked him straight in the eye and responded:

"Don't knock it until you've tried it."

So he did. But only once. She wanted to go to bed the first night.

"That sounds great in fantasy," he said. "But I found such easy taking to be a bit scary and not too satisfying."

Besides urging newcomers to forget their shyness and take the initiative in making friends, single men and women offered two cautions. The first: Don't approach the singles scene with unrealistic expectations. You will probably not meet your Prince or Princess Charming your first night out, so don't let it spoil the evening.

A fifty-seven-year-old widow said she felt desperate at her first dance as she looked around and saw no one who came close to the quality of her late husband.

"I was dancing with a little fellow who was just my size and looking him right in the eye. He wasn't anyone I would even want to go out with. Suddenly, I just told myself, 'I'm not going to marry him. All I'm going to do is dance with him, and I might as well enjoy it.'"

The director of a large singles organization believes in

giving everyone a chance. Women should dance with anyone who asks them, providing they are not rude or obnoxious, even go out with anyone who invites them, at least once.

"People are hidden," she said. "Both men I married were men I scorned to begin with."

The second piece of advice our singles offered: Be patient. Previous examples notwithstanding, over-fifty singles are not given to impetuous behavior. Women are generally reluctant to give out their telephone numbers until they are acquainted with a man, and men usually want to get to know women before they invite them out on a date.

With a positive, outgoing attitude, a willingness to risk, realistic expectations, and a measure of patience, a single man or woman is ready to make the most of the wealth of opportunities available for meeting other singles today.

Of all the avenues open to them, the most popular among our group were the singles clubs and dances that are proliferating across the country, even though a minority viewed them negatively as "meat markets," "a place for losers," and "a hangout for people with hangups." One woman said:

"I think most singles events are pretty gruesome, and I have yet to meet someone I really liked or who liked me. I think there's something about the act of having to go to a singles function—it's sort of a naked declaration that you're hard up that I find a bit humiliating and that makes me uptight."

To these criticisms, the supporters of singles groups reply: "Give them a chance."

"You have to find out what the organization is all about by attending several times. One time is not enough."

"Become involved in the group. Get in there and help."

"Go to the discussions, the lectures, the picnics. Pay attention to what is said and not said. Learn about people."

110

"Join. Get on the mailing list so you can get announcements of their activities. Become actively involved. Take an office. Serve on a committee. Don't just try one activity once."

A look through the telephone book under the heading *Clubs and Associations* in the yellow pages will turn up two or three of these organizations in most major cities. Once acquainted with other singles, you can easily learn where the best gathering places are.

In addition to public organizations open to everyone for the price of admission to a dance—around $3, or less with a yearly membership that costs about $20—there is a whole array of private clubs, joined by invitation. At one end of the spectrum is Who's Who International, a nonprofit organization that describes itself as a "club of highly screened and then carefully selected unmarried men and women from a variety of interests and backgrounds" and boasts such officials as John Astor, Conrad Hilton, and Contessa Josefina Boyer. Headquartered in Marina del Rey, California, it has branches in eighteen major cities in the U.S. and sixteen abroad.

For a membership fee of $150, annual dues of $50, and an admission price to main events held during the year of around $20, Who's Who offers international travel at reduced rates and visits to "some of the world's greatest estates —including the famous King Ranch of Texas (courtesy of Alice King); Hawaii's only privately owned island (Allen Chase); and Acapulco's La Barenque (Warren Avis)." In addition, to quote from the brochure: "because of the social standing and the caliber of our members, an ever-increasing number of special favors are offered us.... The small, side benefits are over and above the comfortable feeling of knowing when you are wining, dining, dancing, or traveling, you are surrounded by the Who's Who of the unmarried people of the world."

111

A contrast to Who's Who is Parents Without Partners, whose only requisite for membership is proof of your single status and the existence of a living child, no matter how old. Founded in 1957, it now has 1000 chapters in the United States and Canada, and a membership of more than 160,000. The largest singles organization in the world, its stated purpose is to offer education, support, advice, and parent-child activities, implemented by small informal discussions in members' homes and a vast variety of picnics, overnight hikes, skating parties, and other events. Older singles will find that many of the parents' children are gone or soon to leave home and that the primary emphasis can easily be shifted from parenthood to a search for partners.

When looking into any singles group, it is wise to check the age of its membership before attending a function, or you may find yourself in an alien climate. The director of one California organization, in which the median age of members is thirty-five, had this to say about older women who attended its Friday-night dances:

"These ladies in their Enna Jettick shoes and little dresses are making a statement about themselves by their clothing and their Emily Post etiquette; while in this organization, we are interested in taking off the accouterments of culture so that people can be less structured. Women who are comfortable in this kind of atmosphere have no problems, but on Monday mornings I get calls. Some of these women are upset because they got hustled. Others are upset because they didn't get hustled. Some are upset because they were ignored."

Even in older singles' groups, women are encouraged to forget their traditional ways.

"Sitting and waiting to be asked to dance is an old-fashioned ego trip," said one of the men, a regular at the dances of two organizations. "A woman should take a chance and ask a man herself.

"And man or woman, if you haven't danced for thirty years, brush up. Take lessons. This may sound obvious, but around here good dancers are only one in ten. Dance well, and you're bound to have a nice time."

Perhaps the person who most effectively follows all the guidelines for success at a singles event is Lollie J. Lollie is a widow with a relaxed, friendly manner, a trim, curvaceous figure, and an infectious chuckle that goes off frequently because she finds humor in any situation, even in her own first venture onto the singles scene at the age of seventy-four.

At the urging of her daughter-in-law, also a widow, Lollie got out her sewing machine and stitched up a long print dress. On the evening of her first singles dance, she tied a frothy chiffon scarf around her neck and went out with her daughter-in-law for the big adventure.

In the lobby of the hotel where the dance was held they met a casual acquaintance, a pretty woman in her forties, younger than either of them, who greeted them cordially and offered some words of advice.

"Don't mind if no one asks you to dance," she said. "You may have to come a few times until you get to know people."

"Well, we'll just see about that," Lollie whispered and chortled again. They bought tickets, had their hands stamped with an inked symbol to signify they had paid, and entered a room full of tables surrounding a dance floor. At one end was the bar, around which were clustered almost a fourth of the men there. The women outnumbered them about three to two.

"That's okay," Lollie assured her daughter-in-law. "We can share."

At the table they chose sat two aloof ladies who presented a solid, unapproachable front to the world and a plump, not unattractive woman in her middle forties, who confided glumly that she had been attending for three weeks

113

and no one had asked her to dance. Lollie was amazed, then after a moment's thought, she said:

"I think we're all making a mistake sitting way over here in the corner when the men are all over there by the bar. Why don't we just go over and buy a drink?" Jumping up, she led the way.

"Do you see anyone you like?" she whispered to the younger woman after they had bought their drinks.

"Yes," the younger woman replied. "That one in the red coat."

"Where?"

"Behind me."

"Well, you should turn around and look at him," Lollie admonished.

The woman turned, saw the man looking at his watch, asked, "Do you have the time?" and the man answered, "Would you like to dance?"

"It's so simple," marveled Lollie as she watched them dance off. "To think she sat around here for three weeks."

Then Lollie moved to the edge of the dance floor. When the music stopped, her glance swept the room and engaged the eye of the tallest, best-looking man in it. Her own eyes danced as her lips silently formed the word: "Next?"

Without hesitation, the man shouldered his way through the crowd and presented himself.

"May I have the pleasure?" he asked with a slight bow. And Lollie's experience as a single had begun.

Not every Sunday evening was a glittering success for Lollie.

"It was difficult being in the same role I was in as a young girl and not having the fellows all gathering around me for dances," she admitted. She did not dance every dance, and some evenings she did no more than participate

114

in the mixers, in which the women formed a circle around the men and seized one of them for a partner when the music stopped.

"I used to play forward on my high school basketball team," she quipped, "and that really helped."

But each Sunday she went back. In time, she developed a circle of friends and admirers and the dances became the high spot of her week.

Second to singles gatherings, the most popular way of meeting the opposite sex among the men and women in our survey was through activities and classes that were in themselves stimulating and enjoyable, yielding as a bonus an interesting male or female friend. These people liked the idea of creating and doing, savoring and enriching their lives, and wanted to meet others who shared the same outlook.

"People who are winners take classes. People who value their bodies are outdoors exercising them," one of the most popular women in our survey maintained.

"It's hard to imagine anyone who loves the outdoors being too bad," a vibrant female member of the California Sierra Club declared.

Those who favored the outdoors agreed that for women it is a hunting ground that's hard to beat. That's where the men are, with prizes going to those who keep themselves in good enough physical shape to take full advantage of it, they say.

"I go on the more advanced hikes with my mountain club, and there are always more men along than women," a glowing fifty-five-year-old Coloradan said. On Long Island, a married woman who works in an office full of widows and divorcées wonders why they never go along with her on the Sunday-afternoon bicycle rides she and her husband take along the shore.

"The women are always outnumbered," she said.

"Besides, it's a marvelous ride in the salt air, in full view of the pounding surf and the great long stretches of beach. You feel wonderful when it's over."

In California, a fifty-year-old woman attracted one of her most dedicated admirers as she bounced around on the tennis court next to his, beating her twenty-four-year-old son in a vigorous game. The same woman's sister, two years older, intrigued a millionaire as she regularly swam lap after lap at the same public pool he used for his morning workout. He later became one of her closest friends.

Outdoors or in, our singles met interesting people by doing interesting things. Some found encounter and other self-help classes a way to instant intimacy. A New York woman who thought it would be interesting to serve on a grand jury found she was one of two women among ten fascinating men. An engineer who had always wanted to spin a potter's wheel became the darling of his class, the only male in it.

"The more things you do, the more men you meet," a slender, sixty-year-old woman said. She met her fiancé at a cocktail party and has kept him running hard ever since, even though he's seven years her junior.

"I'm a Methodist, but now I'm singing in her Episcopalian choir," he said with an air of disbelief. "I spent one whole Hallowe'en evening working in a spook house for the March of Dimes just so I could see her that night. She's so full of energy that I can hardly keep up, but I love it. I love her!"

The old, traditional way of meeting the opposite sex—introductions by friends and relatives—placed third in popularity among those we interviewed, but there were some strong dissenters. More than one woman had the feeling after a small dinner party that men don't like to be programmed into choosing a partner. More than one man felt his friends' judgment was questionable.

"I don't understand how they do it," a particularly ungrateful but much-sought-after businessman marveled. "A friend who knew me *well* arranged a dinner at his home for me to meet a woman who was at the opposite pole. She loved football. I abhor it. She is Catholic. I'm an atheist. On all fronts, it was all wrong. I got away as soon as I decently could."

Another man recalls friends who arranged a date for him with a Lithuanian opera singer while he was traveling in Belgium.

"She wanted to marry me that night," he recalls, still becoming a little agitated at the thought. He departed early too—from the country.

But despite such fiascoes, many of our singles were deeply appreciative of introductions by friends and considered them the very nicest way of meeting someone. A never-married woman regularly reminds her married friends that she is available. One widower regularly gives parties that include his married friends and their families as well as his new single friends, in order to give his new friends a chance to know and judge him better.

The same widower turned one Thanksgiving from what might have been a dreary holiday into a memorable event.

"We had always been a sit-down turkey-dinner family," he said. "That year, two years after my wife had died, my older daughter was married and it looked as if my son wouldn't make it home from college. That left my younger daughter and me to look at each other across a table filled with missing persons. The very thought spurred me into action. I called all the single people I knew who might be in the same boat—there was the divorcée across the street with her son, a writer I knew with his two boys—before I'd finished I had a group of twelve delightful people. Each one brought a dish, his own specialty, and we sat down to a magnificent feast. Not only did the adults enjoy meeting each other, but the experience of all our young people was expanded, because the generations meshed beautifully."

Don't discount your children as a source of introductions, some of our singles said. Two years after her husband's death a widow's son got together with a fraternity brother whose father was single. The two boys were determined that their parents should meet, and when they did, they got along so well that the relationship continued for six years.

Sons and daughters who visit their parents and older relatives in retirement communities open a door to meeting other singles visiting their own parents, while older parents visiting their married sons and daughters meet each other as well.

"My Uncle Charlie was visiting his son in Pittsburgh," a woman said, "when his son's mother-in-law dropped in. There must be an attraction between families, because the two of them liked each other immediately—so much so that now they're married."

Old friends can take on a new look when they become single. A sprightly little widow, who had been seeking a new mate by attending dances and joining clubs all over town, answered her doorbell one day to find a former neighbor standing on her step. He had lost his wife, he told her, and since he just happened to be in the neighborhood....That, too, ended in a second marriage for both.

Another woman, scanning the obituaries, noted that the wife of a man she had always admired had died. She spent two days composing her letter of condolence, and six months later married him.

Ranking close behind singles groups, activities, and introductions by friends and relatives in the singles marketplace was work, although many cautioned against office romances that could explode, raining fallout on the whole staff.

"I'm a supervisor, and the single women in my office are all working for me," one man said. "I don't need that grief."

There is no hazard, however, in other types of work-related contacts, notably in selling and other occupations that bring people into touch with the public. One man dated the interviewer at an employment agency where he went looking for a job. When it became apparent that they had little in common, she arranged several introductions with women clients who might suit him better.

Considerably farther down the list was church, which many felt was too youth- and couple-oriented to be of much use as a meeting place for the over-fifties. Some churches, however, are beginning to recognize singles as a distinct life-style and offer the kind of sociability that can meet their needs. A few are even developing reputations as singles churches.

One of the most widely used stamping grounds, perhaps the first retreat for the newcomer on the singles scene, was viewed by our men and women as the least likely place to start a worthwhile relationship.

"Stay out of the bar scene," a woman warned. "Too many people there are wearing a mask and playing games. It's too easy to get hooked on a married man who lies a lot."

"Avoid bars," echoed a man. "There is no salvation in booze. It is great, but not as a tool towards an end."

A savvy never-married New Yorker observed that the caliber of women in a singles bar seemed to be much higher than that of the men.

"A creepy guy can be lost in a crowd," she said. "He can pick up a girl there when he couldn't if he were any-where else."

119

"Too noisy, too fiercely competitive," a man commented.

But for some, the bar scene works, and these offered guidelines for those who want to try it.

First, pick a bar in a good neighborhood and become a regular. That way, you will see the same people and get to know them. Sit or stand up at the bar, particularly if you're a woman. It will give you a choice of companions on your left or your right, and any man in the room can approach you. A woman should never go to a bar with one other woman but go instead in a group of three or more or alone. That way, a man who wants to talk or dance with her does not feel he's leaving her companion with no company.

One woman who has used bars to advantage is Joanna T., fifty-four, of Miami, who has been single for twenty years.

"Ten years ago," commented Joanna from her perch on a barstool, "ladies in this town just didn't come into a place like this. But today, if you want to be where the fun is, where the people are, you've got to get out, know where to go, and how to handle the scene when you get there."

For Joanna, the bar she frequents feels as natural and comfortable a place to meet men as any other in Miami. It is one of the "right" bars. Although married couples and people of all ages drop in, they are all people who like to listen to the same kind of music: "Star Dust," "Deep Purple," the favorites of World War II. It is a place where a single woman over fifty can feel at home. Moreover, when Joanna goes in, she is reasonably sure she will see people she knows in the course of the evening.

While she almost never goes into a totally strange bar, Joanna has no misgivings about visiting her familiar haunts alone, arriving about 10 P.M., an hour later on Sundays, and taking a seat at the bar to start out. Then, as her friends drift in, she joins them at one of the small high tables in the back

120

room, where the seating accommodates four cozily, with just room on the table to put a drink. There the conversation may expand to include those at the next table, and soon, she's meeting new people and expanding her circle of friends.

Even in Savannah, Georgia, where it has only recently been possible to buy liquor by the drink, Ralph M., fifty, finds bars a natural hunting ground, much more compatible with his tastes in that Bible-belt city than church. The bias against such meeting places is beginning to disappear, and women of middle-class background can be found there. Younger women, that is, which is okay with Ralph. He likes to date women at least ten years younger than he is. Like Joanna, he is a regular at his bar, where he knows the bartender and the people and has made a few warm and lasting friendships among the women he has met there.

"There are, of course, all kinds of women in bars," he says, "and to begin with, it doesn't really make any difference whether they're hustlers or just women who are lonely."

Priscilla T., fifty-eight, likes to combine bars with conventions because she finds that men who attend conventions are usually safe, substantial people out for a good time.

"I have accepted dates with strangers under safe conditions, taken chances other women wouldn't, and found many good friends," she said. "I guess I'm either a very good judge of people or very lucky."

When she is traveling, Priscilla keeps a sharp eye out for banners that say WELCOME STOCKMEN or SHRINERS or other conventioneers and finds her motels in towns where the action is. Sometimes the men she meets are married, a fact they usually make clear.

"As long as I know that, I can date them without becoming involved. We both have a good time, and that's that. No guilt. If they're going out with someone, it might as well be me."

121

Only two of the singles tried commercial dating services, and both found them unsatisfactory. Applicants seemed to be screened poorly if at all. One woman, divorced from an alcoholic, specified on her application that she did not want anyone who drank too much. Yet the first man who arrived to pick her up was drunk when he reached her home.

"You only meet the freaky people who don't have enough personality to meet someone on their own," the other woman said.

A handsome, successful Greenwich Village sculptor who had neither time nor patience for the bar scene, the dating game, or any of the other hunting strategies, went right to the heart of the matter and advertised for a mate.

"I'm very busy," he said. "All these dates, evening after evening—it was time I could be spending with my sons or doing many other things." Choosing the *Saturday Review* because of the professional quality of its readers, he placed the following notice:

Widower/artist, 59, mature, sincere, with a lovely apartment, seeks warm, caring, stable, childless woman (40–50). Share joys of intimacy in living-together arrangement, sailing, travel, concerts. No chain smokers. Write by your hand.

A serious graphologist, he screened out all but ten of the more than a hundred replies he received by analyzing the penmanship of the writer. These ten he interviewed by telephone, narrowing the number to five, each of whom he took out for coffee.

For those who didn't seem right, he had a pleasant but vague "I'll call you sometime" or "Keep me in mind." But at last he found the one with whom he was able to establish a close and loving one-to-one relationship.

The one-to-one sharing and caring relationship this man sought and found is the goal of some—not all—of the men and women who are meeting each other in the multitude of ways our times have to offer them. At this stage in their lives, some are still healing from the wounds of widowhood and divorce and are cautious about making a hasty and perhaps ill-considered alliance. Others, farther along, feel that they have passed that danger point and are settling down to enjoy single living in all its rich variety. Few are looking for the one-and-only they were conditioned to search for in their youth, and more and more are beginning to accept the idea that no relationship, even another marriage, is going to be forever.

Instead, they are enjoying the day-to-day companionship of those they meet, discovering in the process that what they really need is not men, not women, but people, a support system that will not, like their last one, fail them if they lose the keystone. In the process, too, they are building interests, developing abilities and strengths that are making each of them, in the words of the most self-sufficient of our sample, "the very best company I know."

CHAPTER 8

Across A Crowded Room—I
what men find attractive
in a woman over fifty

"My God! What a woman!"

The comment was made by a handsome, thirty-five-year-old bachelor as he returned to his bridge table in a crowded Chicago banquet room. It was made not about a meltingly beautiful young girl but about a woman in her middle fifties.

"I'm not sure what there was about her," he said later, "but I went out of my way to walk right past her chair. I guess it was her eyes. She had sparkly eyes that convinced me she really cared about people."

What qualities are there in a woman over fifty that makes her enduringly attractive to the opposite sex? Can that "intangible something" that draws glances from across the room be defined? Does it have holding power?

To find out, we queried more than a hundred men, including a retired banker, a vagabond, a company president, a car mechanic, a writer, a butcher, a television producer, a schoolteacher—in short, men from many and varied social and economic backgrounds. They told us in detail what they liked and what they didn't like about the women over fifty they had known. They described the ones they had loved and those they had shunned or had, after loving, left. From their comments some patterns emerged; and from these patterns we have designed a composite picture of all the qualities an attractive older woman should have, in the words of the men we interviewed.

Our men said emphatically, repeatedly:

"I hate fat!"

"Fat turns me off!"

Individually, they commented:

"Women think they can hide fat by the way they dress. They can't. We notice. It just shows they're more concerned with what they eat than with how they look."

"If a woman lets herself go physically, she just doesn't care about herself, and it shows in everything she does. If she doesn't like herself, how can anybody else like her?"

While a beautiful body was a definite plus, few men expected perfection.

"It's great if she has a good shape, but I'm satisfied with a reasonably nice figure."

"She doesn't have to have thirty-four–twenty-four–thirty-four measurements, but she should look trim."

An attractive woman need not be beautiful in the classical sense, but most men agreed she should be meticulously groomed:

"Frumpiness makes a woman look older."

"No one over twenty-five can get away with looking unkempt."

"I always note a woman's fingernails. If she takes care of her nails, she usually takes care of her whole self."

Although wearing the latest style did not seem important to most of the men, they liked women who were well-dressed, not only for dates, but for every occasion, looking their best in Levi's or in lingerie.

"I'm thinking now of a woman in her midfifties. She's a woman you would remember even if you saw her only once in a crowd. She not only knows how to dress, she knows how to dress for everything, even down to the way her hair flows in an open car. If you took each individual part of her, there is nothing outstanding. It's the way she puts it together—like wow!"

So much for the exterior, which the men always mentioned first. Shining through and clearly visible, however, should be certain key personality traits: vitality; a young, positive attitude; and a lively interest in life and other people.

"The vibes are there right away. You know immediately if a woman is happy, likes herself, and is still living to the hilt. Age doesn't matter. It's her attitude."

"Still learning, still living, still growing, no matter what her age."

To most of the men we talked to, *old* was a state of mind. More than fat, it was the quality they found least attractive and at which they hurled their sharpest barbs. *Old* meant a woman who felt she was over fifty, looked as if she felt it, acted as if she felt it. It was a woman who was "staid," "jaded," "extremely in a rut," who had lost her interest and involvement in life, who was tired, afraid of change, the woman who had given up.

"There are women who follow a clock that says it's time to quit, time to watch TV—to hell with activities. It's time to stay home. They have died."

"Some older women have lost their youthful outlook and spontaneity. They are so totally hung up in the adult and parental mode that they can't live for themselves. They're still living for their children, who don't give a damn about them any more."

A young outlook, however, was not to be confused with obvious attempts some women make to look younger than they are:

"Trying desperately to be too young."

"Miniskirts when they are out of style."

"Trying to act like twenty."

"Too heavy-handed with the makeup."

"Using colloquialisms of the young when they don't know what they really mean."

In some ways, many of the men thought, older women can spectacularly outclass a girl.

"I wouldn't know how to relate to a twenty-year-old. She's a child compared with a mature woman. Older women are more in league with my feelings. There's a bond of understanding."

"She's more independent and free than a single mother in her thirties because she has her children raised, or nearly so."

"If she's widowed or divorced, she's weathered a hell of a storm and learned more about herself because of the crises she's gone through."

"Older women know themselves, their likes and dislikes, therefore it's easier for them to empathize with others."

"They have more compassion. Their experience shows through."

The visibility of all these qualities was summed up by one remark:

"If a woman reaches that platform or peak of herself and finds that elusive having-it-all-together quality, it shows on her face—her strength, her humor, her ability to live with her world."

Another area in which older women excel, it seems, is in the sexual arena. The general opinion was best expressed by a rugged and magnetic middle-aged man who had been living for three years at sea on his twenty-six-foot sloop:

"Put a child in a swing and what happens? The swing goes back and forth and the child thinks it's great. But put a forty-five- or fifty-year-old woman in a swing and she kicks up her heels and makes it go around and round.

"Take my ex-wife and me, for instance. We went into

the sexual aspect of marriage as novices. We knew one position and that was it. But just about the time we started to get bored with sex, we found we could do something else—like cross our fingers or turn on a light. It takes time to develop variety. A twenty-year-old has just not had the men in her life and the experience to do it the way an older woman can do it."

Nearly a fourth of the men objected to women who were unladylike, coarse, aggressive, loud, antifeminine.

"I can't stand a woman who chews gum."

"Foul language in a female—yuk!"

One man reserved the right to use colorful language, however.

"Most women think chivalry is dead," he said. "I took a young woman on a date last week, and when we got to the show, she started to open the car door. I just told her, 'Keep you ass on the seat, lady. That's my job—to open doors.'"

Men are attracted to women who are direct and open. They say:

"The thing I like about my woman is that she has the courage to say what other women wouldn't have the courage to say. I know exactly how she's feeling."

"When I first met my girlfriend, I was impressed when she looked at me and said, 'I really like you.' That's something I don't think a younger woman would have been able to say."

For many men, athletic is appealing.

"It's not unfeminine to work up a sweat. It actually gives a woman a glow that makes her radiant. I have a fifty-two-year-old friend who skis well, swims competitively, is a good dancer—better than I am. Does it bother me that she's better than I am in some areas? Certainly not, when all that exercise makes her look more like thirty-six than her actual age."

"Physical vitality is at the core of everything. I want

129

someone to hike and ski with me—someone who can keep up."

A backpacker in his early sixties wrote this comment in the log of a mountain-club cabin, where he had spent the night alone.

"How wonderful it would be if I could get *her* in here to share this with me."

Some men thought that money made a woman over fifty attractive.

"My wife was a credit-cardaholic. I look for a woman who is obviously able to take care of herself financially."

"I don't want to assume a financial responsibility. I spent years having to consult with someone else about how to spend my money."

"Yes, money is certainly an added attraction. It could mean a lot more fun for both of us."

"I would want a woman who was financially independent. I want to leave my money to my children."

"I want someone who will be willing to share what she has with me."

Other men, however, avoided the woman who looked too expensive.

"I couldn't afford to take her out."

"She wouldn't be interested in me."

"I wouldn't be anxious to get involved with a wealthy woman. If a man doesn't have money too, he goes second class. I don't want to be a lap dog."

Inherent in the men's evaluations of what they wanted in a woman over fifty was an appreciation of the woman who was independent, a whole person. One man put it concisely:

"One thing I *don't* want is a cripple. People who make me too important in their lives are terrifying. I like to think of a relationship as two tall trees standing side by side, instead of one overshadowing the other, and I think most people feel the same way."

These are the facets, then, of what might be called the Ideal Older Woman. To find out how these qualities could be developed, we sought out women who possessed them. One of these is Nora J. of Los Angeles.

When Nora's husband flew his private plane into the side of a mountain, she was left abruptly alone, penniless by virtue of bankrupt business holdings, with four small children to support. She was terrified.

Today, as she approaches fifty, she heads her own publicity and literary agency. She is a creative, energetic, dynamic woman, immensely attractive to men; and life, in her own words, is "a gas."

When we talked to her she had just returned from lunch with three other women, all of whom were vibrant, excited, having fun. From neighboring tables, men were looking—handsome men, interesting-looking men, prosperous men.

"Why not?" she said. "If you're having a good time, people want to be there. They're thinking, 'Why can't I be part of that crowd?'"

This kind of vitality did not just happen to Nora. Traveling from the days when she despaired over the clouds that cloaked the mountains, preventing rescue parties from searching for her husband's missing plane, to the exuberant and fulfilling life she leads today was a painfully hard trip.

"We women have a martyr complex bred in us," she said. "I decided from the very first that I was not going to feel sorry for myself. When bad things happened, I made up my mind to view them as a negative and move in another direction, a positive direction.

"Pain has to come into everybody's life. Instead of allowing myself to feel defeated by it, I chose to regard it as a testing. If life becomes milk toast, what is there to reach for? It's the reaching that makes you grow. There are so many women who don't reach. They're the ones who are in the bottle, five ax-handles wide, bitchy, unhappy, cantankerous old women."

Age, Nora thinks, must be accepted and fought at the same time: accepted as a place where a woman is, but making the very best of what she can be at that place.

"Do you see these lines?" she asked, leaning forward so that the fine creases that carved her high forehead would be more visible in the light. "I used to worry about them in my twenties, until someone told me, 'Nora, you talk with your forehead.' These lines are part of my personality, part of my beauty. I've earned them!"

Nora's slender body and porcelain skin are the result of regular disciplined routines. Sitting behind her desk wearing an immaculate white suit, her dark hair pulled severely back in a chic bun, with a crimson flower fastened behind her right ear, she looked as if she had stepped out of a fashion advertisement.

"And to look this way takes work," she said.

However, her greatest efforts, and they are made consistently and consciously, are directed toward attaining inner beauty.

"It's cost me money, heartache, time, energy, and pain," she said, "but the best things that have happened in my life happened because I've cared about people and they cared back."

The look of self-assurance and serenity that shines from Nora's blue eyes did not come easily, either. An Irish Catholic, she derives strong support from her religion, but she believes it is within the power of anyone, religious or not, to sit quietly as she has done at weekend retreats, and assess the good and bad within themselves, determining to strengthen the good and abate the bad.

When does Nora think she will stop being attractive to men?

"Never!" she replies emphatically. "People seem to say to older women, 'How dare you be romantic?' Well, I intend to be romantic at sixty or seventy or until that final second comes. Love actually gets better as you get older. It's more penetrating and exciting, more tender, because you understand all the innuendos it takes to come to that relationship. When love comes later in life, you're more careful with it. If someone sends you flowers, you appreciate them deeply, instead of saying, as you might have done as a girl, 'Why didn't he send any last week?'"

Nora's experience, while it involved shock and grief and even a sense of abandonment, did not carry with it the shattering blow that is dealt by the calculated rejection of divorce, particularly when a woman has been deserted in her later years for a younger woman. Those women who have suffered through this trauma attest to a shattered image of themselves as a desirable woman and an almost total loss of confidence, complicated by overwhelming feelings of rage and jealousy and panic. From such a point, how can any woman bring herself to feel and function again as an attractive person?

When Miriam K. of Westchester County, New York, had recovered sufficiently from the shock of losing her husband of twenty-five years to a woman in her twenties, she took some long, studied looks in her mirror, then spent several days pondering these questions:

"How can I attract men? Who would want me, a middle-aged woman who has been thrown away like a Kleenex? What qualities do I have that a man would want, and how can I develop them?"

In answer, she considered first the kind of man she wanted. She was not going to settle for anything less than quality. He must be attractive, have looks and bearing and accomplishments of which she could be proud, have a diversity of interests, be physically fit, and have enough money to entertain her in the manner to which she was accustomed. Such a man, she reasoned, being her age or older, would have the traditional values with which she herself had grown up. He would want a woman who was first of all a lady, one he would be proud to take anywhere, one who was well-groomed, well-dressed, and well-spoken. She should not resort to outmoded or too contemporary clichés, but should express herself with precision.

"In short, she should be classic in every sense but one," Miriam said. "She should be very modern, very uninhibited in the bedroom." In addition, she should have an excellent figure, look immaculately clean and healthy, and cultivate a positive, optimistic outlook. By intuition and reason, Miriam arrived at the very qualities the men we interviewed had stressed.

Then Miriam made a plan and put it into action. She gained back, on purpose, only part of the twenty pounds she had lost during the agonizing period of her divorce. Hoping to subordinate her own concerns and troubles to those of other people, she took a job in a travel agency. She kept her body lithe by playing tennis, cross-country skiing, and taking long walks in the park.

"Then I did the hardest thing of all. Because my role as a wife had been that of an employee, and because my feelings during the last ten years of my marriage had been protectively submerged, I did not know how to communicate with men on an equal level. So I buried my pride and joined a therapy group.

"It was damned hard. Most of the people in the group were in their twenties and thirties. I was the oldest person there; and in a therapy group, you can't play any games. You are absolutely naked.

"I hated the day I had to go to that meeting. I often

cried with rage and humiliation as all my old worn-out habits were exposed to everyone's view. But I could feel I was learning to communicate and I went into debt to continue with the sessions.

"I never turned down a date, and every time a man asked me out, I practiced my new skills. They worked. It was like magic. I was learning to be open and direct. I was learning to share my feelings."

In sharing her own feelings, Miriam encouraged her dates to share theirs.

"If a man appeared uptight when he picked me up, and he often did because many of them, too, were in the process of a divorce, I would say, 'It seems to me you have something on your mind. Would you like to talk about it?'

"He would usually be astonished. Then he would start to talk, tentatively, and when he found that I listened and accepted and could often relate his problems to my own experience, he would relax and tell it all—and call me again. After this had happened repeatedly with various men, I began to rebuild my confidence as a female.

"The men in my life now tell me they love my sensitivity. I have finally let my sensitivities be exposed, and exposing them helps me get beneath the surface of my men friends and reach the real person.

Having established her own self-respect, Miriam was able to expect the respect of her men friends.

"I believe that men basically like opening doors and taking a protective role with women," she said, "and that's what I expect."

Portraying an elegant lady in today's ambiance is not always easy. Standing firm on the sidewalk when a man forgets to open the car door requires nerves of steel, she admits; and once, when a male friend left her sitting in the seat of his car as he sauntered off, she called after him:

"Aren't you forgetting something?"

He was surprised, but he went back and opened the door and has been doing so ever since.

Today, two years after her divorce, Miriam considers her course of action to have been correct. Besides casual dates, some of which are with men considerably younger than herself, she has meaningful friendships with men, and is squired consistently by two of the most eligible and distinguished single men in town, who shower her with attention, invitations, trips, and presents.

But the greatest satisfaction she finds in her relationships is their depth and the feeling of mutual support and enrichment they afford:

"The ultimate compliment I have recieved from anyone was from one of my male friends who said to me, 'When I am with you, it makes my life work.'"

It has been said in folk wisdom that forty is the old age of youth, and fifty is the youth of old age. Natalie B. began her old age by riding her bicycle 600 miles along the Pacific Coast.

"Why? Because my sixteen-year-old son invited me to join a bicycle-club expedition. I was still grieving over my husband's death. It was my fiftieth birthday, and all I could foresee was a dreary future of being alone with my body deteriorating and my mind atrophying. I thought, 'Why not?' I wanted to see if I could do it.

"I had always loved to bicycle, but that trip was the most fantastic experience, the most strenuous work, the biggest challenge! I ended it loving my body. It felt so lean and full of potential strength. It was a better body than I'd had as a young woman, or as a cookieholic housewife in my thirties and forties, when I had always missed having a good figure by about ten pounds."

Now fifty-five, Natalie looks younger, with a breezy

natural air that draws admiring glances from men. To maintain her slenderness, she exercises thirty minutes a day and monitors her diet.

"I love it when men think I'm forty, sometimes even late thirties. I have more male attention now than I had in college.

"After my bicycle trip, I made up my mind to change my eating habits. The first time I stopped a cookie in midair and put it back in the jar was the turning point. I kept in my mind a picture of the way to feel about my figure. 'Not one cookie,' I said to myself, 'until the needle on the scale gets one point below 110.' I wrote down the amounts of fattening foods I would allow myself each day, and soon I didn't even miss the no-nos.

"Now, liking my physical self, I began to think about renewing my mind as well. Again, I made lists, this time of ways to spark my conversation, to offer a little extra to my exchanges with friends. I worked on expanding my reading, making special note of any item that would interest a particular person. I gathered interesting anecdotes and stories from other people and from my children, and I went out by myself to meetings and workshops that would bring me new points of view. I practiced talking to all kinds of men, getting used to relating to them in my new role as a single. Eventually, what started out as a project became a part of my personality. As a young woman, I realized, I had been a dud. On a date, I was just there. No man ever said then, as one did recently, 'You are a fascinating woman.'

"Five years ago, I thought my future with men was really over. Who ever heard of a Prince Charming for an over-fifty princess? Well, there are lots of Prince Charmings out there, more delightful in fact than those who were there thirty-five years ago."

Sixty has, in the past, had an elderly ring. It has raised

a specter of slowing down, not a vision of dancing and dating. But at sixty-five, Margaret G. in Dallas, Texas, has a calendar studded with engagements. Five-foot-three and 110 pounds, Margaret pays scrupulous attention to her dress and knows exactly what kind of image she wants to project: tailored but colorful with plenty of style. Not outstandingly good-looking, she is petite and perky and maintains a multitude of interests, bringing to her retirement the same zeal she took to her many years of social work.

There have been many men in Margaret's life. Widowed as a young woman after only three years of marriage, she has spent most of her life as a single, with the exception of a brief marriage that ended in divorce.

Margaret's admirers cannot seem to define her attractiveness.

"There is just something about you," they usually say. But Margaret knows what the something is because she's cultivated it.

"I really like the company of men," she said. "I have a woman friend who keeps saying, 'Men never pay any attention to me.' But she never acts as if she were interested in them. When men are around, I always look right at them.

"I smile and ask them questions about themselves, and when I like something about them, I don't hesitate to say so, even if they haven't paid me a compliment first."

Margaret believes it's necessary to take the initiative because many men are shy to begin with and so scarred by bad experiences with women that by the time they have reached her age, it is very difficult for them to be the aggressor. Six months after her retirement, she had two men in attendance. One hovers protectively, making small repairs for her pleasant ranch-style home, taking her dancing at least once a week.

A second gentleman, who was married to one of her good friends, picked up on the correspondence she had with his wife after his wife's death and has been courting her by mail.

"This one is extremely handsome and has a boat as well, and I am seriously considering his invitation to visit in Santa Barbara."

But then, there is the new widower across the street....

A noted psychiatrist has defined sex appeal as the ability to send out a message of acceptance, a message that promises safety, not judgment or rejection. Such a message can be sent only by a person who is himself emotionally healthy, with a vitality that stimulates the vitality of another and makes an interflow of feelings possible.

Of all the women we talked to, seventy-five-year-old Minnie T. is perhaps the best example of that psychiatrist's view. Minnie's soft, warm voice and responsive laughter create an atmosphere of instant intimacy. Still holding down her job as librarian for a medical society in North Carolina, she enjoys nothing more than to produce a book or document that will solve a problem for one of her patrons. She is surrounded by men in her work, some of whom think she is very special.

"It's nice to feel that men think you're attractive and to watch someone's face light up when he sees you."

"You and your ebullient nature," one told her recently. Watching her banter with another, a young secretary remarked:

"Why, Minnie, he certainly has lovelight in his eyes."

Five years earlier, sparking lovelight was the farthest thing from Minnie's thoughts. She had just lost her husband after nearly fifty years of marriage, a loss that was followed within a two-year period by the death of her only daughter. Minnie's sparkle was dimmed. She grew frail and absent and began, in the truest sense of the word, to grow old.

Then, remarkably, the aging process seemed to come

to a halt and reverse itself. The miracle came about through Minnie's sheer determination and design.

"The worst time of every day used to be in the evening, when I came home to an empty house," she said. "It was unbearably quiet. So I decided to fix my dinner in the morning before I left for work. Then, when I came in the door, I could pop into the kitchen, heat up my dinner in a jiffy, and take it on a tray to the living room, where I had TV for company. At night, when I awoke with those terrible feelings, I'd turn on the radio to a talk show and become engrossed in all those fascinating conversations. It's impossible to think about two things at once, so my trick was to replace a negative thought with a positive one."

Two years after the death of her daughter, to add spice to her life, Minnie joined a singles group for people of fifty and over. She has already made a conquest of what she believes to be the most attractive man on the scene. The gentleman, who was delegated to call for her on the first meeting she attended, now presents himself regularly to escort her. Meanwhile, she is branching out, looking over other singles and church groups, adult education classes, and doing some entertaining herself.

"Not just to meet men," she says. "Everything I do expands my thinking."

Making her own clothes is to Minnie therapeutic and a creative expression of her own femininity. She loves to alter patterns, add a saucy sash, change a neckline, or embroider a spray of flowers, and the results are individual and becoming.

"Besides, dressing nicely makes me *feel* attractive," she explained.

Minnie maintains her trim figure by walking to and from the bus that takes her to work and running briskly up and down the stairs during the day instead of taking the elevator.

Minnie pinpoints her own appeal when she says she believes in "sharing the other fellow's joy."

"It may sound like bragging to some people, I suppose, when a man talks about his sons' achievements all the way to town on the bus, but I really like to watch his pleasure, and it makes me feel good to know, when he leaves, that our conversation made him happy."

Minnie, Margaret, Natalie, Miriam, and Nora—all have the qualities the men we interviewed said would attract them to an older woman.

Their figures range from pleasant to superb. Not one of them is fat.

They dress well, if not always expensively or even stylishly. Their clothes are youthful, but not "young." They are well groomed, even for a trip to the grocery store.

They all have a relish for living and learning. They accept themselves and other people. They have a confident outlook and look as if living were fun. Not one of them is "old."

They are sexually experienced.

They are ladies.

They are financially independent, though not rich.

They are personally independent—people in their own right who have learned to live with their singleness and like it.

All of these women have a common bond: each suffered a crisis or several crises, which precipitated a reassessment of her approach to life. Each charted a new course toward self-chosen goals, a course built on daring to assert herself and on developing new habits of thought and behavior. The very length of time they had lived provided them with the experience and insight necessary to make the moves they did.

As that philosopher movie star of the twenties, Marie Dressler, once said:

"It's not how old you are, but how you are old."
Recognizing and acting upon this difference, they are the women who can still attract a man across a crowded room.

CHAPTER 9

Across A Crowded Room—II
what women find attractive
in a man over fifty

"Gray hair turns me on!"

The words, spoken with feeling by a beautiful woman in her thirties, were echoed in thought by most of the women we polled to learn what qualities they find attractive in men over fifty. The consensus is that older men at their best, with or without hair (and almost no women minded baldness), have attractions seldom found in their younger competition, attractions that in many cases make them more desirable as both friends and long-term sexual partners.

Maturity, stability, self-confidence, acceptance of themselves and of life, consideration, compassion, experience, wisdom, having it all together—these are the phrases that recur time and again when women talk about the assets of older men.

"They are not preoccupied with where they are going because they are already there."

"They have had time to understand and master their feelings."

One sensitive twenty-eight-year-old beauty, who had been living with a man in his early fifties for four years, sharing expenses equally, had this to say:

"The thing that arrests me in an older man is his presence. How he feels about himself, if he's standing proud,

143

standing tall. It's almost an aura about him. He's got charisma.

"Thirty-year-old men just don't relate to me in a mature way. I seem to have more in common with those who are older."

For our composite Ideal Older Man, designed from the comments of the women we interviewed, we found seven basic qualities:

To begin with, he is interesting: a man who can talk about a variety of subjects because he has a variety of interests.

"I like a good conversationalist, someone who's not a single-subject person. At the very minimum, he should read the newspapers."

"A sense of humor is a big plus, but he should be able to have a serious conversation, too, about things that are going on in the world. The person who is always joking creates a barrier. There's no way of really relating to him, and I soon lose interest."

"Older men, the ones who attract me, at least, have a sense of aesthetics: art, music, poetry."

"There's got to be a meeting of minds. I want to be on the same wavelength. Sometimes I run through all the topics of conversation I can think of, and they just get plumped on the floor, like air going out of a balloon. I finally give up and start to get tense."

A fail-safe way of being interesting, some women advise, is to follow the advice mothers used to give their daughters: Be interested. Talk about *her*. Get her to talk about herself.

"It is so refreshing, after years of boosting a man's ego, talking about him and everything he might be interested in, to find someone who is interested in *me*—who even wants to hear about my work and my problems."

Another woman concurred:

144

"A man who gives me all his attention brings out the very best in my conversation."

More than one woman liked the feeling of being singled out by a man, and many think the best way for a man to communicate this feeling is through eye contact.

A brunette of flashing beauty, who felt immediately drawn to the man who later became her lover, still remembers the look he gave her on their first meeting: "He seemed to look right through me and then he looked away—as if he'd had a wicked thought. It made my knees weak," she said.

"But please, no pie in the sky," begged one. "I want an honest man, not one who makes me think I'm the most attractive woman on earth and then doesn't call me all week."

On the other side of the coin, nothing turns a woman off faster, they said, than to have a man's gaze stray over her shoulder to see who is coming in the door.

"The very end is for a man to comment about another woman's looks when he's talking to me. To stop his conversation and say, 'Wow!' or 'There goes a gorgeous chick!' It makes me think he's got a lot of junk hidden inside him that he doesn't know how to handle."

A willingness and ability to communicate not just his thoughts but his feelings is a basic part of being interesting to many women:

"I want to know what makes him happy, what makes him sad, when he's lonely, when he's feeling loving towards me and why, when he's angry with me and why. It's the only way you can really feel close to somebody. Otherwise, you communicate at such a superficial level that your relationship is dry, empty, with no substance; and no matter how many things a man has to talk about, no matter how many experiences he's had, no matter how many neat things he does, he gets tiresome."

One woman, however, cautioned against the overzealous graduate of the pop psychology classes who brings all the vocabulary with him, who is so in touch with his feelings that he has changed "from macho to musho."

Honesty, sincerity, stability, dependability—all the old-fashioned qualities mothers used to call "sterling"—are prized more than ever by today's women. They are qualities, women believe, that older men have often developed with their years.

"Young men get all excited and throw temper tantrums," an attractive young psychotherapist said. "Everything that comes up is a crisis. The older man knows the difference between inconvenience and catastrophe."

One woman could remember her present lover as a young man. "He would have been tough to be around for very long. I can still see him patiently gnashing his teeth as he waited for one of his wives. Today, he is a different person. He takes everything in stride."

Women seeking a more substantial relationship stressed tenderness and consideration as qualities they would look for in a man and were more apt to find in one over fifty.

"Older men know how to treat a woman," a woman said, recalling a former relationship. "I would just mention something I needed to do—change a light bulb, fix my windshield wiper—and before I knew it, it was done."

Men to be avoided, on the other hand, were those who had not matured in other ways: the ones who lost their tempers, were poor sports, had overpowering egos, sulked, were dictatorial, the braggarts and smart-alecks who gave themselves compliments—the men who were completely absorbed in themselves.

"I hate to see a man who's so immature as to blame everybody else for what happens to him. I'm thinking now of a fellow who lost his first game in bowling the other night, put his ball in his bag, and went home mad."

While most of the women liked men who had a

young outlook and kept up with the times, they considered it a sign of immaturity when an older man became obsessed with holding onto his youth. They shun the "middle-aged hippie," the long gray locks that fringe a bald head. One woman cited a man of fifty-five who embarrassed everyone by trying to be one of the boys, when the boys were his teenage sons. He outdid his efforts to maintain his image of virility, she thought, when only three days after getting home from the hospital where he had undergone heart surgery, he went back to work.

"Nobody thought he was macho," she said. "We just thought he was a fool."

The third quality that attracts women to an older man is his zest for living. They want a man who is warm and alive, friendly and fun to be with, who lives life with enthusiasm, who likes to do things and does them well.

"I like a man who smiles, who looks as if he's ready to make friends."

"Remember Mae West? How she used to say, 'It's not the men in your life, but the life in your men'? Nothing's changed."

At the top of the list of what women like to have a man do well is dance. "Any man who is a good dancer can have the singles world by the tail," an officer in a singles club commented. And to make things easier, some dance studios offer men a special rate of two lessons for the price of one in order to attract partners for the women who flock there.

Rather far down the list of assets that turn women on, but the number-one quality that can turn them off, is a man's appearance. Like men, women notice size and shape.

"Pot bellies are out! How can you have sexual intercourse? That's a big thing to be in the way."

"A fat man sitting on a desk with his bottom hanging over the edge is not a pleasing sight. And he certainly should not be wearing skin-tight pants."

147

The sexiest look is healthy: "tanned," "outdoorsy," "in good shape," "a vital, healthy look, as if he cares for himself in mind and body."

And like the men also, women are conscious of grooming.

"It's a put-down when a man comes to see you looking sloppy or soiled—and that goes for his car, too. It's as if he doesn't think enough of you to care about cleaning up."

Dirty teeth, stained teeth, missing teeth were commented upon with distaste.

"Blackheads in the wells of a man's ears—ugh!"

One woman always notes a man's shoes; not the style, but the shape they are in. In short, what women like is a nice, clean man, without spots on his clothes, one who might look a little rumpled, but who has shaved. And clean of body, breath, and armpit, without the addition of perfume, is enough for most.

"What can we say about men's perfume? We can say 'Phew!' Not Old Spice nor Brut nor English Lavender can take the place of clean. Some men are simply laying it on too heavily."

One woman vowed she was going to visit a men's cosmetic counter and smell all the perfumes until she discovered the one that smelled like a barn, so she could advise her men friends against using it.

Clothes that enhance the man and are in style are a definite plus, and most of the women we talked to like conservative taste.

"The best-dressed man I know has only a few clothes in his closet. They are plain, multipurpose, good-quality, and masculine."

"I adore wools and tweeds."

"Please, keep it dignified. No necklaces, square-toed shoes, or open-to-the-navel shirts."

"I guess you can say I like a man to be looking good," a

woman said, summing up a variety of comments. "That's not the same as good-looking. Looking good is something anyone can achieve."

For better or for worse, a reality on the American singles scene is that richer is better than poorer, and the women we surveyed were plain about money, particularly the younger ones.

A beautiful mother in her early thirties with two children to support and a very square sense of values looked straight at us with her honest blue eyes and said:

"Younger men usually have children of their own, and they're pinched for money. I don't want to go through all the hassle again that I had when I was married."

Others commented:

"He should be willing to take me to a nice place once in a while, perhaps once a month, and do the whole works—not pick out a cheap dinner. I guess I think of it as an affirmation of his esteem."

For some women, stinginess on the part of their escort, particularly stinginess in tipping, is a real humiliation.

Imagination, originality, and thoughtfulness, however, are a good substitute for lavishness. A personable New Yorker remembers with affection a man who "always knew the cute little out-of-the-way places. They might even be kind of poor in a sort of funny way—a mom-and-popper, where you'd go next door to the liquor store to buy the wine for dinner."

Another woman was moved by the thoughtfulness of a friend who brings presents, not to her, but to her small daughter, presents that, while inexpensive (like a box of Magic Markers), always thrill the child and give her a tool with which to be creative.

For some, money is linked with accomplishment.

"I must confess, a certain amount of success is important. He doesn't have to be a company president or a

millionaire, but I like a man who, at age fifty, is doing something with his life—isn't still bumming around. If you've
worked hard to do a good job in your own field, you'd like to
find someone who has done something in his, too."

Another aspect of the male-female roles that has not
changed is courtesy. Listen to what women are still saying:

"I'm terribly impressed by men with manners—men
who hold doors for me, who stand up when I come to the
table, who light my cigarettes."

"I still like men to keep their roles. I like to be thought
of as an equal person, but also as a female person."

"I love to be pampered."

"The kind of older man I'm talking about is the one
who has impeccable manners, who knows what to do and
how to do it if he needs to."

"I like to be treated kindly, respectfully, generously
—and very carefully."

Even the more independent younger woman finds it a
nice surprise to be taken care of. One of these who had been
invited to go skiing by an older man said she'd be out in front
of her apartment waiting for him when he came to pick her
up. She confessed to a little thrill of delight when he replied,
"Oh no! I'm going to go up and help you down with your
skis."

All of the women we talked to said that they are, if
anything, turned on by the man who defers his sexual advances. Few appreciate the public lech and most did not
want to jump into bed with someone they didn't know very
well.

"I've never perfected a way to say no," a forty-five-
year-old writer said. "I really like it when a man doesn't push
you the first time, even the third time. And guys who feel
you up and down in public are too crass for words. It's dumb
of them and scares you off because you think if you get in the
car with them, too bad for you."

The men who proffer even milder attentions—kisses and hugs—too indiscriminately at a party lose their dignity in the eyes of many women—and, perhaps more important, their challenge.

"It's just like my mother used to tell me. He can make himself cheap."

Many feel there is something extremely sexy, in this age of quick rolls in the hay, about a man who does *not* make a pass right away.

"I think it explains the popularity of many ministers. You can sit there in church meetings—which are mostly women—and just feel the vibes going his way."

In a class with the touchy-feelies was the man, usually loud of mouth, who touches everybody, men and women, slapping them on the back, roughing up their hair, not the touches of friendship and communication but locker-room roughhouse.

Finally, women are attracted to a man with self-confidence. Many considered it the hallmark of the man over fifty, the one who has weathered all the storms and come out stronger and more tightly knit as a result.

"He accepts things as they are. He's at peace."

"If he likes himself, he's going to like me. More important, he's going to let me *be* me."

"He doesn't have to impress anyone with who he is. He *knows* who he is, and that's enough."

From the group of attractive older men who responded to our survey, we chose five who represented a variety of ages and backgrounds, yet who all had the essentials of magnetism specified by the ladies.

The youngest of the group is Kevin L., fifty-two, a journalist who two years ago for the first time in his life had to handle rejection. After twenty-five years of marriage, he and his wife had been amicably divorced, both realizing that, with the children grown, their personalities were incompatible. She was an introvert who wanted to stay home. He was an extrovert who wanted to get out of the house, meet people, experience life.

What he experienced, three months after his divorce, was a tremendous longing for a wife and family, not for the one he had left but for a richer, fuller family unit with the kind of man-woman relationship he had always missed. Then he met Enid, twenty-eight, beautiful, talented, a commercial artist, and such a relationship seemed at last possible. He fell deeply in love, but when he proposed marriage, Enid laughed coolly.

"You're great fun, Kevin," she said, "but I could never be serious. You're a lot—well, older—and my career is just taking off. I'm not ready to get involved with anybody."

In one shattering moment, Kevin felt himself change from a revitalized lover on the threshold of a new and exciting life to a graying and somewhat shabby man of more than middle age.

"I felt that if I had owned a bank, things would have been different," he said.

But Kevin did not own a bank. He could not even afford a psychiatrist. Instead, he did a lot of reading and talked to himself, sometimes out loud.

"I convinced myself by saying it over and over that rejection did not mean there was anything wrong with me. Some people prefer carrots to peas, which doesn't mean there is anything wrong with peas. I examined my attitudes towards money, which had never been a high priority in my life, and decided that I could not compromise them. I would have to find someone who could share them. Then I focused my mind on making the best of my life as a single."

To take his mind off his loss, he plunged into his hobby of photography, joined an amateur movie group, worked and studied with such single-minded purpose that he won two national awards.

"In Memphis, Tennessee, that made me a kind of celebrity," he said, "and it did a lot for my morale. I began to feel like somebody again."

He also became aware of the admiring glances cast his way when he was introduced at local performances of his films, and once again he began to take an interest in women. This time he approached them more cautiously, experimentally, trying techniques, telling stories and jokes, and listening for feedback.

"As a single in middle life, I had to find out about women all over again," he said. "It's not the old high school gym."

Among the things he found out was that women respond when he tells them how he feels, when he shares his hopes and his disappointments with them.

"Men would have better relationships with women," he thinks, "if they got rid of the John Wayne syndrome and made themselves sensitive to women's responses.

"When I'm with a woman, even our silences are productive. Having learned to let go of my fears of rejection, I don't worry that she may not like me if we can't find something to talk about. I simply relax and enjoy being with her."

Despite his erect, lean stature and Gaelic good looks, Kevin thinks that most of the women attracted to him are interested not in him but in what he represents: stability and fidelity.

Kevin now dates women his own age and somewhat younger.

Old-fashioned in his approach to sex, he believes in staying on his feet, literally and figuratively, until he's gotten to know a woman.

"I can have seven or eight dates with the same person over a three-week period, and guess who becomes the aggressor. Sex will happen, if it's the right thing to do, but I don't think it's the main cake."

When Dwight G., fifty-five, was a boy in high school, he learned about women from a girl who later became a successful madam. Sitting on the sidelines with him at a dance in the gym, watching the adolescent boys, all hands, try to arouse the girls, she commented, "If they only realized it, Dwight, none of them can make a girl as fast as she will make herself."

Remembering her insight, Dwight has never in his life propositioned a woman, or found it necessary.

As an attaché in the American Embassy, Dwight's job was to make foreign dignitaries feel at ease at parties and to dispose them favorably toward the United States. In the process he learned further useful skills—for one thing, about eye contact.

"Today, everybody is talking about the importance of eye contact," he said. "People are staring each other down. If you get locked into one of those stares, smile and direct the other person's attention—and gaze—to something else."

When Dwight was invited to a party to meet Susan, his beautiful, thirty-year-old girlfriend, he followed his old protocol procedure: he found out five or six things she was interested in and made a mental dossier on her. Susan was impressed, and she grew more impressed as she found out more about Dwight.

A survivor of widowhood and a devastating divorce, Dwight forged his recovery in the out-of-doors: backpacking, fishing, hunting, and by plunging into new projects that presented a challenge. After his retirement from his job, he turned his hand to a variety of enterprises: farming, real estate sales, contracting.

"He's such a doer," Susan says, "and he does everything methodically and well, even if it's just fixing my refrigerator."

Surveying the singles scene and the contrast in treatment women receive from younger men (some of whom introduce themselves with "Hi, wanna fuck? My name's Joe"), Susan also appreciates Dwight's courtliness.

"The very nicest thing about him," she said, smiling reflectively, "is the way he treats me in public. He makes me feel like his lady."

Ten years ago, after three marriages, Vance T., fifty-nine, still felt uneasy around women. They were one of his many uneasinesses, despite his secure job as an economist for an oil company in Iran, an exotic standard of living, and an overseas salary that was making him rich.

"I used to wake up each morning with a list of things to worry about, and I'd be halfway down it before I was fully awake. It was my most treasured possession," he recalls.

When his third wife left him, he did not grieve. He had done all the grieving several years before after he came home to a silent apartment, his first wife and two daughters gone, leaving him alone in a foreign country. This time, he looked around and found a good psychiatrist, a woman, and went to see her twice a week for thirty weeks. In the course of his treatment, he discovered in a hot flood of insight that he did not have to please his parents, who had always been unpleasable.

"Knowing I did not *have* to please them left me free to please them," he said. "In fact, it left me free—to quit the job that was going nowhere, to come back to the States, to retire in the middle of my life instead of at the end of it, to enjoy the company of women."

Vance relished his midlife four-year retirement.

"I'd always been a sit-around, drink-a-lot personality," he said. "But in this period I discovered hiking, skiing, tennis, bicycling. I cherished the dream of climbing Mount Whitney, the highest peak in the Sierra Nevada, and when my doctor told me I had arthritis in my knee that would only get worse with time, I decided I'd better climb it right away. I did, and the arthritis disappeared."

The leanness of body, the toughness of spirit, even the weatherbeaten lines in his face that are a legacy of Vance's retirement years are immensely appealing to women. Not insensitive to the magnetism of money, he decided after going back to work as a consultant that his image needed burnishing, and so traded in his Ford for a sportier car. He goes courting in clothes he would wear for a client, either a business suit or a conservative sport coat, "no loudness, no white or two-tone shoes."

An omnivorous reader, Vance can relate to women of any background, at any age level, devouring *Rolling Stone* and Hunter Thompson as avidly as *Playboy,* as voraciously as *The Wall Street Journal.* "You can be interested in young thought without acting like a twenty-year-old," he believes.

Today, he has evolved from the painfully shy youth who counted himself lucky to have a girlfriend—any girlfriend—past the uneasy man of forty into a self-assured veteran, who, in the words of one attractive admirer, "could have anybody."

Watch him, in a crowded room, as he establishes instant intimacy with the woman he has singled out. When there is laughter in the group, his eyes catch hers and he shares the joke with her privately. Later, as he engages her in one-to-one conversation and finds a common interest, his surprise and delight are open. The unmistakable impression left with the lady is that Vance has found a treasure, a woman at last who can share his thoughts, his humor, his dreams. And when, at the end of the evening, he bends over her chair and whispers into her ear "See you later," he is reasonably sure that he will.

In the eyes of one of his beautiful admirers, Gene T. at sixty-three is a man with panache. She loves his wavy silver hair that is combed slickly back to his crisp collar, the way his muscles ripple beneath his pants when he crosses his legs, his active interest in every topic.

Yet ten years ago, after his divorce from an alcoholic wife, attracting women seemed like the last thing Gene was ready to do. He had suffered financial catastrophe in his forties and was struggling sixty hours a week with his new advertising business. What free time he had was occupied with the raising of his three children, of whom he had custody. On top of it all, his friends—mostly couples—had dropped him, and no one was clamoring to introduce him to eligible women.

"I decided I would just have to establish priorities, and the top ones would be my business and my children," he said.

Because the failure of his first business had been caused by the unrealistic monetary values of his partners, Gene was determined to maintain scrupulous integrity in building this one, a decision that not only paid off in his work but also made him feel good about himself. It had a further spinoff benefit, too, when a few years later another businessman confidentially told a woman Gene loved:

"You are out with one of the finest gentlemen in the state of Florida."

In the next few years, Gene's agency grew and thrived, his children left the nest, and he had more time to think about his own development. A New Englander, he was naturally quiet and withdrawn, but to further his business he made himself meet people, serve on boards and committees, give speeches. The confidence and poise he gained in the process served him well as he got back into circulation socially.

Today, it is evident by his lithe movements as he walks across a crowded room that he is in top physical condition. He stays that way by jogging from one to two miles three times a week, swimming a periodic workout of twenty-four laps, playing a fast game of tennis, and skiing. He takes his sports seriously, playing to win, to improve.

While he has little time for reading, he keeps current with two local newspapers, *The Wall Street Journal,* and *Reader's Digest,* all back-up material for his conversational precept:

"A bore talks about himself. A gossip talks about others. A brilliant conversationalist talks about you." When he meets a woman, he finds out about her, talks about her interests more than his own. If the friendship develops, he tries to remember what was happening in her life the last time they were together and inquires about a problem she might have had.

"I also think it's a compliment to ask a woman's advice," he said.

Money also speaks for Gene. Said one of his friends: "I would be less than truthful if I said I didn't love going to England, receiving expensive presents, going to exclusive dances. But who would want to do even those things with a bore? Gene is like a Renaissance man, a multifaceted human being. He knows about literature, music, art. And he's such a learner, willing to try anything, not embarrassed or self-conscious about it, so he keeps getting better and better."

Cyrus J., at seventy-two, has bridged the generation gap. You can see him any morning jogging around the park near which he lives, his slender figure topped by a thick shock of ash-blond hair, waving to friends. Twice a week he works out with men as young as twenty at an evening gym class. Another night, he learns the cha-cha and the hustle at a dance class a twenty-eight-year-old girlfriend persuaded him to attend with her.

When he was fifty, Cyrus learned that age need not be a barrier to friendship. His divorce had been crushing. His wife, who would have been a European countess had she not been married to Cyrus, a commoner, left him the day his assignment abroad ended and they were scheduled to leave for the States. Retiring from government service, he made an up-and-down living with investments. At one of the down points, he took a room in a college fraternity and found to his surprise that his twenty-three-year-old roommate was so companionable that they frequently double-dated. He has numbered young people among his friends ever since.

Unlike some older men, Cyrus, because of a second divorce, does not presently have wealth with which to lure the women he dates, who range in age from twenty-three to sixty. But his interests and background make him endlessly fascinating. He loves the deep-sea fishing off the coast of Texas where he lives and dreams of taking up scuba diving in order to rummage around some old shipwrecks he's read about in Lake Superior. Books are a passion. He likes to read at least three on a topic that interests him in order to gain perspective on the subject.

"My twelve-year-old daughter adores him," said a dynamic M.D. in her late forties, whom he dates, "and so does my mother. Besides being sexually attractive, he likes women as people. He's a constant friend. When a man genuinely likes you, it's pretty hard not to like him back."

Like the women in Chapter 8, Kevin, Dwight, Vance, Gene, and Cyrus turned from the major upheavals of their lives to a search for renewal, a search that led them to evolve into stronger, more confident men, more aware of their relationships with others. Incidentally rather than by design, they developed the qualities that women find attractive in men:

They became more interesting as they broadened their interests and activities, as they re-examined their associations with women.

They learned to communicate their feelings.

They emerged as stable, mature men, having survived disaster, discarded bitterness, and moved in positive directions.

Having improved the quality of their lives, they lived them with exuberance.

They were clean, well-groomed, in shape, and conservatively well-dressed.

If they did not have money, they cultivated substitute attractions.

They were gentlemen.

They had self-confidence.

And why not? They had earned it.

CHAPTER 10

Be Honest With Me, Dear
making sexual relationships work

"It's going to be very difficult for you, after twenty-five years of marital slumber. It's not the same as it used to be—the dating, the good-night kiss at the front door. Not the same at all."

The urbane divorcé, his voice gently sympathetic, sent a chill through his newly widowed listener. The world "out there" seemed suddenly alien, booby-trapped with future shock.

Two years later, the same widow can look back and laugh.

"No, it's not the same, thank goodness!" she said. "All those boy-girl games we used to play twenty-five years ago—the no-nos about sex, the guilt trips. They're gone and good riddance."

Attitudes toward "new" sexual freedom that meets new singles when their marriages of many years come to an end vary widely among individuals and among different areas of the country. Some people deny that there is anything very new about it, maintaining that the sexes are still doing what the sexes have always done. One widowed schoolteacher in San Francisco, recalling her youth, said matter-of-factly:

"Once I was over the teenage traumas and guilt trips of the culture, I thought sex was great. Jolly good fun. I still do."

In some parts of the country, the freedom has never arrived. In Atlanta, Georgia, for example, two lovers feel constrained. Even though both sense a slow relaxation of the rules, they do not feel free to take a trip together, and she worries what her neighbors, good friends though they are, must speculate about his frequent visits to her house.

"No one ever comes out and says it's wrong to have this kind of relationship," he said. "It's the sum total of how everyone relates socially, how they emphasize certain standards of conduct."

Other singles in other places do see a radical change in the sexual mores, and some greet it enthusiastically. Those men who savor the situation with lusty zest say:

"I *love* it!"

"I enjoy being called to talk, to go out, to date, to make love."

The women say:

"It's about time!"

"Freedom! I don't *need* a husband to have a good social life, a good sex life. I can go where I want, do what I want."

But then there are the negatives. From the men:

"Too many women wanting too much sex. This can be tough on a man who can't really handle that much activity. Why didn't this happen when I was twenty?"

"I don't like to see women surrender their femininity. I want finesse and delicacy."

And from the women:

"Does the new sexual freedom mean I am free or free of charge?"

"I think the new morality is degrading."

"I just wish men would be men and women would be ladies!"

Still others have struggled with the change, trying to

overcome their conservativeness. A retired professor of social work who looked skeptically at living-together arrangements among students when they became popular in the sixties finally concluded that they might be a good idea, after all.

"It gives couples a trying-out period to see if they can establish the kind of give and take required for a marriage," she said. "If it isn't right for either, they can end it without explanations to family and friends and without business and legal divorce arrangements adding to the hurt." Today, this woman is fully in favor of multiple lifestyles for all ages.

"I believe that what we've known is not the only way, not necessarily the best way for everybody," she said.

Choosing from the options, evaluating the hazards and satisfactions inherent in each, developing individual standards of behavior when those of society are uncertain or in conflict can be a troublesome task after a quarter-century or more of living under fairly definite rules.

For men, and even more for women, the rules of sexual conduct that applied in their single youth no longer serve. Many women recall the girl talk that centered on when to kiss a boy good night. There were those who thought first-date kisses were "cheap"; a larger number who thought by date number three a good-night kiss was okay. There had been necking and petting and heavy petting and *then* there had been——.

"I feel like an adolescent all over again," a fifty-two-year-old divorcée said. "I seem to be asking myself, 'Who am I? How do I relate to men? What are my values?'"

The singles we talked to have worked out their personal beliefs, their sexual relationships and values in a variety of ways, ranging from casual sexual encounters, unencumbered with emotional involvement, to one-to-one commitments of a deep and lasting nature.

One-night stands and casual relationships are viewed by many as a stage in their disengagement from an ex-husband or -wife, a part of the healing process. People said:

"When you are still reeling from divorce, you are not ready for a heavy relationship."

"One-night stands are important to both sexes at certain times. They fill their needs without getting them tied up."

Sometimes, though, noninvolvement becomes a habit. The motto of one man, four times divorced, was: "Find 'em, feed 'em, fuck 'em, forget 'em." Said he:

"If I get that detail out of the way, I can sleep and awaken refreshed. I have a big sex drive that I must keep fulfilled."

Many people, a male social worker pointed out, do not want a high-intimacy relationship, and it is a relief that they don't have to have it any more.

"There is less pressure on people today to be the things they thought they ought to be and never really were," he said.

A cautionary note is added by a second social-work authority, who regards recreational sex as a complex matter:

"If a person can truly feel that it's like playing tennis, that it makes him feel good, that it's enjoyable but no big deal, then okay. But there are sometimes other forces at work. Many of us have a lurking thought that sex is wrong to begin with. We feel it's a private business. It is also linked with an emotional relationship and a sense of continuity. If any of these forces is hidden underneath, and one partner begins to think he or she needs more than just the sex act, there is a built-in potential for emotional trauma."

Most do not find casual sex satisfying for any extended period of time. Typical, perhaps, is Sally R., a well-heeled Marin County, California, housewife who divorced her husband because he did not relate to her "at a feeling level." When the man she left him for proved unsatisfactory on a practical and responsible level, she tried the dating game for a period of four months, meeting men in bars and spending nights in motels.

"Out of the four months, I had one beautiful experience with a married man from another city. We talked from five in the evening until 2 A.M., got up and took a shower together in the morning, and had breakfast in our room. It was over breakfast I realized the experience had different meanings for each of us. He didn't want anything more. The emptiness later, for me, was horrendous. Not long afterwards, I woke up one morning and knew this wasn't the image I wanted to have for myself."

A never-married woman sometimes goes to bed with men she can "barely stand" despite a feeling that it doesn't seem "proper," simply because it's easier than saying no.

"You bet we're no longer the alabaster saints we were brought up to be," she said. "It's a mess."

The feelings of most women, however, were expressed by this one:

"Casual sex? I couldn't. To me, I'm still giving myself to him. I may need it as much as he does, but I'm not going to give it away that indiscriminately."

Most of the men, too, want something more than calisthenics. As one New Yorker said:

"I've never wanted to go to bed with someone I didn't want to have breakfast with."

Another man echoed the question many women used to ask themselves:

"Does she want me or *it?* I find out by seeing how I'm treated *out* of bed."

While almost all of the women and most of the men want a personal relationship to accompany sex, ranging in commitment from friendship to monogamy, they vary widely in their judgment as to how soon in a relationship sex should begin. Some men think it should precede friendship; most women think friendship should come first. Some follow the rule of three dates. Most, however, refuse to be bound by a formula. As two women pointed out:

"If you feel that way about someone and it clicks, the heck with trivia—how many steak dinners he's going to buy you, how many times he's going to take you dancing. Why wait? It's getting late."

"Some relationships advance very quickly. It depends on who the people are. If you really dig each other, there is probably no question about what you'd do on the first date."

One woman reflects the opinion of many, both male and female, when she comments:

"I think the man should still do the pursuing. A man likes to feel he's in command, and if you jump into bed first and say, 'Come on!' you've got a reverse chase. It's better for a man, especially an older man, to do the pursuing and pick the time when he's ready."

To which a number of the men say "Amen!"

Establishing the sexual nature of a ralationship, however, is only the beginning. From then on, the questions of involvement—how deep, how permanent—and exclusivity loom perplexingly for many.

After Sharon B. filed for divorce because her husband's long and torrid love affair with another woman showed no sign of ending, he said to her:

"Without me, you will be nothing—an old, worn-out nothing. The only thing you will be able to catch is an old, crippled man."

With the words still ringing in her ears, Sharon at fifty set out to be the most glamorous divorcée in town, and despite twenty-five years of unwavering marital fidelity, the sexiest.

"I had a lot to learn," she said. "In my marriage, sex

had been only to gratify my husband, and I had none at all in my last three years as a wife."

Les, her first lover, was eight years younger than she, and from him she learned a lot.

"I would certainly recommend a younger lover to any woman who wants to develop expertise in sex," she said.

Since Les wanted marriage and Sharon didn't feel he was right for her, the relationship broke up. Sharon then met Paul, who was attractive but alcoholic, so that ended, too.

Then came Ralph, handsome, urbane, rich—a catch by any woman's standards—who did not want to be tied down to a one-to-one mutually exclusive relationship.

"I really wanted Ralph," Sharon said. "But that whole first year after my marriage, I looked upon every man as a potential husband, and sex without any kind of commitment seemed wrong."

Sharon's psychiatrist helped her develop perspective on her problem. Women brought up in the Victorian tradition, as she had been, who were virgins at the time of their marriage and who remained faithful to their husbands, had never had an opportunity to discover themselves, he explained. Now was her chance to do what she should have done in her twenties: try out different kinds of experiences, find out her needs with no sense of pressure or desperation.

"What is the benefit of marriage for a woman in your situation?" he asked. "You don't have to be married or unmarried to have successful relationships. You should be selective, certainly, but you need not limit your experience to one man."

So Sharon said yes to Ralph and then felt free to say yes to Larry as well, and the relationship with each man deepened into, if not love, something "very special."

Both lovers know about the other, although they have never met. They shower Sharon with attention and both have proposed marriage. While they are disappointed when she can't accept a date because she is going out with the other, they accept her other commitments with grace.

At first, Sharon hated it when either of her lovers spent an evening with someone else, but with practice she has changed her thinking, so that now when she says "I hope you have a wonderful time," she means it.

"It seems only fair to let them have the same freedom I have," she concluded.

Not only do two lovers make her feel alive and desirable as a woman, each offers complementary qualities.

"No one in the human race fulfills everything you want and need," she observed. "Emotionally, Larry nourishes me. He doesn't criticize. He's a marvelous lover and lots of fun. Ralph, on the other hand, does criticize. He wants me to smoke less, take an interest in politics, handle my finances better; and by expecting more of me, he helps me get more from myself. How wonderful it would be some day, if and when I'm ready to be committed to someone again, I could find a man who is a combination of Larry and Ralph."

Like Sharon, the singles who opt to explore their opportunities find stimulation from the variety of partners they have as well as a safety precaution against overinvolvement with any one of them. The option is not without problems, however. Men sometimes feel drained of time, energy, and money.

"Just making arrangements—planning ahead to find a woman who will be free and will fit the occasion—takes up a lot of time," one said.

And those women who were still conditioned to put a man's needs ahead of their own often find the going rough. One of these enumerated the problems:

"Strained phone calls when the other person knows that you have another guest. Juggling of schedules in an attempt to meet the needs of two lovers. Rushing with the mellow times in order to be available for the other one. Placating each to avoid undue jealousy."

The worst problems, jealousy and possessiveness, are best dealt with by a straightforward agreement as to the nature of the relationship and by respecting each other's privacy.

"Let him know, by casual allusion, that you are dating others," advised a woman.

"Shun statements that imply more than good friendship," said a man.

By far the greatest number of the singles, both men and women, want just one person with whom to share their lives lovingly and intimately, for now, for longer, and some of them, tentatively, for always.

Some are prompted by practical considerations, such as a fear of venereal disease or a desire for the convenience of one available partner. Others want more depth, greater fulfillment than they find in numbers.

"I suppose you go through stages where you want to have sexual intercourse with everyone you meet, but eventually you just want someone to come home to," one man said wistfully. One psychiatrist said he is seeing many men who have left their marriages, had their first fling at being single, and come to his office pathetic and unhappy.

"They're hungry for a good relationship," he said, "either with the spouse they left or with someone new."

The greatest single complaint comes from women who could not find an acceptable man. These looked around and saw no one who compared in quality with the husbands they had left or lost.

"The top-flight men are either snapped up in marriage before they've had a taste of the good single life, or they've been so burned they're afraid of another deep relationship, or they're dead," one of these said.

Woman who were virgins at the time of their marriage and faithful wives for its duration, found it repugnant to have a sexual relationship with someone who did not meet their standards. One who had been married to an eminent psychiatrist looked upon her chiropractor lover as an underachiever and never experienced satisfactory sex with him. But when women do find presentable and attractive men, most quickly discard their inhibitions.

"By the time the opportunity came, even though it was against my morals and my faith, I decided I was going to grab every minute of happiness I could," one said. "I was hungry for it. I loved the attention, the phone calls, feeling like a desirable woman again."

Problems arise, however, when men and women have a different understanding about the duration of the relationship or the degree of commitment to it. Said the men:

"Committed. I have trouble with the word. I don't like it. It's not an appropriate word for people who are involving all the courage they can get together to do what they're doing."

"I want the freedom of sex and the chance to stop dating a person and to begin with someone new. I might get married some day if I met someone I'd want to marry, and I don't want to cut off the avenues."

Said the women:

"Where are we going? That's a dangerous question in the single world, and a lot of us are afraid to ask it, even though a sense of no fulfillment is setting in. When a relationship isn't going to work, you find out right away. If it might work, it takes longer to find out that it's not going to."

"I'm always afraid I might miss someone I'd like better. I really enjoy my life the way it is."

The best way of handling the question, many of our singles believe, is to bring it out into the open and discuss it with scrupulous honesty. Even an agreement that there is no clearly defined goal for the relationship is better than mistaken assumptions. One man put his marriage intentions in writing. Another couple signed a ninety-day renewable contract in which they simply promised to "love, honor, cherish, and be awfully damn nice to" each other.

These kinds of statements, with periodic reviews and redefinitions of the situation, if necessary, can help prevent the kind of entrapment that happened to Peter T.

When Peter became single, he resolved to do the exploring he had not done as a young man. Barely had he started, however, when he met Sandy, vivacious, interesting, with lots of ideas about places to go and things to do. Before he knew it, Sandy had become a habit and nine months of an exclusive relationship had gone by.

Then along came Joan, svelte, sexy, younger, very aggressive, and soon his dates with her had pushed Sandy into the background.

This time, Peter decided to make matters clear at the outset to avoid the reproaches he had just suffered from Sandy. He wanted no commitment, he explained, and Joan said she did not want a serious involvement either. But again, Peter slipped into a mutually exclusive relationship, partly because he had no time for anything else.

"I was just too busy taking care of all the repair jobs at her house, doing her gardening, helping discipline the kids, and fulfilling her staggering sexual needs," he said.

By this time Peter felt that he had all the disadvantages of marriage with few of the advantages, but he was unsure of how to break things off. The nature of their association had never been reviewed. They were drifting.

"Some day," he said hopefully, "she's going to throw one of her tantrums, and I'm just going to walk away from the whole thing."

Such hesitation is not the rule with most singles, however. When the satisfaction and pleasure die, when the com-

171

munication ends, when the involvement of one or the other becomes out of balance, when they no longer look forward to being with their partners, the end comes quickly. Men usually just stop phoning, start dating someone else, and let the affair fade out. Women are more likely to end it conclusively, spelling out the reason or making one up to avoid hurting the man's feelings.

One man found that by writing a letter and taking a day or two to go over it, he could say a positive goodbye that freed him up for another experience. One woman, who was dissatisfied but who could not bring herself to let go because she had no other prospects on the horizon, found help at a group therapy session:

"No relationship is better than a bad relationship," the other members of her group insisted.

"I don't want to hurt him," she objected.

"Cop-out," they responded.

Some thought it only fair to state the problems first and give their "other" a chance to correct them.

"But once out, don't look back or moon or mope," said a woman. "That's masochism. Instead, buy a new dress and set out to look for somebody better."

Out of the unstable, try-it-on, all-right-for-right-now intimacies come the ones that withstand the fire and settle into a union that both sides consider permanent. These are liaisons of love, companionship, or both, free of the strains of day-to-day domesticity. The partners involved have chosen to retain their individual households, their independence, and their identities. The choice, among the people we interviewed, was made by the woman more often than by the man.

One of these was Barbara P.—who, when she became a widow at the age of fifty-two, had lived so sheltered a life raising her six children that she thought a lesbian was somebody from Lisbon.

After two unhappy interludes with men who turned out to be married, Barbara P. met Tom, a handsome engineer. Their relationship has lasted for four years, and for Barbara it is "the last time around." It is full of fun and excitement, kept alive by a variety of mutual interests, with Barbara setting the pace. They play tennis, bowl, ride horseback along the Oregon shore near which they live, go out to dinner, take trips. Each meeting is an occasion, each sexual encounter a romantic interlude.

Accustomed in her years of marriage to "being raped more than loved," she finds that Tom's lovemaking makes her feel "a whole person."

"I dearly loved my husband, and I was always begging him to return it. I didn't want to be just a housewife, a housekeeper. I wanted to be as special to him as he was to me. I wanted a joining of minds, hands, and body."

And she gets it, now, from Tom.

Tom, on his part, presses for marriage, but Barbara wonders exactly what marriage has to offer her. There are hints of its offerings when Tom comes for dinner and takes a nap while Barbara—after a full day's work—cleans up alone.

"I had so much of that when I was married. I don't want to get locked into it all over again," she sighed.

Nor does marriage offer the security it might have provided in the past. Not only is it easily dissolved, but under new divorce laws it's often the woman who pays the penalty for the mistake, particularly if she has more money than her mate.

Does it ever get lonely for Barbara, in her own house with Tom across town in his? Not really. He calls three or four times a day, sometimes just to report on a Saturday that he's washed his socks. For Barbara, who likes her solitude and time to herself, it's all the togetherness she wants.

The key to success in making a relationship work is open communication. For Dorothy and Hugh, both in their midfifties, developing and maintaining this skill has not been easy.

"I would drive clear across town to be with him because my teenage daughter still lived at home, and he wouldn't even get out of bed to see me to the door when I left. He hardly ever took me to dinner, never sent flowers. I felt like a convenience, used. I blamed his indifference upon my having been too hasty, too 'easy,' which only reinforced my guilt feelings about going to bed. But I never could tell him how I felt. Instead, I simmered in frustration, nourished my hurt, and then, one day abruptly ended our relationship, saying only that it didn't seem to be working out. He said nothing at all."

Two days later, feeling bereft and remorseful, Dorothy wrote Hugh a letter, pouring out all her grievances, and he answered it, expressing his anger and his hurt. She phoned him. They met for coffee, and for the first time discussed their deeper feelings.

Since then, they have learned techniques for dealing with their differences.

"The magic sentence that has really worked for me," said Dorothy, "is this one: 'I feel _____ when you do _____ because _____.' Fill in the blanks with your grievance, such as 'I feel unloved when you don't tell me that you love me because I'm not sure you do.' You are giving expression to the problem without attacking or laying guilt on the other person. You're assuming responsibility for making yourself feel the way you do."

Some monogamous couples find that their relationships benefit from constant renewal, and allow each other the freedom to maintain their individual friends and pursue their own interests. One woman thought the best time in her single life occurred when she had one lover and fifteen men friends, all platonic, whom she dated for lunch, bowling, and skiing.

Said one man, a veteran of two divorces:

"All that terrible togetherness we used to have when I was married—the same friends, the same activities, the same vacations. We never had anything to tell each other because we'd both done it."

The best kind of relationship, our singles agreed, was one in which there were two givers, people who showed their affection by doing nice things for each other, not from compulsion, a sense of "goodness," or to create indebtedness in the other, but for the sheer pleasure of making the other one happy.

When Philip takes his Harriet out for dinner, he double-dates the next evening with her nine- and ten-year-old son and daughter. One day, after a particularly hard day at work, she moaned that she hadn't had a bubble bath in months. The next night, she came home to an empty house and a note from Philip:

"I've got your children," it read. "We're not coming back until 10 P.M. Sit and soak until you're shriveled."

Harriet, for her part, will spend hours in the kitchen preparing steak-and-kidney pie, a dish Philip relishes.

"And if you've ever spent an afternoon smelling a cooking kidney, you know that's a labor of love," she said.

In varying degrees, many single men and women are disturbed by the absence of commitment to which they must adjust in today's single world.

"I fear that I may not ever be able to relate to just one person again as a lifetime partner," one man in his midfifties said. Another found the prospect of living the rest of his life without a permanent partner "frightening."

Sociologist Richard Sennett has said, "Something about making a lifetime commitment of marriage doesn't work any more. . . . The idea of a permanent commitment to another human being has lost its meaning."

For those who are happy and relieved to be done with

years of tedium, stress, and misery, the lack of commitment is a joyous change. For others, who have given their hearts unreservedly once or twice or even three or four times before, only to have them broken, it is not surprising that they are slow to offer them up again.

"I'm afraid it will get dropped on the floor," one man said.

Instead, the singles who are dealing successfully with their lives are learning to relax and make the best of what comes along, be it casual sex, multiple relationships with meaning, a one-to-one relationship that is temporary or very deep. They are doing so by being open and honest with each other, expressing their feelings when it is appropriate to do so, and giving thought and effort to make their relationships work. At the same time, many are retaining a certain separateness, shrinking from involving themselves totally in each others' personalities and lives, determined to retain and improve their own identities. As one woman summed up for most of them:

"I cherish what comes my way, when it comes my way, for as long as I have it. But I've got to think of myself, because I'm the only one who will never leave me."

CHAPTER 11

Money Is Sexy
in today's marketplace

Alan is a ruggedly handsome bachelor who is sixty and doesn't look it. Fastidious and sensitive, he is at ease only in familiar situations and surroundings. The very highly paid manager of a successful business, he has been the faithful lover of a number of most attractive women about his own age, one after the other. Each of them left him to be married; his current partnership is of nearly five years' standing.

"I'm essentially monogamous," he said, "but marriage is something else."

He explained why he had to think whether or not women's money attracted him, although every one of his women friends had been well-off or even rich.

"My first thought was no, or course not," Alan went on. "But when I asked myself why I'd never fallen for a poor girl, it occurred to me that while I'd never put it to myself just that way, a woman's money does help make her attractive, even seductive. I'm sure this is not because I want any of it. But the world I live in is a world of moneyed people. I'm more comfortable with those who have it, especially women.

"But that's not the whole story. Deep down I suppose I feel more outgoing when my attraction for her isn't my money, and could I ever be sure of that if she's poor? Then it's important for me that we share the same affluent background. Money becomes like the sparkle in her eye; I don't want to take it from her, but it sure is alluring. So I have to say for me money is sexy."

Some women, particularly those who have handsome divorce settlements or inheritances, begin their new lives with a fear that men will be attracted not to them but to their wealth. Many will. But that does not mean, if you're one of these unfortunate fortunates, that you should live in a hovel and wear rags so that men will love you for yourself alone. Love of money and loving someone who has money turn out not to be the same thing. Consider your financial assets, instead, as a part of your charm, which they are. Half of the men we interviewed said so.

"Of course I like a woman with money," a handsome and rich older divorcé said. "I like to be seen with someone who is beautifully dressed and styled, who mingles with the kind of people I'm used to, and who has the same background and tastes. I don't feel I'm buying her."

Another man, just as handsome but not as rich, said:

"I don't date a woman just because she has money, but if she does have it, I look hard to find other good qualities."

That men should feel this way no longer bothers one well-endowed divorcée who experienced initial misgivings about her wealth.

"Just because men are attracted by your money doesn't mean you're going to give it to them," she said. "It doesn't take an explanation for men to see, by my dress, where I live, the clubs I belong to, that I've got it, but I always *tell* them 'I haven't a farthing.' Money is something that can bring you benefits sometimes without having to spend any of it to get them. I never lack for dates, and while money alone would not get them for me, I'm not so naïve as to think it doesn't help."

Women who think money is sexy were quicker than

Alan to realize it. Most of the women were more direct in their expressions, especially if they were in business or a profession.

Other things being equal, about half the women in our survey would take a man with money over one without.

One of the "yes" respondents was Geraldine, a strong-minded, deceptively mild-looking widow who even before her husband died achieved a successful career as an executive secretary. She had since been given larger responsibilities that broadened her contacts. She said she was attracted only to a man she could respect. One of the things she respected him for was money, but in terms of what money stands for, not what it buys.

"I guess I feel that way because I'm really a go-getter myself," she mused. "I don't think I'd feel the same about a man who merely inherited money and did nothing with it. It's the achievement wealth represents that gets to me."

Geraldine apparently never even considered dating any man whose income did not mark him as an achiever.

While some singles feel that money shouldn't make a difference, they concede that it does. These point out that wealth is so interconnected with power, status, self-esteem, ability, self-confidence, and all those good Puritan virtues of thrift and hard work that it's impossible to separate it from sexual desirability, at least in our society.

The common denominator among all who found money sexy was expressed by one of them:

"It makes both parties to the relationship more comfortable with each other, and therefore more natural."

Singles saw this as a stimulating prelude to a satisfactory sexual partnership. The reason these usually well-to-do people gave for their preference was that they enjoyed members of the other sex who were more or less of their own financial standing and lifestyle—or gave that impression.

A stockbroker, for instance, teaches an investment

class for singles so he can meet women with the same interest in the market, and the same reason for it, as his. They are all over fifty, as is he, and have enough money to take investing seriously. He argued that women of wealth possess traits he admires—distinctiveness, intelligence, taste.

"But a woman has to care what is done with her money to fully interest me," he said emphatically.

A divorcée who lived well in tasteful, well-appointed surroundings, traveled luxuriously, and relished expensive entertainment put it more simply. She was used to her standard of living, she explained, and is attracted only to men who have as much as she.

Singles who denied the sexiness of money ranged from those who said they were indifferent to some who considered it a negative factor, which goes to show that there are no universal guidelines to sexual desirability. Here are some explanations:

"Money positively turns me off, probably because I grew up as a poor boy. Besides, women with money are more demanding, while not having money makes relationships deeper, less superficial. Finally, I wouldn't want to become a lap dog." (This comment comes from a man whose own income is modest.)

"Picnicking, hiking, and biking are much more fun than the things that cost money. So a man's money doesn't matter to me at all." (A part-time designer, a woman who loves the outdoors.)

"I wasn't attracted by his money in the first place, and in time it spoiled our relationship. He thought too much of himself just because he was rich, and treated me like a thing instead of a human being. So I broke off with him. I don't think that would have happened except for his money." (A sixty-one-year-old widow who likes what money can buy but has a sense of her own value.)

"If I met someone to whom I'd really be attracted and

180

she didn't have a nickel, it might even help our relationship. It would make me feel more protective, I guess you could say more masculine, and frankly I like that." (A widower who described his late wife as a wonderful girl who relied on him for everything.)

Sometimes the possessor of wealth is regarded with awe rather than passion, and few feelings are more calculated to chill sexual ardor. Men especially, in the course of frank interviews, admit they are afraid to date women much wealthier than themselves. Pinned down, they are likely to reveal that they were brought up to believe in the power of money, and never found any reason to doubt it. They fear being dominated by rich women.

Everyone is not so decided as those quoted. Some who started by saying they could never be influenced by "the stuff" ended up by "guessing" that yes, they supposed they did find money sexy.

"It all depends upon the individual," one of the ambivalent women concluded. "It comes down to how he treats *me* as a person. Perhaps his money could influence him in more directions than one. I'd have to see."

These singles usually added that for them money meant security, which in turn had a sexual allure.

The wealthy who thought their money made them attractive to those of the opposite sex proved to be fewer than those who said they were attracted by another's money. Men who believed their wealth lured women were especially rare. One who did have faith in the glamour of his assets brought his complete financial statement as the owner of a string of motels to impress a new feminine acquaintance on their first date. He was bewildered when she politely declined to show hers on the second date. He did not report whether there was a third.

About one-third of the singles said they were quite open in discussing salaries, property, insurance, even wills.

Rather more singles were not sure whether or not they should volunteer such information and ended by deciding it should be left to the time when the two involved were planning to combine their assets in preparation for either living together or marrying.

"Whether or not to divulge finances depends on how much money means to the individuals," a banker of wide experience and considerable wisdom advises. "It could influence judgment when one of the parties has a tendency to appraise the other's success as a person on the basis of earnings or holdings."

"There's more to be lost than gained by it," commented a man to whom this advice was repeated.

When disclosure is decided upon, nearly all agreed, it should be mutual and complete. A lawyer pointed out that partial revelations can breed false hopes, manipulation, deceit, and disappointment.

The allure of money can be so very strong that it may impel a single, usually a man, to an obsessive, even intrusive curiosity. It is a sort of financial sexual perversion, akin to voyeurism. It is no more likely to appeal to the target than does voyeurism, especially among singles. What happens when the party of the first part can't restrain his inquisitiveness and the party of the second part won't satisfy it was told by a decorator who had received a small inheritance.

"I dated a man who kept trying to find out what I owned," she said, adding that up to then she had found him excellent company. "It made me skeptical when my friend asked me about my stocks and bonds and said he would expect to manage my holdings and income if we married. I felt he was not only crass but stupid, and I terminated the romance."

In dealing with money at a social level, men and women in our survey have these guidelines to offer:

Money Is Sexy

If you have it, don't flaunt it. Big-time spenders impress people with nothing but their bad taste.

Don't be curious. Leading questions make people suspicious.

Don't allude to it. It can be mortifying, especially to a woman, to be identified as rich, particularly if that appears to be her most important attribute.

"I could feel my face get hot when my *host* at a party introduced me as a woman who owned property," one said. Another recalled a male friend turning to someone she barely knew and saying, "Isn't she lovely? Beautiful, talented, rich—"

"Had he just left out the 'rich,' I'd have felt really flattered," she observed. "As it was, it seemed to color everything else."

Don't be stingy. If you're a man inviting a woman out for dinner, take her to a nice restaurant that caters to couples or fix something epicurean at your place. If you're a woman, don't impose on your date the economies your mother taught you. One man said he has women friends who will pick up and pocket the tip if he doesn't linger behind and keep a sharp eye on them.

Don't keep accounts. In buying a present, for instance, pick out the right thing, the one the other person would like to receive, instead of "paying back" with something that has the same price tag as the present you got.

If you don't have a lot of money, no need to worry. Half of the people in our survey said they don't think it makes a man or woman more attractive. Some even believe it can have an adverse effect on relationships. They maintain:

"Other things are more important."

"Relationships can be deeper when money doesn't get in the way."

Many people think that staying within your general

183

economic status when you date makes for a more comfortable relationship. A well-to-do widow who dated a postman had trouble with his easygoing philosophy.

"My husband and I had been hard drivers, and I just couldn't cope with someone who didn't want to improve his position at *all*," she said.

A train brakeman finally decided his romance with a legal secretary was not going to work out:

"My kids would think yours are snobs, and yours would think mine are slobs," he concluded.

An attractive male who had deliberately shed the accouterments of wealth and was touring the country on a motorcycle found out that the woman he had moved in with was a millionairess.

"One day she started talking about estates and investments and the whole tiresome, complicated business. It blew my mind. I jumped on my motorcycle and left," he said.

When the man has more money, however, relations may proceed more smoothly, perhaps because men are "supposed" to have more. Plenty of women count themselves fortunate to have a man with a *lot* more money than they themselves have. But many are no longer willing to put up with put-downs or any other kind of mental or physical mistreatment for the amenities such a relationship provides.

Singles who had not had any such money troubles as have been described while they were dating reported that money became a problem as the relationship settled into an ongoing, day-to-day affair. When the couple was, as the teenagers say, "going steady," it put a strain on their attitudes toward money, a strain that casual companionship did not.

Half of the singles said they had had a steady association with someone who was in a substantially higher or lower income bracket. And half of this group declared that dissimilarities of goals, cultures, and tastes led to differences that expressed themselves in terms of money. Doing things that did not cost much became impossible. The one who paid the larger share for what they did do wearied of it or began to question the worth of the relationship, again in terms of money.

This was more emphatically the case when the woman had money. They developed a tendency to regard their men as underachievers. When men had the money, they slowly became disappointed in their women, complaining of trifles —appearance, behavior, extravagance, speech.

One such pair worked out a schedule of sessions to discuss their problems freely under a code of rules such as "don't interrupt" and "stick to the point." The scheme worked for a while. But difficulties kept piling up, and the disparities in their incomes at last proved too much for them.

One or the other in some ongoing relationships came to feel exploited in a money sense, and an often stormy break followed. It also happened quite peacefully. Men who were turned down when they asked to move into a woman's apartment, men whose requests for loans were refused, simply disappeared. One pair split when he discovered that their steady patronage of expensive places, which she had said "are good for your business," were in fact due to her desire to be seen.

"It wasn't me she wanted, but just the exposure," he complained.

The greatest confusion on the new singles scene centers on who should pick up the tab.

Back in the days of your first courtship, rules were simple. Men paid. They kept right on paying, generally, for the next twenty-five or more years because they were the ones who made the money, or most of it. Now, on your second time around as a single, you may find that the role money plays in sexual relationships is as blurred and confused as the shifting roles of men and women themselves. That confusion can place a burden on your associations with the opposite sex—if you let it.

"I *never* know when I ought to volunteer to pay my share," said a New York public relations director. "I admire and wish to be like women who never burrow into their purses when there's a man around to pick up the bill. I'm always worrying about whether he can afford to, or whether he *meant* for me to pay."

Janet P., an Ohio schoolteacher, still remembers nervously checking her billfold while waiting for her first date after becoming single. Her son and his girlfriend, living together since college, always split every expense meticulously down the middle. Did a dinner invitation now mean "Dutch treat" and if so, how should she go about paying her share?

When her date arrived, she offered him a drink and decided to clear up the problem.

"This is my first date in twenty-five years," she said frankly, "and I don't know how things are done now. I'll be happy to pay my way."

Smiling broadly, he assured her that he'd invited her, and she would be his guest.

"Things haven't changed that much," he said.

But as the relationship progressed into friendship, Janet found that things *had* changed, that she was paying far more of mutual expenses than she ever would have done in her twenties, both because she wanted to do so and because her reciprocity was accepted with grace and appreciation.

Of the men we talked to, the overwhelming majority said a woman should share expenses, at least sometimes, and more than half of the women agreed. Of those who did not, half said they would reciprocate in other ways than picking up the bill, such as with dinners at home, at the club; for symphony, theater, football tickets, where no money openly changed hands. The day of the man as total provider for the woman's needs and entertainment seems clearly to be drawing to a close.

Said the men:

"A woman should contribute. If she doesn't come up with cash, she should develop ideas or tokens."

"Men should not have to carry the whole load."

Those women who agreed said:

"I'd rather go Dutch than not go."

"Nothing wrong with a woman paying half or all expenses if she is in a good position to do so."

"Her half, okay. Both halves will eventually be bad for the relationship. He will be weak, and she'll resent it."

One strong advocate of home cooking had this to say:

"Women should never underestimate the value of their own cooking just because they have been housewives and it was expected of them for so many years. A carefully prepared, home-cooked meal—gourmet, with wine, the works—will outclass any dinner for two in town. In terms of expense and effort that goes into buying, preparing, and cleaning up, it gives dollar-for-dollar value."

Even though most of the people in our survey believe men and women should share expenses generally, a funny thing seems to happen in a restaurant when a woman reaches for the check. In this situation, only half of the men and women approve of her paying, and among those who do qualifications can be heard, such as: "if they eat together frequently," "if it's a nondate situation, such as business, platonic, or in a group," "if the woman has invited the man." A number of men like to have it clearly understood ahead of time if the woman is going to pay. Said one:

"If she springs it on me when the bill is presented and insists, I would simply leave her money there as a tip."

There are those, both men and women, who like the payment to be discreet. A woman can use her credit card, excuse herself to go to the ladies' room, and pay the check privately. One woman entertains at her club so there is no question—the only way the bill *can* be paid is for her to sign it.

And there are others who think the simplest way is for a woman to open her wallet, take out the money, and give it to the waiter.

Then there's the substantial number of men and women who frown on a woman picking up the tab in a restaurant at all. Said the men flatly:

"No way!"

"I'm old-fashioned and proud of it!"

"What if any of my friends saw her pulling out her money?"

"I would lose all respect for her."

Said the women:

"Not in good taste."

"I would never go out with a man who doesn't pay the bill."

In the absence of an ultimate authority on modern etiquette for singles over fifty, here is what comes close to a consensus of the survey sample:

If a man invites a woman, he expects to pay.

If a woman invites a man, she expects to pay.

If their relationship is an ongoing one, they talk out methods for sharing or reciprocity that avoid burdening either.

If the relationship is platonic or they are dining or entertaining for business reasons, they should decide beforehand who will pay the bill.

If they travel together, a woman can share expenses by paying the hotel or motel bill, buying dinner, or splitting total costs, including air fares.

If they are living together, the one with the larger income expects to pay the larger share of expenses.

The freedom to share expenses makes it possible for a companionable or romantically involved couple to go places that they might not otherwise be able to afford.

"I could never have taken Helen to Europe," a college professor said, "so I simply told her how much I'd like to have her go with me if I could afford it. She immediately offered to pay her own way, and by sharing accommodations, it was cheaper for each of us than if we had each gone separately."

When they are invited on a trip, most women offer anything from a token breakfast or dinner to half of the total bill, with the man keeping the account and woman reimbursing him at the end of the trip. In between, there are women who pay for their own ticket when air travel is involved, pick up a motel bill from time to time, or buy their host a nice present afterward.

Some women think that sex alone is reciprocity enough. The idea that a woman is giving a man something when she goes to bed with him dies hard.

"I just don't need it as much as a man does," one woman said. "In fact, if I get really involved in what I'm doing, I could go on indefinitely without sex. Yes, I think I'm doing him a favor when I go to bed."

"I was raised with the idea that men are animals and all they really want is a woman's body," said another. "It's hard to overcome that conditioning. My mother always told me she could get anything she wanted from Daddy if they had sex, so I was programmed to think that if sex is what he's getting, then he pays the expenses."

A minority of both sexes thought it their right when they had provided lavish entertainment—an expensive dinner and theater, a weekend of skiing, a trip to a big city. When the man or woman who was the beneficiary of such generosity failed to oblige, that usually was the end of the relationship.

189

Men who rebuffed a woman's advances after accepting her hospitality expressed greater repugnance than women under the same circumstances. One gentleman left abruptly when his hostess began French-kissing him ardently. Another said he more gently repulsed his lady by telling her he wasn't in the mood.

Plenty of members of both sexes accepted—and often enjoyed—the convention that a good provider of fun and games in public is entitled to a sexual reward in private. About a third of the women reported that regardless of how an evening ended, the question of whether or not she would go to bed with her date was in her thoughts all the time.

Some men said they would resent receiving a woman's sexual favors just because they spent a lot of money on her. As one put it:

"I would feel demeaned if I got sex for any other reason than that I was attractive to her."

Another view was expressed by an engineer who bluntly said he "wouldn't hang around" unless he got sex. His notion was that only old-fashioned women thought they were giving anything when they slept with a man. He supposed this was a holdover from the days when they weren't supposed to enjoy intercourse. He was surprised at the suggestion that his own attitude dated back at least as far, to a time when men supposed they had to buy sex from anyone except their wives.

Some men and women say that using sex as a form of currency is in a class with prostitution. A majority of both sexes said that who paid for what is irrelevant. Sex, they argued, should be based entirely on mutuality of desire. Even more general was the opinion that when a woman paid her own way, she should be able to choose sex or leave it alone.

Most of the men and women we talked to feel that there is no *obligation* on anyone's part to have sex in return

190

for anything. But if the desire is not there, if not at the moment, at least at some time, invitations for dinner and dancing, to go on trips, are generally not given or accepted.

One of the nicest things about money is that it can buy presents, and many singles delight in finding just the right gift with which to surprise and thrill each other. One woman's lover, poor though he was, helped pay her way through secretarial school, then celebrated her graduation by buying her a beautiful white storm coat, so she would look "like a real secretary." The presents may be big in money, like the color television a woman bought for a friend's new apartment, or big on time, like the material a woman bought for her lover and then stitched into shirts and ties. Pure maple syrup from Canada, a beautiful turquoise necklace, a gold pendant set with diamonds, a sweater from Neiman-Marcus—even an unexpected windfall inheritance from a lover's estate—are all ways in which they say "I love you."

It's not always the big, expensive presents that make the most lasting impression. The nicest gift one woman ever got was in a small package her lover gave her as he put her on the plane after an idyllic week in Hawaii.

"Don't open it until you're inside," he said. "I'll be on the runway, waving." When she opened the box, she found a small plastic statue of a kitten. On its cheek was a red tear and on the base was an inscription that read: "I miss you."

The two biggest surprises among the gifts received by singles of the sample came to two as different as people can be. She had been for years devoted to a businessman, but had refused to marry him. During his last illness, she was assiduous in her attentions but had the impression he could not quite forgive her for rejecting his proposal. She was overwhelmed to find herself the chief beneficiary of his will. The story of the other surprise gift is told by the man who received it.

"I'm an alcoholic," he begins, "and she made me take a

look at my drinking. She poured a drink over my face when I was being ridiculous, and I thank her for that lovely and very unexpected gift. I no longer drink."

In spending—or not spending—their money on each other, singles today have no Emily Post rules to fall back on. The determining factors of yesteryear—the dependence of women, the male's superior economic position, the woman's pedestal, the male macho—all are in a state of uncertainty and change, and new patterns have not yet stabilized upon which to build a new set of standards.

But many of the older singles are enjoying the freedom to create their own styles, based on their own individual circumstances.

"As an older single today," said one, "you can meet and have a relationship on the nicest level, rather than worrying about your pocketbooks."

CHAPTER 12

Courage and Candlelight
the contemporary sex scene

"When I got married, the whole of my sex education was summed up in my father's admonition: 'Satisfy your woman.' I wondered what in hell he meant, but didn't have sense enough to ask. So on my wedding night, we had intercourse and *I* had an orgasm."

This is John recalling the callow young man he had been and the failure of his marriage. Youth and the marriage are well behind him. He is fifty-five years old now, chief accountant of a nationally known corporation, a lusty single more than a dozen years after his divorce.

"My wife wasn't happy," he acknowledges. "We bought books that described and even illustrated complicated positions. But I was under the impression that as a man I must know all about sex. So I had a block when it came to understanding what the books really said—if they did say anything useful.

"Fifteen years later when we got divorced, I still didn't know how to bring satisfaction to a woman, according to my wife. I didn't know any more than the day we met which breast she liked to have kissed, where she wanted to be stroked and where patted, or for how long. She never told me; of course I never asked."

The sex side of John's marriage could have been a car-

193

bon copy of countless others. Those in the survey sample who had thoroughly enjoyed their legal mates in bed were a minority. Most of them were no more successful immediately when they were single again. They had to adjust to the intense sex scene of which they now became a part. Today these middle-aged nymphs and satyrs learn to revel joyously in a tempo and style of sex behavior that in their youth they associated with the orgies of Rome at its most decadent.

"I had sex with any female, and I found plenty of them available," John says. "But it wasn't any better than it had been with my wife. Most of the time after intercourse with them, I'd wish a TV screen would drop down from the ceiling and the Super Bowl or World Series would be on. Of course it never happened, so I'd get up and leave. I wasn't very kind to those women, but they always were there when I went back."

Gradually John learned the first requisite of the good sex life. It is communication, verbal and tactile. John speaks for many singles when he goes on to explain how he progressed from wishing for a television set after sex.

"I got educated by talking, listening, and trying. If she said 'Use your finger,' I'd use my finger. If she said 'Use your thumb,' I'd use my thumb. But I was so naïve I'd ask 'How?' and she'd move my thumb for me. I had sex several times a day with several different women. I wanted to learn the differences in women, but more than that, I was angry with women. I was thinking about putting something over on someone. I had conquests but I had no satisfaction from them. Any orgasm I had was an orgasm of learning."

John says it was several years before he could hold off his own climax long enough to give a woman satisfaction. Again, this was a common discovery. The greatest concern mentioned by the men who completed the sex part of the questionnaire was a desire to gratify their partners—to make sure they were "happy," "pleased," "experienced orgasm." It was an idea that had seldom occurred to them during marriage.

"I began a serious study of the art of lovemaking," John continues. "Later I found a woman who was extremely attractive to me. She came to my apartment every Friday night. We'd start by caressing, kissing, having a drink, and winding up in bed. She seldom left bed except to go to the bathroom, make coffee, or eat some crackers and cheese. I studied what brought response, what would make her moan or groan with pleasure, what made her feel good. She would leave Sunday night. These long weekends went on for about a year. All my previous screwing came into focus.

"I learned women are constructed differently from each other—larger or smaller clitorises, vaginas, nipples, bottoms. I learned that I like a woman to say 'Touch this,' 'Do that,' 'Move your left hand,' 'Softer,' 'Harder,' 'Good.' I learned when they were bluffing. I learned to touch each woman where she could be aroused, fondling the breast, holding the nipple up with one finger while gently flicking down with the other finger, stroking her body all over, kissing and nibbling up and down her torso. I learned that I don't like a woman to say 'Ouch' or 'Don't do that.' It turns me off, reminds me of my unsatisfactory sex with my ex-wife."

John also learned that women did not care to hear about other women, and that he should never ask a question unless he really wanted to know the answer.

"Things have changed since I came on the singles scene," he says. "Any man who thinks a woman is at his beck and call is going to be disappointed. A man can't ignore a woman's needs for gratification. If he does, he won't be asked back.

"I like screwing in a circular motion, not just an in-and-out thrust. I go back and forth like a pendulum, too. Since studying the anatomy of women, I can bring them to

195

orgasm, and enjoy staying hard while she climaxes. I do this orally, the woman lying on her back with her knees drawn up. I face her with my head at her genitals. I rub her clitoris with a stiffened tongue, at the same time using my hand, palm up, with the middle finger in the vagina, the index and ring fingers running alongside the lips to stimulate the vulva. I increase the pressure with tongue and fingers as she becomes excited. The secret is to be able to breathe so I can continue to bring her to orgasm. I find it necessary to arouse a woman so she begins to open naturally, her whole being opening like the petals of a flower. The wetness is like dew, and her second orgasm is with me in her, a natural succession that brings mutual pleasure."

John expresses what many singles over fifty discover but feel guilty about—the delights of what they were brought up to consider wicked perversions. Cunnilingus, the oral stimulation of a woman even to orgasm, and fellatio, the similar act for a man, are words many never had heard. They often are surprised by their reactions when introduced to the practice. Breaking the bonds of old sexual taboos, singles learn the truism that nothing both partners enjoy need be regarded as sinful—oral sex, mutual masturbation, unorthodox positions. This attitude is a result of recent changes in sexual mores, and singles make the most of them. The rule observed by much of the survey sample is: "Anything goes so long as it pleases both and hurts no one."

Not all singles take as great care as John to explore the best paths to ecstasy in bed. But his story of how he learned about a woman's body and how he used that knowledge in ways she found most arousing was repeated during other interviews in such terms as:

"A woman's needs are paramount. It doesn't take long to find out what they are."

"I take time to find out about the woman's body, my partner's body."

196

"I make sure she's completely relaxed and free. I ask her to tell me what feels good."

"I've learned that because of the position of the clitoris, it's often impossible to stimulate it while I'm in there. Now I do it manually or use a vibrator."

"I try to hold back until she has reached her apex. Then my own enjoyment is increased."

Among all the men surveyed, this theme of satisfying the woman was given as the man's first concern, proper caressing and foreplay his second, and only then worry over attaining erection. Cumulatively, they have these suggestions to offer other men:

Make sure she's completely relaxed and free. Make her know you're happy to have *her* with you.

Take time to find out about your partner's body, its individual rhythms and timings, what particular caresses and movements excite and thrill her.

Read sexy books or watch sexy movies together.

Use lots of foreplay. No nightgowns or pajamas to block the way. Lots of snuggling and kissing.

Fondle breasts and nipples.

Don't hurry through the sex act. Try to hold back until you feel she has reached her apex.

Lie gently side by side, facing each other, using your fingers effectively to massage her clitoris until she is ready to come, then go in.

Say her name.

Don't worry if your orgasms are not simultaneous. Sometimes that's not possible because of the position of the woman's clitoris. Either manipulate it manually or use a vibrator.

Such effort bears rich fruit. As one man said, "After they get used to me, they don't want anyone else."

On the receiving end of all this patient attention, women began to unfold and blossom sexually, some for the

197

first time in their lives. After years of "faking it," of feeling left out and sad, of thinking that the fault that they did not enjoy sex was theirs, many now say they feel "reborn."

These women sample more than one method of reaching the heights of sexual feeling. They shed shame and guilt as easily as they discard a torn slip. They speak of their feelings with complete honesty. They almost broadcast their joy in touching and exploring their naked bodies, and the bodies of their lovers. They exult in their ability to laugh and have fun in bed, to make love in the moonlight, to keep wine and fruit on the night table without being self-conscious.

The reasons for their erotic abandon are varied, cumulative, leading them from one level of enjoyment to another.

One reason for the newly found thrill of sex is that they now savor all the pleasures of coition without nagging fears of pregnancy or the fuss of contraceptives. Men also note this sense of freedom; it is an explanation some give for preferring partners near their own age.

Another reason for their new enjoyment is discovering new delights in their own bodies. This smooth skin, these soft curves are their very own, and for the first time in their lives they derive voluptuous pleasure from the fact. It enables them to throw themselves into a man's embrace with unaccustomed ardor. They find that a fit, shapely body improves sex. Men who got rid of a paunch and women who eliminated unnecessary bulges gained in self-esteem and in the admiration of their coital partners besides enhancing the enjoyment of sex. Women who in marriage were dissatisfied with their bodies now find a supposed blemish can be a blessing on the singles scene. One woman whose husband complained that her breasts were too small boasts happily that lovers admire her lithe, girlish figure.

The first revelation that the act of coitus not only can be far more than a routine coupling in which the male "takes" the female but also can be designed for her satisfac-

198

tion seems to be almost as much a surprise to widows as to divorcées. Half of the widows who filled out the sex portion of the questionnaire had been less than ecstatic about their physical pleasure during marriage.

In fact, two-thirds of both sexes in the survey sample reported that their marriages had been less than happy, and sex problems were placed high on the list of reasons. They blamed themselves as much as their spouses. One woman explained that she had acquired her attitude toward the carnal relationship between husband and wife from hearing her mother say of her father that she could get anything out of him if she gave him sex.

"So I thought that's what sex is for," the daughter recalled. "That concept ruined my marriage. Only after my divorce did I find out the truth, and then I guess because I was free to talk about it."

The conclusion seems to be that if these mature people had known while married what they learned about sex afterward, many of the divorced (if not most of them) might not have become singles after fifty. Also it is a reasonable conclusion that to be single and fifty in today's free and easy world of uninhibited carnal pleasure can be a liberal, rich, and rewarding sex education.

Mary, for example, is quite sure she is happier and a nicer person as a single than she was as a wife. Then she was nervous, irritable. Now she is tranquil, at ease, and sex makes the difference. With a husband it was shackling; with lovers it is liberating, exhilarating. Her experience as a single has emancipated her from ridiculous conventions and doubts, she contends, adding:

"I grew up thinking all men somehow knew how to handle intercourse and if I didn't appreciate it there was something wrong with me. Now I know better, but when I was married I was reluctant to say what would bring me to orgasm. So I would fake it, and have no satisfaction. I'd feel left out and sad. One of the bonuses of being single is

199

that I have everything to gain by talking openly about what he can do to make me feel good.

"I have a close relationship, about two years now, with a man dear to me. When I masturbate, I pick up the phone and tell him about it and what I thought about him while I was masturbating. He responds warmly, glad I had a good sexual experience, and says, 'Incidentally, I am free for lunch today.'"

The pleased surprise of single women to find men who are as concerned for their arousal as for their own is reflected in the rhapsodies of a woman who speaks of herself as being fifty plus and just discovering the varied delights of oral sex, clitoral orgasm, copulating at odd times in odd places—such as in front of the fireplace, in the middle of the afternoon, on a loveseat. Jane is statuesque, her appearance belying an inner timidity.

"Such a nice surprise," she exclaims, "to find men so changed! They're much better! I can tell them exactly how I feel and they're not intimidated. Right now I have a big physical affair going with the first man I dated since my divorce. It would have been impossible to admit this ten years ago. I mean that I love sex with him. He is so careful and patient, and it's marvelous to be able to say I like it so much."

Jane is not alone in her lingering doubts about the morality of sexual pleasure. The notion that sex is somehow dirty dies hard in people who were raised in puritanical backgrounds. Although they consciously reject the teaching of the past, old fears crop up, as when Jane says:

"I asked him if we were taking a terrible chance being so involved in sex, and he said, 'Just enjoy it and see what happens.'"

Mary and Jane are not unusual. These extracts from interviews indicate the new attitude of single women over fifty:

"Splendid, not being dominated any more! He does it *with* me, not *to* me."

"The very best lover I knew whispered my name as he was climaxing. I knew he was making love to *me* when I heard that!"

In general, the women avoid sexual relationship with any married man. Asked why, they usually shrug and say it isn't worth getting involved when the liaison can't lead to anything.

Of course sex for singles over fifty is not invariably a crescendo of delights. Not all men and women revel in their freedom from fear and shame or in an expanding horizon of varied and mutual tenderness. They encounter such problems as flagging potency, especially but not exclusively among men nearer sixty-five than fifty. They worry or argue over suitable methods of arousal and fulfillment. Not all of them are rid of old inhibitions against masturbation, oral sex, and enjoyment of intercourse.

Today's new sexual imperative, too, often gets in the way for both men and women in finding fulfillment. To men, that imperative says "Perform." To women, it says "Have orgasms, the more the better."

The men ask themselves:

"Am I old-fashioned and rusty?"

"What do I have to offer?"

"My God! The new morality is here. I should be running around humping seven or eight women!"

The women wondered:

"What if I don't have an orgasm? Am I abnormal, an underachiever, an outmoded Victorian?"

"Will I be able to relax and enjoy the delights I read about?"

"How do I measure up against all the up-to-date and younger women? Am I mediocre—or worse—in bed?"

The more they talk about such questions, the more

201

obvious it becomes that the basic answer is communication. Nearly all who have brought themselves to frank exchanges with each other obtain satisfaction for themselves, whatever others might think of their methods. But those who fail in candor remain frustrated, unfulfilled.

A classic case of the importance of plain speech between sex partners was related by a woman psychiatrist, a pioneer in counseling the sexually disturbed. A couple she dubbed Paul and Pauline, recently turned fifty, came to her in distress. Neither ever had married. He had retired early from the Navy after the traditional sailor's life of a girl in every port.

They had met shortly after the death of her aged mother, for whom Pauline had cared for years. It was the attraction of opposites, and they confided to the psychiatrist that she had given up her virginity to Paul on their second date. The first night went off quite well: "I was real gentle, Doctor; I'd never had a virgin before." But ever since she had been cold and he impotent. Although they still professed great affection for each other, he was furious with himself as much as with her; he fancied himself a stud.

When Paul was alone with the doctor, he described the difficulty. "Of course I'd never had any but paid whores," he explained. "But that's not it. You see, Doctor, I get awful hot during the act, so hot I can't stand covers over me, so I throw 'em off. Every time I'm just reaching my climax, she reaches down and pulls the covers back up. Dammit, it throws me off. I have to start all over again. I get up to the climax and she pulls the covers up again. I'm going crazy, and I think she is too."

"Have you told Pauline how you feel about the covers?" the psychiatrist asked.

Paul was horrified.

"My God, Doctor, you can't say things like that to a nice girl!" he cried.

"Why not?" she demanded. "You just told me and I'm a nice girl."

Paul went out shaking his head. Pauline, informed during her session with the doctor of Paul's idiosyncrasy, laughed in relief.

"Is that all!" she exclaimed. "Oh, Lord, I just want him to be happy. I don't expect anything for myself. I guess I reach for the covers without thinking; maybe it seems more decent."

A month later Paul and Pauline called to report progress. He had regained his vigor—"Three times last night," he gloated. Pauline confided that thanks to his gentleness and enthusiasm she was experiencing "the most wonderful, exciting sensations"—she didn't know the word *orgasm.*

Perhaps the most important thing the singles we surveyed learned was to communicate with a sex partner, and do it before as well as during intercourse.

"Talk is no substitute for sex," one of the more philosophical of the men interviewed declared. "But it can help a lot in the intimacy of the bedroom. I suspect anyone who is always sounding off about sex in public. They're usually pretty poor performers in private. Anyway, when it comes to sex, words are not the only medium of communication. A touch, a movement, a look—all these are important too."

Ability to communicate and the mutual satisfaction it brought gave women a new sense of dignity. They pointed out that for the first time they were equals in a partnership of sex. Men discovered in this equality a degree of fulfillment for themselves never before experienced.

Most singles over fifty have a great deal to communicate. Men complained that the exigencies of daily living make it difficult to get into the mood for intercourse. Among their rationalizations were:

"Sex can't be forced. When you're young, nature

makes you excited, lusty, and lovemaking can be quick. When you're older, it takes time to get it up, and it helps to set the stage."

Settings varied with tastes. Nearly always a sympathetic partner was stipulated. Women frequently were instructors and guides in the art of coitus, and what they provided usually was a tactful exercise in communication.

A physician in his sixties who had not had intercourse with his wife during the last twenty years of their marriage could not attain an erection for a year after he became a single.

"The first sign of success came when I slept with a woman who seemed so unworried, so relaxed, so understanding as we talked about it that within the hour I became quite hard. We had the best sex I had known in twenty-one years, all because she showed confidence in me and I was imbued with her confidence."

For one man in his fifties, reading sex books with a woman restores potency. For another, lying naked next to a naked woman and talking—"I'm vocal if it's okay with her"—stimulates him so that if he can't make it this time, he will next, and "If we communicate, that's better than nothing." But a third asserts:

"Love and liking are still the best basis for sex. If it's too easy, you lose interest. Put a high value on sex but mix love lightly with humor."

Women reported that it was not only a challenge but fun to put men in a mood to forget business or sports and enjoy sex. They offer many tested techniques that women can use to help their partners, since an understanding and reassuring woman is what it takes to help matters.

First, set the stage. Flirt a little. One woman builds a fire in her fireplace, takes the phone off the hook, makes sure her children will not be coming home, and lets him know there will be no distractions. Then she serves dinner with wine and tells him how really great he is, how close she feels to him.

Read sex books together: *The Joy of Sex, More Joy of Sex, The Sensuous Woman* are good starters.

Have dinner in bed.

Watch sexy movies. One man has a collection that he watches with his girlfriend on the ceiling of his bedroom.

Try a warm bath with a citrus scent. Some couples take turns in the bathwater. Others take a bath together and make love in the tub.

You might prefer showers. One woman likes to wait outside and dry her lover off with a big bath towel. Another said:

"We shower together, lathering each other with a fluffy big sponge, acting like kids, washing each other's elbows, behind the ears, between the toes, giggling, teasing, and laughing."

"There's something about warm water, the stimulation and massage of washing the body, and the joy of doing it together that is very erotic," said another.

Use lotion or oil in the shower, so both bodies glisten, another recommends. "It's sort of a damp, not slippery feeling—like having a thin film of a costume on."

Tell him how the sight of his naked body arouses you.

Once in bed, relax. Have some pillow talk. Share your affection. Touch. Caress.

Fantasize together. One man reached back into his memory and brought out his sultan fantasy, in which he raped all the women in his harem.

Masturbate—each other or yourselves. Some men get turned on by watching a woman, and learn in the process what excites her.

If it doesn't happen, don't panic. As one man said, "A

man in his fifties can't be expected to score a hundred percent of the time. If you don't, relax and rest and try again.
The trying is fun."

The men in our survey found that, with an understanding and supportive partner, one who helped rebuild
their confidence, sex came back, if it had been a
problem, with a big bang—often the best it had been in
years.

Women themselves, as the earliest sex studies in this
century showed, are most aroused sexually simply by men.

"When I see my lover take off his Jockey shorts, it's
very stimulating," reported a vivacious brunette, "and I say,
'I like seeing you erect. It's exciting to me. I begin to
lubricate just watching you.'"

A stumbling block and part of the communications
problem is that many a man in this age bracket is unable to
speak endearing words at appropriate moments. He proves
by his acts that he loves a woman, but he doesn't say so. He
may explain this is a holdover from a day when the strong,
silent hero was the idol of youth, but this fails to meet
women's objections. They express such views as:

"Showing his love by actions is wonderful, but it
doesn't do what actually hearing the words of love does."

"When he whispers 'I love you,' a wave of happiness
floods through me. It's an essential nourishment to our relationship."

"We need to hear it and we need to say it. Why is it so
hard for some?"

Most women said that in order to enjoy the sexual experience fully, they had to be told, usually over and over,
they were loved. They said:

"Without that reassurance, I have to keep my feelings
superficial. Sex can be fun with someone you like, but the

total feeling of happiness that comes with unreserved surrender and sharing of emotion can never be there. No matter how you try to compensate, something's missing."

"Sometimes I feel dried out inside."

"What makes me feel alive is to be reminded I am a
beautiful, lovable human being."

Supplying that missing ingredient is extremely hard
for men who have been trained from childhood to believe
that expressing their feelings is weak and unmasculine or
who have experienced rejection and don't want to risk it
again, whose attitude toward women is often soured by years
of unpleasant marital associations. Hostility and suspicion
are far more natural to them than words of love. These
explained:

"I worked very hard to rise out of grinding poverty to
a position of success. While I was doing it, I was taking dinner home every night to an alcoholic wife and trying to compensate to my children for their mother's neglect. I still look
upon women with distrust."

"Once as a child, I said 'I love you' to my father and he
laughed. I'm still afraid of being laughed at."

"When you say 'I love you,' you lose control, and we're
raised to think we should be in control at all times."

Men point out that they express their affection in
other ways than talking about it:

"I help her with her income tax, shovel her sidewalk."

"I took her to a stop-smoking seminar, even though I
don't smoke."

"I helped her buy a new car."

"She knows she can call me at any hour of the day or
night and I'll rush to her aid."

"I listen to her problems, support her emotionally,
offer help with her children."

And then there are some who have learned to say the words, like the dour New Englander who had always found it hard to express his feelings:

"It was damned hard, but I did it, because I knew it would make her happy."

In their efforts to please or just from their own hunger, women can become overly aggressive and defeat their purpose, sometimes making men fear they might be called upon to perform and found lacking:

"A lot of times a man doesn't want to have sex, and women today are too aggressive. I may have to perform, and I can't. I still think it's nice to take my time. The tendency is to hop into the sack, and I'm not sure that's right. A little restraint is still very alluring."

"I like aggressive women, but a little fifty-fifty goes a long way and more is something else. A woman who expects it all the time and never lets up is too much. I'm in the middle of an affair now with a woman who wants sex two or three times a day. Well, I don't have time. Even every other day is getting to be too much. She will call and say she just wants to come over and read the paper, and then my whole evening is shot. I'm a working man trying to do two jobs."

"Maybe the last thing I want some nights is sex. What I want then is comforting reassurances, quiet understanding, and not to be rejected next time I try."

The secret of success for singles is to find partners whose desires match their own. One of the advantages they see in today's sex standards is that they can flit from flower to flower until they find the right one.

"Fantasies and fantasizing together bring results," said a genial extrovert who after some searching found a woman who liked his dreams. "When she asks me to reach back into my memory for bizarre sex adventures, I recall wanting to make love to several women at once, walking down a street undressed, or being raped by a woman. I begin to turn to stone, and we're off."

Singles who enjoyed a technique in marriage want to carry it on with their new partners. A prosperous businessman of distinguished appearance and his wife relished mutual masturbation to the point that when he was on a trip, they engaged in it while talking on the telephone.

"I still use that technique with women I date," he said a few years after he was widowed. "If a woman masturbates in my presence, it really turns me on. I love watching her use her fingers. I am involved now with a woman who never masturbated before, and I am showing her how. When I see her do it, I can get it all up. Last night we had sex three times. A lot of affection accompanies our relationship. I have learned from her to eat less, no sugar, no salt, and I think that is helping my sex."

Masturbation practitioners maintain that what used to be called self-abuse is now considered helpful and healthy, although some say it was not easy to overcome childhood inhibitions. Reasons they like it were expressed as:

"A marvelous release when I feel uptight and can't seem to get started on something difficult confronting me."

"It's a better way to keep healthy than finding someone, just anyone, to sleep with."

"Excellent training. I like being nice to myself."

"Another way of exercising my body."

Descriptions of masturbatory methods were occasionally long and detailed. Men and women explained the virtues and effects of the state of dress or undress preferred, ointments, positions, pictorial props such as magazine art, which fingers to employ, mechanical aids such as vibrators. The resulting sensations also were recounted with enthusiasm. This is the account of a divorcée:

"I lie in bed, naked, lubricate my genitals or my

fingers with water-soluble lubricating jelly. I use two fingers, the index finger of my left hand inside my vagina, pressed against the bone, rubbing gently back and forth. Meanwhile my index finger of the other hand is manipulating my clitoris—side to side with a soft rhythm that grows and gains momentum as the excitement rises. In a few minutes, my nipples harden, my body contracts, and I feel bliss."

Others talk about their vibrators:

"I ordered mine from an ad in a woman's home magazine that had a picture of a girl holding a phallic-shaped vibrator against her cheek to 'relieve tension.' It really does, too." Others got theirs from notions counters in department stores or ordered catalogues from advertisers in men's magazines.

A few suggested discretion in using a vibrator if others are living in your house: "Mine makes a noise like a B-29 coming in for a landing," one woman said, "so unless I'm alone in the house, I turn up the radio in my bedroom."

Another suggested testing it out to see what effect it might have on a TV set in another room: "I had a friend whose set went berserk every time she used hers, upsetting and mystifying everyone in the living room."

Even though oral sex is as old as time, many older singles regard it as part of the "new" sex scene. Some view it with revulsion. Others, who had always wanted to experiment but whose mates were unwilling, are now free to try.

"It's so great to find partners who are willing to do new things, who don't regard any kind of variation from the same, tired old way as 'wrong,'" said one.

A woman who had always thought of oral sex as perversion was introduced to it by a younger lover shortly after becoming single: "He was so relaxed and matter-of-fact. Now I love it." Other women, while less enthusiastic, were equally flexible:

"My first reaction when I heard about it from my kids

was: 'You've got to be kidding!' I grew up on a farm and it seemed so animalistic. Now, I think that whatever gives a couple pleasure is okay, and while I don't enjoy it, I don't dislike it either."

"These days when sexual freedom gives men so many opportunities, the older woman has to learn contemporary ways to bring a man satisfaction," one of these older women argued. "If she won't, younger women will."

"My lover told me that the genitals are cleaner than the mouth," remarked one who up to then had not known what cunnilingus is. "Now, if the man has skill at this, I can reach orgasm in a short time."

"Oral sex? I find it repulsive. I don't and won't participate in it. With all the jackets I have on my teeth, it would give me gum infections. If it's done to me, it's exciting, but I never initiate it."

Men's storehouses of sexual memories often hold relics of former oral experience. Members of the survey sample expressed these opinions:

"Sure, some women are allergic to oral sex, probably if that guy hasn't been circumcised and has bacteria under his foreskin."

"Cunnilingus . . . I like it and enjoy it. It turns me on. When I do it to her, it brings her pleasure. It's really exciting to see my woman climax. My wife never climaxed in our nineteen-year marriage."

"I'm a varied type. I never do something the same way twice, never go to the same place on her body twice in the same night. I had thought about fellatio and cunnilingus for years, but my wife would never let me get close to trying. Thank God, that hangup isn't part of my sex life now."

Curiosity led a few men to invest in water beds. Those who said they did it because it was good for a bad back or because they heard hospital patients had fewer bedsores on

211

such mattresses seemed satisfied. Those who hoped for some sort of miracle of sexual bliss were not so enthusiastic. The image was sexy, they reported, and the bed a great conversation piece. But when it came to performance, women did not swoon with delight. One man who said his water bed helped his aching back added disconsolately that when it came to sex he had to move to a more conventional couch.

A number of men and women in our survey are leading perfectly happy lives without a sexual relationship, some abstaining temporarily until they meet the right person, others deciding they would be more content without the hassle and complexities of a relationship. A few of these, particularly those who were raised to believe that masturbation is unhealthy or morally wrong, fill their lives with interesting activity and simply don't dwell on their lack of sex or allow it to make them tense. An author declared almost proudly that he had reached a period when he no longer got satisfaction from sex.

"My celibacy at the moment might be called a "tragedy," he reflected. "I call it a chance to gain greater insight and to know what I want so I won't be rejected again. I concentrate on other things, work hard, write, turn my thoughts and energy elsewhere."

Another man tells how he handles sex when no partner is available.

"I relive great moments in humping history, fantasize about doing it with two—humping one, eating the other; eating one while the other's eating me. Or it may be something I did just once and which is better in retrospect, like a hitch in the Navy."

"I stopped having sex relations because I believe my productivity is better," said another professional more prosaically. "I am happier without it. I made that decision consciously."

"I seem to be quite happy and not at all uptight about

my lack of sex," said a woman who had been widowed for several years and admitted she still thought a great deal about her husband although she didn't talk about him much. "I must be getting undersexed, but I don't seem to have any physical problems. Maybe if I meet the right guy all this will change."

One woman simply said the satisfactions of celibacy were enough for her, and another explained that since she was a Catholic and widowed, of course she was celibate. Still another summed it up:

"I find that sexual fulfillment is no problem if one doesn't dwell on it."

Casting away with their marriages the inhibitions of a lifetime, many single men and women over fifty are finding that sex has dimensions they had never explored. Men are becoming innovative and skilled in giving their partners pleasure; women are responding in imaginative ways of their own. Together, they are finding that making love can be a creative and carefree pastime, another enjoyable facet of single living in the "golden years."

CHAPTER 13

Where You Live
and with whom

"When I walk into a person's home, it speaks to me." So said a divorced businessman who left the large and solid house that spoke for him as a family man to live in a condominium that conveys a very different message.

As a single you can, perhaps for the first time in your life, live in a place that speaks for you alone.

"When I was married," said a physical therapist, "everything was a compromise. We had to consider schools, make room for my mother-in-law who lived with us for a while, and be close to my husband's business, which took precedence over my job. Even decorating had a common denominator. The only color we could all agree on, the one we had in almost every room, was gold—not because anyone was crazy about gold but because nobody hated it. Today, I've got my very own house, small but cozy, tailored to my comfort and needs, reflecting my taste, enhancing my personality."

ARE YOU SURE YOU WANT TO MOVE?

Before pulling up roots and selling the family homestead, however, it's advisable to give the decision careful thought for at least a year after you become single. It's bad for your health, as we have already seen, to pile change upon change, and such a major move should be made in a calm, controlled state of mind.

Think about the advantages of keeping your home, especially if you still have teenagers who are happy at the school they attend and whose friends are a stabilizing influence. A mother who managed to hold onto her family home at some sacrifice asked her eighteen-year-old son several years after his father died if he had ever been tempted to take advantage of the disappearance of the main authority figure in the home.

"The thought occurred to me," he replied honestly, "but the kids around here all look down on drugs and drunks and dropouts."

Even when children leave for college, their home still provides security the first year or two after they have left.

"My kids never appreciated their home so much as when they came back from college that first Christmas in their freshman year," said a mother of three. "They seemed to soak up the familiarity. They kept saying. 'It's so good to be *home!*'"

Even if your children are gone, do you really *want* to move? Are the memories so pleasant, your home so convenient, the neighbors so compatible that another home might suffer by comparison? Then ignore the urgings of friends and relatives and stay where you are, or if you're doubtful, rent out your house and try someplace else without burning your bridges.

How much money are you actually going to save by moving? Look at some of the places that interest you, then sit down with paper and pencil and make the following calculations:

Amount of capital gains tax you will have to pay when you sell your present home.

Difference in the percentage of interest you will pay

on the mortgage for your new house as opposed to what you are paying now.

Cost of moving.

Cost of redecorating or remodeling the home you are considering.

Cost of buying new furniture or appliances when yours may not fit.

Projected increase in the value of the house you now have as compared with the one you are considering, thinking not only of the houses but also of the neighborhoods.

Differences in real estate taxes.

Differences in cost of utilities.

Relative value of each home, by the square foot.

Estimated maintenance costs, based on the construction and state of repair of each house.

You might have some surprises. One woman found it cost less to heat her present home by steam than it did the much smaller one she was considering, which had forced-air heat. Another homemaker, after looking carefully at all her options, decided it was only slightly more expensive to live in her $90,000 home with its $28,000 mortgage than to move to a more modest one. So instead of moving, she got a job.

If, however, you do decide to move, either through desire or necessity, you'll want to ease the uprooting as much as possible.

Only you should make the decisions about what to keep and what to get rid of, and you have to be hard-headed, sometimes hard-boiled. A woman whose children wanted her to take most of her furniture into her smaller home, so they could have it when they had their own homes, said she'd be glad to pay storage on the pieces that didn't fit if they would reimburse her when they claimed them. After some thought, they decided they didn't really want them that much.

Most parents don't mind storing smaller heirlooms. A grandmother who moved from her family home into an apartment divided her good china and linens into four cartons, wrote the name of a grandchild on each, and put them in her storage locker in the basement.

Expensive pieces of furniture are best advertised in the newspaper or placed with an auction house, while lesser items can be sold at a garage sale, and that's where you should get lots of help. Take everyone up on their offers of "If there's anything I can ever do—" One divorcée who tried to run a garage sale herself was overwhelmed. When her next-door neighbors saw the crowds of people swarming all over the driveway and lawn, the whole family stayed home from church to help her.

In some towns, you can locate help for such sales through secondhand and antique stores, professionals who will conduct the entire sale for a percentage of the receipts while you take the afternoon off. The very last shreds of junk can be disposed of via the Salvation Army or Disabled American Veterans, which will not only send their truck to clean out the garage but will also give you a form on which *you* estimate the value of your donated items and deduct it from your income tax.

Some singles, of course, have only to leave their home with the spouse and family in it. Many found it easier to do so when the children are in school and their spouse is out of the house.

A HOUSE

Where you go depends upon your pocketbook and your taste. There is much to choose from. Well over half of the singles we interviewed prefer a house. As an investment, it's hard to beat: a place to live that generally goes up in value while you get a tax writeoff on your mortgage. Square foot for square foot, it's cheaper living than an apartment or condominium of comparable quality.

In a house you have space. When children return to the nest, it represents a home where they feel comfortable and offers them a place to entertain their friends. When your friends visit (and many singles like the way it breaks up their lives when they do), they have rooms to which they can retreat, backyards to sit in, so they are not right *there* with you at all times. You have space for yourself, too—an extra bedroom or family room for your hobbies or den.

"I fill the whole place, where four of us used to live," said one man.

And there in the backyard is your own bit of ecology, something most homeowners would not trade for the top of the highest high-rise in town.

"Anytime I get depressed, I go out and work in my flower garden for an hour and I'm back to normal," said a sixty-two-year-old widow.

Rick W., an accountant, has made the half-acre surrounding his house into a small woodland to attract birds and wildlife. In it he raises butterflies, protecting the larvae on the branches of bushes and trees from birds by wrapping them carefully in cheesecloth. Summertime provides a flower garden in flight. He also grows his own vegetables and fruits—raspberries, strawberries, apples, and plums.

"I can go out, come in. I don't have to follow any rules the way I would in an apartment. It's peaceful, quiet, secluded," he says.

No matter how secluded a house may be, however, when it's in a family neighborhood there are certain limitations on privacy. When her first date arrived to pick her up after her divorce, one woman recalls seeing a finger in the window across the street separating the slats in the Venetian blinds. A man reports that each time he brings home a new woman friend, a neighbor stops by to borrow or return

219

something. Another woman, sitting in her date's car outside her house one night, was startled to have a police car pull up to investigate. It had been summoned by an interested neighbor. For this reason women often feel reluctant to have a male friend spend the night, while men usually put a woman friend's car in the garage out of sight so as not to flaunt their habits.

It is this very sense of community responsibility, however, that you appreciate when you leave town for the weekend. There is usually a neighbor willing to pick up the newspaper, take in the mail, keep an eye on the house, a favor which of course you will later want to reciprocate. For longer trips, you might find an apartment-dwelling friend who would be glad to stay in your house for a change of pace, even at the cost of watering or mowing the lawn.

When you buy a house, look for a neighborhood that's on the upswing, and don't get the best house in it. Its real value is depressed by the lesser homes around it. Consider the sun. Trees add a lovely touch and a protection against the wind, but it's a real downer if day after day your place is dark. Think, too, about the future. One woman who loved two-story houses, because of their association with her childhood and because she feels safer in an upstairs bedroom at night, is beginning to wonder if she will still want to run up and down stairs in another fifteen years. A man said he wished he'd thought about the possibility of remarriage and bought a home with bigger closets in the bedroom.

APARTMENTS

About a fourth of the singles we interviewed live in apartments. One of these is Bonnie G. The year that Bonnie became divorced, her last child left for college and she found herself alone in an oversized house, terrified at night. Seeking the security of a high-rise, she canvassed forty-nine apartments before she found the one that suited her. She has these suggestions for apartment-hunters:

If safety is your thing, look for inside parking and note how many doors there are to the garage. The more doors, the harder it is to guard them, and muggers can just walk in and take the elevator up.

Notice how far you have to carry your groceries from your car to your apartment. In one building, Bonnie would have had to walk up two flights of stairs before reaching the elevator.

Look to see if hallways are clean, grounds well-maintained. Such care indicates good management.

Check the parking facilities for visitors.

Note the location of the laundry room. It's nice (and safer) to have one on the same floor as your apartment, instead of in the basement.

Ask the manager what the occupations and ages of people who live in the building are. Also their marital status. They will be your neighbors, friends, and who knows what else.

Bonnie loves the apartment she found. It's close to a park, where she goes jogging, and to highways and thoroughfares that makes it accessible to every place in town she wants to go. She loves the convenience of having someone on hand to receive packages, of picking up the phone and calling the manager when a repair job is necessary, of being able to lock her door and go on a trip whenever she wants to without having to worry about break-ins or mowing the lawn. Its biggest plus is the people who live there, a wide variety ranging from a poor artist to a millionaire, many in her own situation: single.

Contrary to popular belief, most urban singles who

live in apartments not only know their next-door neighbor but also usually know as many people in the building as they care to.

"There is always something to bring you together," a New Yorker said. "Maybe it's just a problem with the manager. There's an unwed mother in our building now, and everybody got together in the lobby the other day to celebrate the baby's first birthday. Then there's a couple who met in the elevator who just got married."

Said other apartment dwellers:

"I love the sense of life all around me."

"I always see someone I know in the grocery store."

"There's an instant camaraderie when you meet in the pool. I've made some super friends."

THE TOWNHOUSE AND CONDOMINIUM

A compromise between apartment living and house owning is a townhouse or condominium, either a high-rise or one with its own patio and piece of sky. The difference between the two is a legal one. In a townhouse, you own the roof over your head, the ground under your feet, and part of the walls you share with your neighbors; in a condominium, you own an undivided interest in all common elements. Every condominium and townhouse complex has its own distinctive character, so check as you would in renting an apartment to see what the tenants are like. If everyone works and you like to play bridge in the daytime, there will be no one around to play with; and there's no sense in paying maintenance on a clubhouse and swimming pool if you're not going to use them. Before buying your condominium, you might talk to some of the owners, whom you can contact through the association that every condominium owner joins when he buys his condo. Find out, if you're interested, whether you can bring your pet cat with you, whether children are allowed, whether you can rent out your condominium, what the rules are governing maintenance, and what type of security there is. Some places offer twenty-four-hour security guards and patrol. Others offer only your neighbors.

The big advantage of a condominium, of course, is the maintenance-free living—no walks to shovel or lawns to mow, a chore that can be burdensome for a busy single.

Selma J., who at first thought she should maintain her family home for her college-age children, got some straight talk from her friends.

"It's time," they said, "to think about you. The children will be around, when they're home from college, for only a few more years. Plan for yourself and you won't be a worry to them."

Selma first moved to an apartment, but had a feeling of "semi-shame, of not being as good as people who were homeowners." The condominium she settled on gave her a sense of ownership and roots but had only two bedrooms; Selma worried about Christmas, when her grown son and two college daughters would all be visiting her.

"When they came, Andy brought his sleeping bag, Cindy took the guest couch in my study, and Nancy shared my bed. It was the best Christmas we ever had. It was fun being crowded. We had a sense of intimacy, a joy of sharing, and where everybody slept was the least important matter."

HOUSE BEAUTIFUL

Whether you elect to stay where you are or to move into a new setting, give way to your impulses, the way so many singles have done. Most of those in our survey disregard the dictates of decorators or the principles laid down in *House Beautiful* and follow their own great tastes. Consulting a decorator can save costly mistakes, particularly in your choice of color combinations, and you may gain many useful ideas, but don't let decorators dominate you. The richness of more than fifty years of living cannot be bought in a decorator's studio, and you should capitalize on it.

One woman, who values her Danish heritage, has adorned her apartment with lovely Scandinavian bits of art, combining them with self-restored walnut antiques from back-road barns in New England communities. A man who finds status-symbol furniture offensive, decorates instead with things he likes: "Snapshots stuck in the corner of frames, old army junk, a straw spirit house from Siam, a scrap of a rug from Turkey, a piano, books, postcards from friends set out on the mantel, and a nice-looking blanket a friend wove thrown over the end of the sofa in case somebody gets cold." Artifacts, souvenirs, pictures, trophies—anything that makes you smile and feel good—are what belong in your living room, or anywhere in your home. A geologist has beautiful pieces of agate, turquoise, and curiously marked rocks that he's picked off the ground in the course of twenty-five years scattered by the sink in his guest bathroom. A banker who "loves history and erudition" punctuates his townhouse with old maps, old pewter, Portuguese glassware, mugs from Germany and France.

This is your chance, if you're talented, to create a one-man or -woman show of your own art and craftwork, hanging your framed and lighted paintings throughout your house, displaying your own pottery or crewel work to delight yourself and your friends.

One thing you should *not*, if you're widowed, display in the living room or too prominently anywhere else, are pictures of a deceased husband or wife. Said a widower who had loved his wife dearly:

"I dated a girl once whose deceased husband looked out at us from pictures in every room, including the bedroom, and I decided right then I would never make anyone feel as uncomfortable as I did that evening. I want my date to feel she's in my house, not the house of another woman."

One divorcée does not even have too many pictures of her grown children around any more, much as she loves them.

"It was a different period in my life," she said.

Others, however, still like to surround themselves with rich and happy memories. One widow's coffee table is crowded with snapshots of joyous moments, displayed and protected beneath the glass cover.

In decorating your house, think about light. It can subtract years from your age if properly used. Warm, incandescent, rose-hued lights enhance colors—and you. Avoid the glare of overhead lights and have instead the softer glow a sidewall fixture offers. Consider dimmers. One woman has them in every room, including the bathroom. Lights on dimmers cast interesting shadows and add enough illumination to a candlelit dinner for a man to see his food. They add a warm glow, even to a firelit living room.

Don't overlook some of the least expensive and most effective decorative accents: plants. They bring the outdoors in and freshen the air. One green thumb has a dramatic curtain of greenery cascading from his second-floor balcony and reaching in places to the floor of his living room.

Warm, upbeat colors—yellows and earth tones—are important for maintaining a cheerful atmosphere when you're alone. One house, whose owner is a native of Mexico, is an explosion of vibrant color, created by a dozen cushions of different hues and brilliant wall hangings.

Or you may, like some, prefer soft muted tones: "white and cool and quiet"; "any color so long as it's blue, but highlighted with bright accents"—the colors you feel good with, or the colors that set you off.

"No more muddy feet or salivating dogs," a statuesque

blonde said. "So I chose white. When I give a party, I wear a brilliant dress, and I stand out anywhere in the room."

Most people, however, decorate for their own pleasure and comfort rather than for impression.

"When I can afford it, I get some cut flowers—just for me. It's a real upper."

"I display nothing I don't want to look at twenty-four hours a day."

"I can appreciate beautiful woods in furniture—let others worry about polishing it; I will take chrome and glass tables."

"A home should please the person who lives in it," said a woman who had been single many years. "It should be delightful just for her or him, so that it's a real haven, not just for show. I've known bachelors who have never bought a stick of living-room furniture—just left it bare for their whole lives. It's as if their comfort and need for a pleasant place to live doesn't count. Even women, especially after a divorce, neglect to make their beds in the morning because 'nobody will see it,' as if they can only do those things for others—not for themselves. If, like me, you've been single a long time, you realize after a while that you're not 'nobody' and you deserve nice surroundings too."

ROOMMATES

More than three-fourths of the singles in our group live alone, and most of them love it. They said:

"I live by myself, thank God! After all the years of living among others, I can now make my own decisions, sometimes on the spur of the moment, and come and go as I please."

"Just me and myself. We get along fine."

"I think all my life this is really what I wanted to

do—live alone. The confinements, the confusions, the concerns, the pressures to meet everyone else's needs—it's all over."

Some who felt lonely at first grew to like it.

"The hardest thing to get used to, when things started going wrong, was to have no one to turn to. But it makes you stronger when you learn you can do it."

One woman, not entirely satisfied with her solitude, said:

"I've thought about roomies, but I'm probably too fussy today. I would expect to find my best knives where I want them, my towels in the drawers, and I might growl if they weren't. I've run my own show for so long that I think I would have trouble adjusting to a girlie-type roomie. My dogs live with me and they are charming friends. I recently met a man who hates dogs, likes cats. We'll see if he adjusts. If not, too bad."

There are those, however, who find that for company and economy a roommate is a good answer. One man maintains a "halfway house" for friends who are in the process of getting a divorce and enjoys the constant flow of new companions.

When you have a roommate, plenty of space is essential for good relations. Each person needs a bedroom big enough so that it is not filled by the bed, a retreat where it's possible to spread out and pursue a project.

"Otherwise, you're both in the living room a lot and you see too much of each other," a woman advises.

Respecting each other's privacy, giving each other breathing space, is another essential. A woman who shared her apartment with her best friend also got her a job in her office, went out with her socially, and discovered that too much togetherness destroyed the relationship.

Most people with roommates advise that an agreement should be reached ahead of time on major issues: division of household chores and expenses, particularly. Any such agreement should provide for flexibility so that no one has to stay home to cook dinner just because it's his or her night to cook when something more interesting is happening.

"And you should never allow a dependency relationship to develop," a woman said. "If you have a date on New Year's Eve and your roommate doesn't, that is not your responsibility, unless you just want to be nice and can get her one."

Or maybe you're thinking of a living-together arrangement with the man or woman you love, an arrangement many endorse as a proving ground for marriage. Before you enter into such a situation, find out what constitutes a common-law marriage in your state. In some places living together and reputed to be married will make you man and wife, especially if there is written evidence such as a joint bank account to support the idea of marriage. You should also have the same kind of agreement about sharing housework and expenses that you would have with a roommate of the same sex. Finally, be sure, particularly if you're the woman, that you can stand the heat you may still get from more traditional friends and neighbors.

Wilma G., fifty-three, thought the taboo about facelifts was the last Victorianism and made no secret of hers. But when she decided on a living-together arrangement with her lover instead of marriage, she let people assume he was her husband. The relationship did not last, and now, when people ask about her divorce, Wilma tells them candidly that there will be no divorce because there was no marriage.

"It's like my facelift all over again," she says thoughtfully. "Maybe the disapproval some people feel about living together is *really* the last Victorianism."

In the case of Wilma, whose friends are mostly non-Victorian people, there is no problem. But for Martha K., who lives in the corporation-executive atmosphere of an exclusive residential community outside St. Louis, things are different. After Burt, her lover, moved in with her, her son Donald looked out of the living-room window one summer evening and said:

"Oh! It looks as if everybody's having a party on the tennis courts. Why weren't we invited?"

No one in her development openly disapproves of Martha and her lover; neighbors even do small favors for them occasionally. But they are not "included" any more. Martha is also uncomfortable at PTA meetings, never quite sure of how to introduce Burt. Donald, however, has no problem. When friends visit, he simply says, "This is Burt. He lives here."

For their own social life, Martha and Burt are independent of the neighborhood, meeting weekly with a couples group of all ages, some married, some not.

"The people we're interested in knowing accept people for themselves," she said, "not for the way they lead their personal lives."

SAFETY—LIVING ALONE

One of the major concerns many singles have when they first begin living alone is safety, a fear that usually diminishes as time goes by and there are no encounters with robbery, mugging, or rape. Most finally adopt reasonable precautions and dismiss their fears.

Gretchen P., who lived in Manhattan for twenty-four years, has been threatened only once—not in New York, but on the main street of a college town.

"I'd have been ready for it in New York," she said,

"but when a young girl came up to me on the street in Ann Arbor, Michigan, and asked me for a dollar, I was flabbergasted. She was better dressed than I was, and I started to laugh—until she pulled a knife. It's foolish to argue with that. I gave her the dollar."

Gretchen's safety precautions for life in Manhattan could be employed anywhere. She stays on well-lighted streets when she must be out at night, walks on the curb side of the walk, away from alleys and building entrances. Once she crossed the street to elude a man who seemed to be following her, and when he crossed, too, she screamed at the top of her lungs. He abruptly turned and hurried away. Since several people have been held up in the doorway to her apartment, she always has her key at the ready when she gets out of a taxi and checks the entrance for loiterers before she goes in. When getting into an elevator, she looks into the mirror in the back corner to be sure there's no one hiding out of sight, and she never gets into an automatic elevator alone with a man she doesn't know.

"I don't make any excuse. It's a common problem here, and I don't see any reason to be embarrassed about saving my life. If he's okay, he'll understand."

Whether out and about or at home, Gretchen believes, you should stay alert and conscious of what's going on around you, just as you do when you cross the street.

"It gets to be a habit after a while," she said.

Gretchen's habits check out well with police and other safety officials, who have these rules to add:

On the Street. Always lock your car, even if you're going to be gone for no more than a few minutes, and take a quick glance into the back of it when you return before you get in.

At parking lots, leave only your car key. Your house key could be duplicated, and your license plate can lead anyone to your house.

Keep your car in good working order, filled with gas, so you won't be stranded in scary places.

If you do have car trouble on the highway, put on your flashers, raise your hood, tie a handkerchief to the aerial, climb back into the car, and lock yourself in. If someone stops to help, open your window a crack and ask him to report your difficulty to the police.

If you are robbed on the street, quickly give your money. Police say victims who do not resist generally do not get hurt.

At singles dances—or anywhere else—don't accept dates until you get to know the person. One woman *married* a stranger. He borrowed $5000 from her to settle some business in another state, and she never saw him again.

Don't accept rides from strangers, either home from singles dances, from night school, or from anyplace else.

At Home. Lock your doors. A fifth of all burglars walk right in. Don't forget the cellar door, the tool shed, and the garage.

Use good locks—a dead-bolt lock in which the bolt extends at least one inch into the strike plate; and for added protection, a double-cylinder lock that you can lock from the inside at night or when you leave home.

Lock your windows. You can buy locks that will secure them in partially raised positions for fresh air at night.

Have a lock on your bedroom door, a phone by your bed, and emergency numbers by the phone or in your head.

Put a peephole, not a chain lock (which can easily be wrenched loose), on your front door, and don't open it to anyone you don't know. Have him slip his credentials under the door, or check them out by telephone.

Front- and back-porch lights are cheap insurance. Crime rates drop in well-lit neighborhoods.

Clear the shrubbery away from accessible windows and doors so a burglar can't hide when he's breaking in.

If you are a woman alone, list only your last name and initials in the phone book, or on your mail box if you live in an apartment.

Make your house look as if someone's there, even when no one is. Have automatic lights that go on and off at certain times, and a radio that does the same. Halt mail and newspaper deliveries.

On the Telephone. Don't give out any information, even to verify your number, until you know who's calling. If you frequently recieve wrong-number calls or hang-up calls from strangers, notify the police.

If you get an obscene call, hang up. Don't infuriate the caller by blowing a whistle in his ear.

If you have an answering device, leave a message that sounds as if you will be back any minute.

Have Friends. Make friends with your neighbors and involve them in a mutual security system: you watch their house, they watch yours.

Establish contact with a good friend or relative every day, someone who has a key to your place in case they don't hear from you.

In houses, condominiums, townhouses, and apartments, with or without roommates, single men and women over fifty are arriving at a new concept of home. *Home* no longer means the patter of little feet and echo of family laughter, the smell of home-baked cookies. Children and grandchildren are welcome, but no one is waiting around. Instead, home, according to the singles in *this* book, is a haven in which to restore yourself for another day of work or productive activity, in which to immerse yourself in the reading and records and hobbies you've always longed for, a place in which to welcome your friends. It is a place that reflects your individuality and establishes a setting for the creative, tasteful, interesting person you always knew you could be.

CHAPTER 14

The Single Chef
RSVP for one or more

"All of a sudden eating becomes a problem."

That's not the opening remark of a worried patient describing symptoms to the doctor. It is a new single over fifty facing up to the unaccustomed situation of sitting down to meals alone. Judging by their responses to the survey questionnaire, this is a preoccupation that ranks with money and sex, sometimes a notch higher.

One makes the preparation, serving, and consuming of even the simplest repast for one a challenge to ingenuity. The food is cooked as by a master chef expecting a visit from royalty. Much thought goes into the choice of wine, table setting, and lights. Plenty of time is allowed for ingestion.

Another single simply gobbles what comes to hand, standing in the kitchen, reaching into the refrigerator for a leg of chicken eaten with the fingers or spooning the contents of a can from a pot on the stove directly into the mouth.

An outsider who thought "How like a woman" of the first, and of the second, "The poor devil of a man," could be right. But the account of the painstaking diner is that of a man who had discovered the creative joys of the culinary art after his divorce. The second is the description of a once very fastidious woman responding to the necessity for nourishing her body, also after divorce, and not much caring how she does it.

Most singles when dropped from the ranks of the married simply try to ignore food. The men seldom had much share in the planning and preparation of meals anyway, and profess themselves lost in a strange world of pots and pans. The women, sometimes with relief if they had not enjoyed the chores involved in feeding a family, think cooking just for themselves is too much of a bother. Even so, they resort to eating out less often than men.

About half the singles, more often men than women, never get over this initial attitude. It is a tribute to others' adjustment to their single state, and perhaps to healthy appetites, when they stop feeling sorry for themselves and discover the fun of cooking. Once launched on a career of creative chefsmanship, they often place the happiness they derive from culinary skill and resourcefulness on a par with the raptures of lovemaking. In bed or at the stove, some of them will tell you, they are simply satisfying the most natural appetites.

The gastronomic education of Joseph in Houston illustrates this type of success in a new way of life, admittedly achieved only by a small minority. He was divorced while in his early fifties, a handsome, professional-looking man with an engaging Swedish accent. He says of himself that at the time he didn't know how to boil water. But he liked food, so after a brief period of adjustment he enrolled in a cooking school, which he attended assiduously one night a week for six months.

"I was the only man there—a bonus," he chuckles. "I learned how to slice mushrooms correctly, make homemade meatballs for spaghetti, and to thicken sauces the new French way, using puréed vegetables instead of flour. I cook for myself just as if I had guests. I serve shrimp remoulade or curried chicken for a party of one. I decant a nice wine and I feel glorious."

Joseph's smile stretches from ear to ear as he describes the joy of cooking just for himself, a joy shared by only a few men and not many women. He speaks of the even higher joy of cooking for others, especially for one other.

"Food is the open sesame to sexual companionship. Men don't cook because they don't know how and think it's beneath their dignity, not masculine. I don't feel that way. Men should learn to cook at least a few delicious things. They can then entertain a lover or guests." Joseph found that even the best gourmet dinner in the coziest setting is no guarantee sex will follow the dessert. But both men and women reported that good cooking enhanced the pleasures of an evening of love.

Joseph combines a gourmet taste with the busy man's rush to get from home to office in a hurry. He makes his breakfast eggs *en cocotte,* which is as easy as boiling them, and wastes hardly any more time than if he had cold cereal and a slice of toast. He butters an ovenproof custard cup with unsalted softened butter or margarine. He breaks an egg or two into it and sprinkles *very* lightly with sea salt, freshly ground pepper, and dried parsley or sweet basil. (Gayelord Hauser's Spike or Vegit seasoning is also good, he says.) While the eggs bake in his toaster oven at 400° F. for about ten minutes, he dashes into the shower, shaves, and dresses.

On weekends, he takes his egg with fruit and toast back to bed. When he has a stayover guest, he serves also a Bloody Mary or a peeled peach (a well-drained half of a canned peach in winter) in the bottom of a stemmed glass filled with champagne. (Apple juice, white grape juice, or ginger ale for teetotalers.) Each bite is more delicious than the one before as the fruit absorbs the liquid.

Josephine, a dancing teacher in Detroit, is as tasteful

and particular. As a widow of fifty-six, she neglected food until a few attacks of illness warned her to pay some attention to her health. She says she now makes her meals special events and finds each one a "delightful experience." She explains:

"What I do is treat myself as a guest in my own apartment. I am a guest! In the morning, I take a tray, arrange a flower in a bud vase, put on a Rachmaninoff symphony or a Mozart quintet. No matter what kind of a day it is outside, that one hour belongs to me. I put orange juice, a brioche or bagel on my tray with a plate of cottage cheese or bowl of cereal sprinkled with wheat germ, and coffee. Then I take my tray back to bed and read the paper, watch the *Today* show, or just be myself silently and gratefully.

"At 4 P.M., no matter what, I stop and have a cup of interesting tea, jasmine or herb, with an apple or plum. I teach classes at night, so I prepare a good nourishing dinner. I serve myself a meatloaf, broiled chicken breast topped with a slice of tomato and melted cheese sprinkled with bread crumbs and dotted with butter, or I fix a tail of a filet of beef. It's perfect for one person. I cultivate my butcher, and he saves the tail of the filet for me. It looks terrible, but it tastes divine broiled, sweet and cuts like butter."

A snack at bedtime while listening to more symphonic music puts the finishing touches to a day of which Josephine can say:

"I have conquered eating alone."

She did it, though, only after a much less happy experience that is common to singles after fifty.

"One of the first men I dated after my husband died told me that I would soon join the ranks of those who ate their meals at the sink. I thought to myself, 'Never, that's too crass!" So where was I eating in a few weeks? Leaning over the kitchen counter, pulling on my bifocals and sticking my nose in *The Times*. If I had an apple core in my fingers, I just dropped it down the disposal. If I wanted seconds, I ate from the pot on the stove."

All singles who were cooking for themselves with zest noted as an extra savoring that they ate better and at less expense than if they patronized restaurants. They tended to work out stratagems and recipes that saved time and trouble without sacrificing flavor or refinements. They discovered they could get good food on the table quickly by preparing it ahead of time. One woman does it by putting together an oven-ready casserole:

CHICKEN CASSEROLE WITH GINGER BRANDY
(1 SERVING)

$^1/_3$ *cup Uncle Ben's rice*
$^1/_3$ *cup chopped onion*
2 *tablespoons chopped green pepper*
1 *chicken breast, split lengthwise and skinned*
$7^1/_4$-*ounce can ready-to-serve low-sodium cream of mushroom soup*
2 *tablespoons ginger-flavored brandy*
1 *teaspoon instant vegetable or chicken-flavored bouillon granules*
$^1/_8$ *teaspoon dried sage*
$^1/_8$ *teaspoon dried rosemary*
$^1/_8$ *teaspoon poppy seeds*

In one-quart casserole with cover, combine rice, onion, and green pepper. Place chicken breast on top. In small bowl, combine soup, brandy, bouillon, sage, and rosemary. Pour over chicken. Sprinkle with poppy seeds. Cover; bake 45 minutes at 375° F. Uncover; bake 10 minutes more.

When fresh raspberries are in season, this woman sprinkles the casserole with a few as a garnish.

Anita was converted to good cooking when her neglect of balanced meals after her divorce led to a serious illness. She did not want to devote as much time to the kitchen as she had as a wife, so she hit on the device of preparing half a dozen servings at once. A roast, hot the first time and sliced cold for the rest of the week, is one such method. Others find this too monotonous. One greases leftover TV-dinner trays with salad oil, fills the compartments with a piece of meat, chicken, or fish, a potato, and a fresh vegetable, dots them with margarine, covers with foil, and freezes. When she comes home from work, she has a cup of coffee and watches the news while one of her dishes is cooking in her toaster oven.

"Simple and nutritious," she says, "and easy on dishwashing. I run my dishwasher once a week, and I need market only once every two weeks."

Joseph achieves much the same result with trout he brings back from fishing trips in the Rocky Mountains. He places each cleaned fish on a sheet of well-buttered heavy aluminum foil, sprinkles lightly with sea salt and paprika, cups up the sides and ends of the foil, pours a jigger of gin over the fish, seals the foil (leaving a small air space inside), and puts them in the freezer. When he wants to use them, he bakes them in the oven or barbecues them over a charcoal fire.

A low-calorie dish for one was discovered by a single who was trying to recall just how the cook she had before her divorce had made a particularly delectable fish. The result was not quite what the professional had served at a large dinner party, but has other merits of its own.

SOLE FILLETS WITH HERBS
(1 SERVING)

6 *ounces turbot, sole, or flounder*
fillets
$^1/_2$ *cup low-fat cottage cheese*
Dash seasoned pepper
$^1/_2$ *teaspoon dried parsley flakes*
Pinch of powdered thyme
$^1/_{16}$ *teaspoon celery seed*
Paprika

Wipe fish with damp cloth. Cut into one or two portions suitable for stuffing (depending on size of fillet). In bowl, combine remaining ingredients except paprika. Spoon onto fillets and roll fish up. Place seam side down on baking dish, sprinkle with paprika. Cover with aluminum foil and refrigerate. When ready to cook, bake at 350° F. for 15 to 20 minutes, or till fish flakes easily at the point of a fork. Do not overcook.

A heartier solution to dinner for one was worked out by a man who often does not know until the end of his working day whether he will be at home for the evening meal or not. He buys a rump roast, cuts it into four or five serving-size pieces, wraps each piece tightly in foil or plastic wrap, and freezes them. When he gets home from work, he unwraps one piece, puts it in a Dutch oven along with one

239

package of beef gravy mix, a little water, a peeled halved potato, a peeled quartered onion, sprinkles with lemon pepper, and bakes it, covered, for two hours at 300° F.

Drinks before and with meals are a major preoccupation of singles who take their culinary art seriously. They are as meticulous in getting just the right combination for mood and flavor for themselves alone as they would be if they were expecting a group of their special friends. Some of the pickups, they say, add just the right touch of exhilaration to the evening and can be prepared while dinner is cooking. The following recipes are for single drinks:

MINT-PARSLEY TEA

2 leaves lettuce
2 sprigs parsley
2 cups water
2 sprigs mint or $^1/_4$ *teaspoon*
dried mint leaves

Into small saucepan, tear lettuce in pieces. Add remaining ingredients. Bring to boiling. Cover; reduce heat and simmer 10 minutes. Strain. Serve with lemon wedge or honey. Good hot or cold.

TOMATO ENERGIZER

1 cup Clamato juice
$^1/_4$ *cup dairy sour cream or*
yogurt

$^1/_2$ *small ripe peeled, seeded, and*
chopped tomato
1 slice lime

In blender, combine all ingredients except lime. Whirl on medium speed to blend. Pour into mug or glass, garnish with lime.

BANANA NOG

1 cup skim milk
1 small ripe banana, cut in chunks
1 tablespoon honey
1 egg yolk (optional)

In blender, combine all ingredients. Whirl at high speed till smooth.

A physician who reports that wine gives him great therapeutic benefits—"I drink Bordeaux when I'm tired and get a lift from it"—has these favorites:

WINE BRACER

$^1/_3$ *cup light red dinner wine*
1 tablespoon honey
1 teaspoon lemon juice

In wine glass, combine ingredients, adding ice cube if desired.

241

SHERRY ZING

¹/₂ cup orange juice
¹/₂ cup dry sherry
1 cup ice
¹/₂ cup milk
1 tablespoon honey

In blender, combine all ingredients. Whirl at high speed till blended.

AROMATIC TEA

¹/₂ lime
2 cups hot tea
2 cloves
¹/₄ teaspoon powdered allspice
Dash nutmeg and cinnamon
3 tablespoons honey
3 tablespoons rum, claret, or
Burgundy

Squeeze juice from lime; cut rind in half. In small saucepan, combine all ingredients except wine or rum. Bring just to boiling; reduce heat, simmer 5 minutes. Strain. Add wine or rum.

These all came from men. Women seldom seemed to mix aperitifs for themselves alone, but they too had favorites. A divorcée in San Francisco who is generally considered glamorous by her friends thinks part of her reputation may be due to the fact that she keeps domestic champagne on hand. She often sips it by herself or in company.

"A luxurious thing," she calls it, "before dinner, before a trip, before bed, before anything."

Some singles fear that drinking alone, even if only at mealtime, may lead to a habit of blotting out a lonely evening. Others are concerned about the calories. While this was not general, one man offered a suggestion for avoiding the temptation of excess.

"The best way is to have a drink I hate. I then sip it instead of gulping it and I consume less."

Singles over fifty don't talk about food very long before they get into figures. This age bracket, fifty to sixty-five, seems to be the most girth-conscious in the country. Related to this, and used or abused as much as a topic of conversation, is food and health, not without reason. After thirty-five, the slimmest figure has a tendency to thicken around the middle; by fifty, pounds are far easier to put on than take off, and the body is not so adept at defending itself from the damage that can be done by a faulty diet. Among singles, discussions of this sort slide easily into monologue, and here are some extracts:

"I eat about forty-five percent of what I used to and weigh seven percent less."

"I make it my challenge to buy half of what I want to buy, so I'll have an almost bare cupboard and consequently eat less. But I buy the best quality, indulge in every food I desire for myself. Supermarket people are very cooperative about repackaging small quantities for a man who asks."

"I used to walk with two canes." (This is a sixty-five-year-old man who looks fifty.) "My doctor told me two years ago that I would never walk without them. I made up my mind to find out why. I experimented with foods. Within three months, I found my culprits: sugar, salt, milk, lard, and white flour. I eliminated these and soon threw away my canes. My own secret for avoiding the aging process is a daily salad of raw peas, cauliflower, and avocado. I make a dressing out of the best mayonnaise, a dash of sweet relish and Worcestershire sauce, some safflower oil, and stir it well."

Singles are great on salads, praising for both taste and the small number of calories. A slender sixty-year-old in Seattle attributes her ability to keep her weight down to her heavy reliance on salads and her custom of eating them with chopsticks or an oyster fork. This assures her very small bites; she takes longer over a meal and feels satisfied.

Salads that slender singles suggested for varying a mainly vegetable diet included:

BREAKFAST SALAD
(MAKE IT THE NIGHT BEFORE)

*¹/₂ apple and ¹/₂ tomato, washed,
peeled, and chopped
¹/₂ medium stalk celery, chopped
1 tablespoon raisins
4 chopped dates
4 mushrooms, quickly washed,
dried, and sliced
1 teaspoon toasted pumpkin or
sunflower seeds
1 teaspoon lemon juice*

In small bowl, combine and gently toss all ingredients. Cover; refrigerate overnight. In the morning mix it with:

YOGURT DRESSING

$^1/_2$ *cup plain yogurt*
2 slices peeled ripe avocado
1 teaspoon lemon juice or cider
vinegar
$^1/_{16}$ *teaspoon poppy seeds*

In blender or small bowl, mix and blend all ingredients.

This one is from a man who has his own garden and has his lover over for lunch. She sips white wine and chats with him while he gathers the greens and prepares:

CEDRIC'S SPANISH TUNA SALAD

7-ounce can white-meat tuna
fish, drained
1 tablespoon olive or safflower oil
2 tablespoons sherry
1 small onion, chopped
2 tablespoons minced parsley

In medium bowl, combine all ingredients, breaking tuna into small bits. Mix well. Serve on a lettuce leaf with chunks of French bread and softened butter. Top with mayonnaise, if desired.

A widower in Florida submits this:

HAROLD'S SALAD SANDWICH

*2 slices rye, sprouted wheat, or
sunflower-seed bread*
¹/₂ avocado, peeled and sliced
¹/₂ teaspoon sunflower seeds
¹/₂-inch layer alfalfa sprouts
*1 tablespoon chopped onion (op-
tional)*
1 or more teaspoons mayonnaise

On one slice bread, layer avocado, seeds, sprouts, and onion.
On other bread slice, spread mayonnaise in amount desired.
Press bread slices together.

Tossed green salads are a favorite of this generation.
Singles recommend these additions to make the usual combination more appetizing: capers, peeled and sliced broccoli
stems, sliced fresh mushrooms, drained canned Mandarin
orange sections, peeled sliced apple, and poppy, celery, sesame, or pumpkin seeds. For a spicy change, some serve it
with:

GORGONZOLA CHEESE DRESSING

*¹/₄ pound (1 cup) Gorgonzola
cheese*
3 tablespoons half-and-half

$^1/_2$ *teaspoon lemon juice*
$^1/_2$ *teaspoon chopped parsley*
$^1/_2$ *cup good-grade mayonnaise*
$^1/_4$ *teaspoon dried dill weed*

In blender or small bowl, mix ingredients to almost smooth consistency.

Salt and cholesterol preoccupy health-conscious singles to a considerable degree. Doctors and magazine articles tell them that the sodium in salt can increase blood pressure and have other dire effects. Among the foods that contain it are canned vegetables, prepared luncheon meats, salted and smoked fish, bottled salad dressing, most butter and magarine, sardines, anchovies, breads, pastries, over-the-counter indigestion aids.

Cholesterol, a fat that is one of the body's essential foods, may deposit some of itself on the inner lining of the arteries as it passes through in the blood, narrowing the channels and eventually perhaps blocking one completely. This is one of the commonest phenomena of the aging process, happening to some extent to just about everybody over fifty but usually without being noticed. Because of cholesterol's association with heart attacks and strokes, singles in the survey sample were fairly well aware of the desirability of cutting down on foods rich in this fat—eggs, cream, butter, marbled meats, and so on.

Sugar also is anathema to many singles; the majority avoid it because sweets so easily add weight to the body where it is least wanted. Doctors prohibit sugar for some; others whose figures remain slim and who like to keep them that way find it a good rule of thumb to reduce sugar intake by at least half after fifty, unless it was very low before.

Entertaining at home is the supreme test of the gourmet cook, and singles who attempt it concede that it is more difficult alone than when they were married. Because of that, the custom has withered and died for some who used to enjoy having people in for dinner.

Men reported it is too hard to get the place cleaned, they had no proper dishes, they hadn't time to plan and market, they didn't know how to cook anyway. Women cited such complications as no one to mix drinks and help in the kitchen and the embarrassment of inviting couples when they had no man of their own. The only occasions on which many, man or woman, entertain at home is when their children or other relatives or friends visit them on holidays. Then singles stage the traditional feast and enjoy it.

The minority of stalwarts who do more entertaining than that say it is important, just as important as when they were married.

"If you want to be asked to other people's parties, you have to ask them to yours, at least occasionally," explains a pretty widow who has gained a reputation for maxicaloric masterpieces, whether cooking for her son's college debate team or clients of her interior decorating business. "The magic word for a single is casual."

She says she keeps the food simple and usually prepares it in advance so she is relaxed when guests arrive. She insists the meal be attractively presented, and lists a "carrying party" as an example. She was moving next door, and guests were warned they would be expected to carry a lot of things the movers could be spared from handling. With plenty of cold beer and juices on hand, the carrying of pictures, books, lamps, silver, and the rest went gaily, and when the work was over she served, along with buttered Italian bread, a giant tossed salad laced with paper-thin orange and apple slices, and red wine:

BETTY'S BEEF AND SPAGHETTI PIE
(MADE THE DAY BEFORE)
(6 SERVINGS)

6 ounces spaghetti
2 tablespoons unsalted butter
$^1/_2$ cup grated Parmesan cheese
4 egg yolks, beaten
1 pound lean ground beef
$^1/_2$ cup chopped onion
$^1/_4$ cup chopped green pepper
$^1/_4$ cup chopped parsley
8-ounce can Italian-style tomatoes
6-ounce can tomato paste
1 teaspoon sugar
1 teaspoon Worcestershire sauce
$^1/_2$ teaspoon dried oregano
$^1/_2$ teaspoon dried sweet basil
$^1/_4$ teaspoon garlic powder
1 cup ricotta cheese
4-ounce package grated mozzarella cheese

Butter 10-inch pie plate. Cook spaghetti till tender, following instructions on package; drain, but do not remove from pot. Stir in butter. When butter is melted, stir in Parmesan cheese and egg yolks. With fingers or back of spoon, spread spaghetti mixture in prepared pie plate, shaping it up sides to form a thick crust; set aside. In medium skillet, over medium-high heat, sauté beef, onions, green pepper, and parsley till vegetables are limp, about 10 minutes. Spoon off fat. Cut up tomatoes; add tomatoes with juice, tomato paste, sugar, Worcestershire sauce, oregano, basil, and garlic powder. Bring to boil; remove from heat. Spread ricotta cheese over spaghetti. Cover with meat sauce. Top with mozzarella cheese. Bake at 325° F. 30 minutes or till heated through. Let stand 5 minutes before cutting into pie-shaped wedges.

Betty served this on paper plates at the carrying party. For dessert, she put a can of chocolate sauce on to heat. Also in paper dishes, she served a large scoop of coffee ice cream topped with the warm chocolate sauce over which she sprinkled crushed Heath candy bars.

Sam, a longtime bachelor, gets almost as effective results as Betty by giving the delicatessen he has patronized for many years a few days' notice of his plans. A large moussaka or lamb ragout is delivered, and he doesn't worry too much about serving it to his guests because "anybody who walks into my kitchen is put to work." He also premixes his drinks in a pitcher ready to serve as soon as the doorbell rings, so he doesn't lose time from the party mixing cocktails. One of his favorites:

KIR

1 bottle white table wine, Chablis
or Rhine
¹/₃ cup crème de cassis

Combine in glass pitcher or wine carafe. Chill.

A good way for singles to entertain easily and pleasantly for both themselves and their guests, according to Sally, is a "bring your own" party. Sally is a hard-working designer who loves to have people around her but doesn't have time to cook elaborate meals. Each of her guests brings a dish of their own fancying; she supplies beverages and the dessert, something she can make ahead of time—such as:

CHOCOLATE CHARLOTTE
(6 SERVINGS)

16 packaged ladyfingers, split
1 teaspoon unflavored gelatin
3¹/₄-ounce package vanilla pudding and pie filling
2 cups milk
4 1-ounce squares semi-sweet baking chocolate
¹/₄ cup almond paste
1-quart container non-dairy whipped topping

Line 8¹/₄ × 4¹/₄ × 2¹/₄-inch loaf pan with waxed paper, leaving edges of paper on outside of pan. Line bottom and sides of pan with ladyfinger halves, curved sides out. In medium saucepan, stir together gelatin, pudding, and milk. Bring to boil over medium heat, stirring constantly; remove from heat. Add chocolate and almond paste; stir till smooth. Cool. When cool, beat with wire whisk or spoon till smooth. Measure out 1 cup whipped topping; refrigerate. Fold remaining topping into chocolate mixture. Spoon half the pudding mixture into ladyfinger-lined pan; add layer of ladyfinger halves; cover with remaining pudding. Refrigerate 4 hours or overnight. When ready to serve, unmold and place on serving dish. Top with reserved chilled whipped topping.

By contrast, Teresa, a highly paid executive, likes to give the same elaborate sit-down or buffet dinners she did when she was married. So she engages a cook who prepares the meal during the day, and leaves it for her all ready to serve. An example is this "vegetarian mini-cocktail buffet":

SKINNY DIP
(2 CUPS)

2 cups cream-style cottage cheese
1 tablespoon sliced pimiento
1 teaspoon dried parsley flakes
¹/₂ teaspoon dried dill weed
1 tablespoon taco seasoning mix
(shake package before opening)
1 tablespoon drained capers
1 large round loaf unsliced dark
rye bread

In blender or mixing bowl, combine ingredients except capers and bread. Put in pretty bowl, sprinkle with capers; cover. Refrigerate. To serve, carefully cut out center of bread to make a well. Place dip in well. Cut bread into cubes. Surround dip-filled loaf with bread cubes and fresh vegetable dippers: young turnip slices, zucchini, cucumber, carrot and celery sticks, and very young asparagus spears.

RATATOUILLE
(6 SERVINGS)

³/₄ cup olive or safflower oil
2 cups thinly sliced onion
2 cups seeded, thinly sliced green pepper
2 small eggplants, peeled and cubed
2 medium zucchini, thinly sliced
2 cloves garlic, peeled and minced
4 tomatoes, peeled and chopped
1 teaspoon sea salt
¹/₂ teaspoon freshly ground pepper
¹/₂ teaspoon dried sweet basil
3 tablespoons minced parsley

In large heavy skillet over low heat, sauté onions till limp, about 10 minutes. Add green pepper, eggplant, zucchini, and garlic. Cover; cook over low heat 30 minutes, stirring occasionally. Add tomatoes, salt, pepper, and basil. Recover; cook 40 minutes more. Stir in parsley. Serve hot or cold. This can be made the day before and refrigerated.

TOMATO RELLENOS
(6 SERVINGS)

6 large firm tomatoes
2 tablespoons unsalted butter or margarine

¹/₂ *cup chopped onion*
1 ¹/₂ cups drained canned whole-
kernel corn
2 eggs, beaten
1 teaspoon sea salt
¹/₈ *teaspoon Tabasco*
¹/₂ *cup grated Cheddar cheese*
2 tablespoons chopped pimientos

Butter flat baking dish. Cut ¹/₂-inch piece from stem ends of tomatoes; reserve. Scoop out insides of tomatoes (use for tomorrow's salad). In medium skillet, melt butter or margarine. Sauté onions till limp, about 10 minutes. Remove from heat; cool 5 minutes. Mix in corn, eggs, salt, Tabasco, cheese, and pimientos. Stuff tomato shells with corn mixture. Cover with reserved tops. Place in baking dish. Cover with aluminum foil. Bake at 375° F. for 25 minutes, or till well heated through but tomatoes have not collapsed.

Sunday brunches are favorites for singles. They and their guests seem to enjoy the informality; no one notices an uneven distribution of men and women. A particularly elegant menu and an excellent prelude to an afternoon football game, concert, boating or other excursion, or whatever:

CANADIAN BACON WELLINGTON
(SIMPLER TO MAKE THAN IT LOOKS)
(8 OR MORE SERVINGS)

3- to 3¹/₂-pound piece smoked
Canadian-style bacon

2 *tablespoons brandy or Grand*
Marnier liqueur
2 *10-ounce packages unbaked*
frozen patty shells, thawed but
not warm
1 *egg, beaten with fork*
Parsley clusters
4 *ripe kiwi, peeled and halved*
15-ounce jar applesauce

Preheat oven to 325° F. Remove casing from bacon if there is
one. Trim off fat. Place on large sheet of aluminum foil.
Brush with brandy or liqueur. Wrap foil loosely around
bacon. Place on cookie sheet. Bake 40 minutes. Remove
from oven. Cool. Remove foil. On unfloured bread board,
place patty shells side by side, press together with fingers,
then roll into large square. Place cooled bacon in center of
dough; wrap pastry tightly around bacon, trimming and
tucking edges, but not making pastry double thickness anywhere except side and middle seams. Trim excess. Moisten
pastry edges with bit of water, then press seam down with
fork; lightly sprinkle with flour. Use any trimmings for dec-
oration, sealing them with fingertips dipped in water. Line
cookie sheet with foil; lightly butter foil. Place dough-
wrapped bacon on foil, seam side down. Brush with beaten
egg. Prick with fork to allow steam to escape during baking.
Bake at 425° F. till pastry is crisp, flaky, and golden, about 25
minutes. Cover with foil if it is browning too rapidly.
Meanwhile, heat applesauce. Remove bacon from oven.
Cool 5 minutes; remove from cookie sheet with wide spatula.
Garnish with parsley clusters and kiwi. To serve: slice with
sharp knife into $1/2$-inch slices, cover with warmed applesauce.

TEQUILA MUSHROOMS
(8 SERVINGS)

6 tablespoons unsalted butter or
margarine
1¹/₂ pounds mushrooms, quickly
washed, dried, and sliced
³/₄ cup 80-proof tequila
³/₄ cup dairy sour cream
¹/₄ teaspoon white pepper
¹/₄ teaspoon dried dill weed
¹/₈ teaspoon celery seed
8 slices toast, halved and but-
tered

In large skillet, melt butter or margarine. Add mushrooms.
Over medium-high heat, cook till lightly browned but *not*
soft. Meanwhile, warm tequila over hot water. Pour over
mushrooms. Stir in sour cream, pepper, dill, and celery
seed. Heat through, but do not boil. Serve hot over buttered
toast pieces.

Reciprocity in entertaining is of more concern to
singles than it was when they were married. Most of the
men, even those who cooked their own meals, usually took a
date out to dinner, and sometimes the question of who
should pay the check arose. As indicated in Chapter 11,
this presents thorny dilemmas for the woman. But men asserted with fervor that if a woman cooked a good meal for
them, it was more than ample return for any $50 restaurant
dinner in town. A sixty-five-year-old Californian dismissed
the problem with:

"A woman should never pick up the check. But she can feed me peeled grapes in bed after a night of lovemaking."

The most popular form of entertaining among singles is dinner for two, served preferably in front of a fire on a small table in the living room or bedroom, or on snack tables. One enthusiastic male chef insists that any man can prepare a more-than-adequate, an ambrosial repast that will delight the most delicate and discriminating palate. His unusual, luscious menu, starting with the hors d'oeuvre, goes like this:

SARDINES DIJON
(2 SERVINGS)

2 slices toasted bread
2 tablespoons melted butter
2 tablespoons Dijon mustard, or
to taste
1 can good-quality Portuguese
sardines, drained and split
lengthwise
Cayenne pepper or paprika
Lemon wedges and parsley for
garnish

Generously butter toast slices to the edges. Spread with mustard. Cover with sardine halves, skin side down. Sprinkle lightly with cayenne or paprika. Broil till just heated through. Garnish with lemon wedges and parsley.

For the dinner entrée, he makes:

SIRLOIN STEAK WITH GREEN PEPPERCORNS
(2 SERVINGS)

2 tablespoons drained green pep-
percorns
1½-inch-thick sirloin steak
trimmed of fat (reserve fat)
1 tablespoon brandy
¹/₄ cup heavy cream
¹/₂ teaspoon prepared mustard

Mash peppercorns with back of fork. Heat skillet large
enough to hold steak. Rub reserved fat around skillet. Discard fat. Over high heat sear steak on both sides. Reduce
heat; cook steak to desired doneness, turning only once.
Remove to warmed platter. Pour fat from skillet. Add
brandy, green peppercorns, and cream. Bring to boiling in
skillet, stir in mustard, remove from heat. Pour over steak.
Slice steak into serving pieces.

To serve with the steak, this chef prepares:

STUFFED PIMIENTOS
(2 SERVINGS)

4-ounce jar whole pimientos,
drained
³/₄ cup cottage cheese
Lemon pepper to taste
¹/₄ teaspoon each dried chives,
parsley, and sesame seeds
Unsalted butter or margarine

Butter small flat baking dish. In bowl, combine cottage cheese and seasonings. Carefully fill pimientos. Place in prepared dish. Dot with butter or margarine. Cover with aluminum foil. Broil 10 inches or more from heat till heated through and lightly browned, about 10 minutes. Pimientos scorch, so keep a watchful eye.

After the entrée comes a salad and a fruit plate—small clusters of grapes, $1/4$ sliced apple, pear, or kiwi fruit; cherries or strawberries; several slices of gourmandise, Brie, Camembert, or Cheddar cheese, a few nuts or raisins, and either slices of French bread or assorted crackers and a pat of butter. The finale is this extravagant dessert-drink:

PRINCESS GRACE
(2 SERVINGS)

4 scoops vanilla ice cream
1 jigger Grand Marnier
1 jigger brandy
1$^1/_2$ jiggers Kahlua
1$^1/_2$ jiggers dark crème de cacao
Nutmeg

In blender, whirl all ingredients except nutmeg till smooth. Pour into stemmed glasses, sprinkle lightly with nutmeg.

CHAPTER 15

So You Think You Want To Get Married Again
how to know if you should

When Jerry asked her to marry him, Dorothea L. says she was surprised. Not by the proposal (she had seen that coming) but by her answer.

"I'd considered and reconsidered just what I'd tell him. He's very attractive, you know, and we've become extremely close in the last year. I admire him, love him for his gentleness, patience, and humor. Still I said 'No.'"

Dorothea is a self-assured woman of fifty-six. She says her assurance is only recently acquired, since she became a single four years ago after thirty years of marriage. She is a small woman, carefully groomed, with soft brown hair framing an olive-skinned, dark-eyed oval face. In the last two years, she has built a small business as a color coordinator, consulted by top-flight decorators and fashion designers.

"Turning Jerry down may have been surprising," she goes on, "but it was logical. I am living in my own rhythm, in my own balance. I feel good about myself and my work. If I ever do marry again, it will be to improve on what I have. What I have is so much that I can't see how a husband, even as fine a man as Jerry, could do that."

She pauses to survey her strikingly beautiful living room, and continues:

"I'm not at all the same person I was before my divorce. I was a dependent, clinging-vine female. But as the wife of a man with a big salary and substantial property besides, I had a secret. I knew my husband would rescue me from any difficult situation, make all the important decisions, always be the good provider. In return, I kept a nice house, was a good mother and an affectionate wife. Oh, I had it made.

"Then he came home one night and without a bit of warning said he had fallen in love with his secretary, who was thirty, and wanted to marry her. My secret little world just crumbled away. When I walked out of the courtroom the day the divorce was final, I felt tears warm on my cheek but didn't have the energy to wipe them away. What did it matter? My bra was binding me and it was hard to breathe; the air seemed to stick in my throat. I felt the arms of my daughter on one side and my son on the other supporting me, but the corridor looked longer than I could navigate.

"The memory of that afternoon is forever in my brain, and in my heart, too. One of my thoughts then was that I'd be lucky as a single woman fifty-two years old ever to get a date, let alone another husband."

In making up her mind about Jerry, she reviewed the years of experience, risk, and experiment that culminated in her newfound assurance and contentment.

"Men are not the mystery to me that they once were. It took the crashing and crushing blow of divorce to teach me the full value of my freedom and at last produce some of the self-esteem and pride in myself as *me*.

"My life is no longer controlled by someone else. I admit there are times when I would rather be childish, have somebody take care of me. But the adult in me doesn't allow this to surface as often as it used to. I am handling single life very well. Married friends say to me, 'What will you ever do when you're eighty?' Well, if I were married, there's no guarantee I wouldn't be alone and totally responsible for myself then anyway."

Other singles in situations like Dorothea's also react with extreme caution to suggestions they remarry. Only one out of six in the survey sample said they did want to remarry, while more women than men replied definitely "No." They wrote such comments as:

"I almost proposed three times, to three different women, but each time the caution light went on in my head."

"I've been tempted, but there's such a risk, and what do I have to gain?"

"I always had to fit my schedule to that of my husband. When a man begins to talk about marriage, I back away because I am cautious about making all those adjustments again."

Singles give many and varied reasons for being so deliberate in their approach to remarriage. Memories of a less-than-perfect first union are vivid. The "once burned, twice shy" adage applies; "that goes double for me," one remarked forcefully. Others wrote:

"I was demolished when my wife divorced me. It took me five years to pull myself together, but now I can see marriage was more a burden than a joy; I wouldn't want to be tied down like that again."

"Marriage wasn't the be-all and end-all we were brought up to believe. Freedom is better."

"My life was a perpetual calm. But when I got over my husband's death, which took quite a long time, I discovered that the world can be exciting too. I'd think hard before I'd give this new life up for the old complacency."

"I'd have to be sure it wouldn't be a hot-and-cold affair. The man I was living with and did not marry was moody in the morning, and nice in the afternoon because he wanted to get me in the mood for sex in the evening. At this age, who needs moodiness?"

The fact that remarriage is likely to be more complicated than the first attempt also counsels caution. The complications often involve other people as well as the single's own emotions.

"Children have to be considered even if grown up. Their feelings are bound to have an influence, both on the parent and the prospective stepparent."

"It would mean such a readjustment in so many personal relationships—my children, her children, our former in-laws, our relatives, even some of my business associates and my ex-wife."

"I would want to be sure remarriage would definitely improve the life I have now, not just change it."

"Unwed used to mean no social life, no sex life, no happiness. Now it just means you're not married, and you can create the kind of life you like without being dragged back by someone else who may disagree with you. Remarriage can endanger all that."

One who vehemently agrees is Emma J., a nurse, who got married soon after being widowed.

"I was hypnotized," she said. "At that time—about ten years ago—everyone thought you had to be married to be happy, that it was a healthier life, that a woman didn't really blossom unless she were a wife. My friends all thought I was crazy to hesitate when Al asked me, so I married him, and the day after our wedding I felt like running away."

While only one in six singles said they want to remarry, a majority fantasize about it. One of the questions debated was how long they should wait. They measured the time less by the calendar than by the state of their emotions or stage of maturity.

If you are considering remarriage, they advise, you should ask yourself some searching questions. Are you marrying to escape loneliness, to gain security, to find a

wholeness and happiness you don't already have? If these
are your reasons, they say, then you're not ready.

On the other hand, if you are emotionally free from
your past marriage, if you remember your late or ex-spouse
without feelings of bitterness or tears, if you feel happy and
comfortable as a single, then perhaps you *are* ready.

Typical interviews contained these explanations:

"No one can be a good partner until that person has
an inner identity. It is only when two wholes get together,
not two halves, that a sound partnership can be formed."

"The time to remarry is when each person has a sound
sense of his identity, not looking at another to bring him happiness."

"Have a torrid, torrid affair, fall madly in love, but
don't get married for two years." (The advice of a coordinator of seminars on divorce.)

"Six months to a year. Life is shorter when you're
over fifty, and we are getting too set in our ways."

"It all depends on individual needs, situations, and
desires."

"Just as long as it takes to become self-sufficient, self-
secure, stable, and free of old attachments, and when we no
longer feel we *should* remarry."

"It's not the amount of time, it's the amount you have
developed. Wait until after two or three relationships; then
the fantasies you have about yourself and the opposite sex
will have been worked out."

When the possibility of a new marriage presents itself,
take stock of your current situation. Some marriage veterans
found they had gotten used to a good deal of freedom and
solitude while they were single and that they would need
time in their new marriage that they could depend on for
themselves alone. A woman whose second divorce occurred
because of her husband's possessiveness said:

"I never had time to myself, even to pluck my eyebrows in the bathroom. If I were to do it again, I would have my own leisure guaranteed in a written agreement."

Be sure you understand what kind of role you will be expected to assume in a new marriage and whether you really want to fill it. After a year or more of single living, few women want to go back into the traditional, male-dominated, family-oriented homemaker position.

"You may not even realize you don't want it," said Sadie R., sixty-six, a retired public health worker, who accepted the invitation of a widowed suitor to visit him in the town where she had been a young matron forty years before. For a week, Sadie lived in the world she thought she wanted to re-enter.

"I got so bored, I could hardly believe it," she said. "I'd seen all the good movies in town. All we did was visit relatives and walk up and down the malls looking in the store windows. There was no symphony guild, no lunch with the girls, no singles clubs—all the things that made my life exciting at home."

Another woman, who thought it was nice that her fiancé wanted her to quit her job, found that she was expected to be total housekeeper, nurse, and counselor, completely at his beck and call.

"The hand that holds the gold rules the household," she warns.

For their part, few men at this time of life want to be the total support for a clinging vine.

"I found, after I married Clara, that she couldn't even balance her checkbook. The dependency that seemed kind of appealing when we were going together became oppressive after we were married, and I had to help her decide *everything*," confessed an insurance salesman.

Most veterans of two or more marriages urge that you take plenty of time getting to know your prospective spouse very, very well. Instead of crowding your dating days with activities and people, go for hikes and picnics, just the two of you; spend evenings by the fire, give yourselves time to talk about what you think and feel. Notice particularly how you handle disharmony. Can you discuss it and arrive at a compromise solution?

Said a commercial photographer:

"When Cindy and I were dating, we were always partying with our two circles of friends so that we never really talked things over. After we married, I discovered that every disagreement degenerated into a quarrelsome interchange that got nowhere, or she would turn cold and distant and refuse to talk about it."

Meet the friends, children, in-laws, brothers and sisters of your intended, and, if possible, the "ex" if he or she has been divorced, to find out why the divorce occurred.

"Before we were married, my husband kept saying he didn't want to share me. If I'd met his friends, I might have found out that he was an alcoholic," said one woman.

A systems analyst who married a neurotic said that next time he'd date a woman for two years and keep a written diary of any curious behavior.

"A person can hide a neurosis for the first year, but it's harder the second," he believes. "I should have started my record last time when my fiancée, after accidentally knocking a drink out of a woman's hand, angrily told her to watch where she was going."

Children are frequently at the dead center of discord between a couple. They can and often do destroy a union.

"The biggest problem in my second marriage was the attitude of the children, especially when it came to financial matters." This from a financier after his second divorce when he explained his doubts about a third marriage.

"There seems to be a gut-level reaction to the 'intruder' both on the part of the children and of their parent," one woman whose children were still at home said. "I see it in myself. I fly to defend them against criticism, even when I know it's justified."

One stepfather thought he was championing his new wife when he reprimanded her sons for their rudeness and lack of cooperation, only to have her turn on him with "Who are you, telling my kids what to do?"

Before you step into a family situation, then, check it out first. Observe the relationship between parent and children, the problems the young people have, how possessive they are of their parent, how accepting of you. Live in the family for a month and see how everyone reacts to the authority you will have to exercise.

The best way to find out if you and your future partner are compatible, of course, *is* to live together before you marry, and half the men and women in our survey said that is exactly what they would do.

Many, especially if nearer sixty-five than fifty, admitted shock and disapproval if a child of theirs made that choice, yet they believe the arrangement would be useful for themselves as a tryout for marriage. Living together is also an obvious alternative to marriage for singles over fifty.

Marge V., a widow who never had intercourse except with her husband, says she still feels so married to him that she could not marry another man.

"If I fall in love again," she says, "I would live with him, but not marry him."

Marge's sister agrees that such an arrangement would be perfect for her, too, but for a different reason. Her alimony payments will stop if she remarries.

"I feel I *earned* that alimony and I only get it for ten years anyway after twenty-five years of total service and devotion to my husband and working side-by-side to help further his career. Besides, what if a new marriage failed and perhaps under the new interpretations of the law I might not get anything, or he died and left everything to his children?"

Another example of this frustration came from the widow of a schoolteacher who is drawing survivor benefits in the form of an annuity. She would lose those monthly checks if she remarried. "It's ironic," she says, "but one of these days the Board of Education may be subsidizing my 'living in sin.'"

Victor D., who had married his high school sweetheart, recalls that they struggled through twenty-five years together, and adds:

"When she died, I felt sad, but you know there was relief, too. Marriage is a trap really. It would be nice to live with a woman if she had herself all together, the way I do. But I'd be scared of making another mistake that I'd be committed to for keeps."

Fred H. wishes he had been as wise, but he married on the rebound to "legitimize" a sex relationship he was enjoying. He now says he "will never again get a license to get into the same bed with a woman without trying it out for a couple of years."

A minority insisted they would not live in such unlegalized unions. Only two women and one man indicated that they were not sure or had not made up their minds.

Age differences between man and wife are less impor tant in today's world than ever before, according to the sur vey sample. While a majority expressed the opinion that remarriages have a better chance of success if the parties are approximately the same age, it can be "fine, just fine, if the husband is younger." Even so, the trend running through the comments is that the discrepancy puts extra stress on a marriage in spite of the few women who reported having zest for living revitalized by the love of a younger man. Some of the remarks on the subject:

"Men have been marrying women younger than they

for ages. It's time to turn aside another cultural hangup." (A clinical psychologist who is romantically involved with a woman twelve years his senior.)

"Why not? I feel comfortable with him and it's extremely practical in terms of sexuality and longevity." (A woman who dates a man five years younger than she.)

"Nothing good can come of it. It can only lead to unhappiness for the woman if the man becomes interested in someone his own age." (A widower who says he bases his view on observation, not experience.)

Timing is as important as time. With all those reasons for caution, singles may wait too long and then overcompensate by rushing in too soon. A racing fan among them suggests they have to learn to "rate the pace." Don L., an inventor and manufacturer who had all the usual reasons for hesitation to remarry in spite of several satisfactory intimacies, described in an interview the failure of his timing in the matrimonial handicap.

"I was so embittered after my divorce that when I fell deeply in love with Karen, I wouldn't marry her. After a couple of years of living together, she told me she would leave me unless we got married, but I wasn't ready. I came home one evening to find the house half empty, and what Karen hadn't taken with her she had a friend pick up the next day. Within six months, she married a good friend of ours.

"I felt bereft, but it taught me a lesson, I thought. When one is ready for marriage, one can usually find someone to marry. But who? I had several casual love affairs in the next couple of years and then fell in love with a beautiful divorced woman who came to work in my plant. I had reached the stage of self-esteem and respect for others that I think is the foundation for a good permanent relationship, so I proposed. But this time, she wasn't ready. She said my invitation was flattering, but it was too soon for her to make that kind of a commitment."

Even before they are ready to remarry, singles over fifty set down precisely what they expect if they do take the plunge. They are particular because they have attained fulfillment, exhilaration, a sense of accomplishment. Women who could have found security and status only with a husband fifteen or twenty years earlier have earned both for themselves. Men who thought they needed "total" married life—a woman around the house to cook, clean, and care for them—discover keeping house isn't as bad as they had expected, and anyway it is possible to share a home without marriage.

"My marriage was based in part on myths, as I look back at it, and I suspect a lot of others are too," Don commented in justifying his delay in getting ready for remarriage. "Now some of us have investigated the myths and we only hold onto or update those that fit contemporary society."

Broadly speaking, as one did, singles now expect from remarriage "a *human* experience, the beginnings of honesty." But more specifically, they expect, as they tell it in interviews:

They would want communication. If this element was missing in a previous marriage, as it seems to have been for a majority of the singles, they think it is of prime importance to correct the mistake in any remarriage. They say they would speak out honestly to express their ideas, thoughts, and feelings.

Kenneth N., trim and in his fifties, is a good example. He has been single for as long as he was married, but he stayed in the family home after his wife died to raise their four children. Now, staring out of a window at a frozen lake, he speaks of what he considers the key to successful remarriage:

271

"Communication means talking *and* listening. It does no good unless both do it. If one ventilates his feelings and wants, but the other's mind is shut to what is said, that's not communication. My wife used to say, 'I don't want to talk about it,' which stopped the conversation. The woman I am dating now says, 'I would like to discuss that, but could we do it after dinner, or when I'm not so tired?' She shows a willingness to keep lines open.

"I've learned lately it's just as necessary to be alert to the meaning behind words as it is to hear what's said—to watch body posture, hand and arm gestures, facial expression. All these help express what the person is trying to convey."

Marion F., a salesperson in her sixties, reveals as much about her late marriage as she does about how she would handle communication in another, saying:

"I would be more open today. Instead of doing things to infuriate my husband as reprisal for things he did to me, I would say how I feel about what he said or did, and not put the guilt on him. I would bring the problems right out, talking about the emotional frustrations, anger, rather than keeping them until they expanded out of proportion. It's wrong to be silent because you think it might upset your partner. I would want my husband to do the same."

Variations on this theme are abundant in the lines scribbled on questionnaire forms, such as:

"If I didn't understand what she meant, I would struggle to get the meaning. I've learned it's O.K. to feel foolish, vulnerable, and out of character when I'm reaching out to understand her, or to get her to understand what I mean."

"I had the illusion that problems would work out, that time would fix things. I've learned not to let them lie, but to talk to him, maybe not at the moment, not in the heat of an argument, but wait until things are soft again. It always works."

They would want to feel equal partners in a joint venture. They stress "equal." Equal rights, privileges, rewards, equal regard for the other's needs and interests is what leads to the happiness cycle of respect for themselves and for the partner. One might be dominant at one time and the other at another time; one might lean more at one time, the other at another time, but there should be a balance, a sharing equally in the overall picture. More important than agreeing, they feel, would be the ability to negotiate so that each has some of his needs met. One should not be the perpetual giver and the other the taker.

Many men no longer feel they would be entitled to control the purse strings if they were the breadwinners but would make financial decisions a mutual responsibility.

"I would now acknowledge my wife as a human being of equal stature, not a madonna who could never understand what went on in the pressures of my job or the little girl who shouldn't be worried about finances. I might point out where she was off base but I'd not make her feel she was less of a person."

How they would each spend their time as married couples (what they would do together and what separately) would be a joint decision. Some men said they would no longer feel entitled to freedoms they would not allow their wives, such as the extra-marital affairs many had enjoyed during their first marriages.

Finally, some felt they would be more tolerant of each other's habits. "I was so critical of my ex-wife's hair curlers and her habit of driving with one elbow on the wheel and her hand in her mouth. Habits are part of a partner. I'd allow her to keep hers and I'd expect to keep mine."

They would want companionship. Even those singles who

273

have become masters at enjoying their own company prefer a genuine rapport with someone of the opposite sex. They want "the one person" with whom they would share their interests, be they bowling or needlepoint; upon whom they could rely for support; with whom they could sit and talk; and whose company they could enjoy under any circumstances. Good sex would no longer be enough; they would want enjoyment and satisfaction while living all the other moments they would spend together.

One person defined this kind of companionship as "A feeling of unity about the partnership, a comradeship with one another, a meeting-and-matching of minds and hearts —not just a sharing of interests but an easy and comfortable togetherness."

They would be more realistic in what they expect. The remarriage standards set in these interviews may seem high, but singles modify them as they realize what they can and cannot do without; what they expect of themselves and their partners. "We've all lost our rose-colored glasses. Prince Charming isn't coming and I'm not Cinderella. My partner wouldn't be all in all to me, which should take a load off his shoulders."

Many agree they could now marry one of several people they know and have a successful union, providing both partners have realistic expectations. They would not expect, for example, the constant attention they gave and received in courtship. Having had an opportunity as singles to try the sexual experimentation they had missed in their youth, many women said they now realized that men don't know everything about sex—as their mothers had told them when they were growing up. If they were to remarry they would be patient with their partners as they learned to bring each other pleasure.

Singles are aware too that after living alone they would have to adjust to married life all over again. Said one

274

woman who has a live-in relationship after six years as a single:

"No more staying in town for dinner with a friend or taking a weekend trip on the spur of the moment. Even turning out the lights and going to bed at the same time has been an adjustment."

They would be firm about things they do not want. For all their professions of adjustment and mutual tolerance, singles set strict limits on what they would expect of a new spouse. They did not actually say *demand,* but the connotation was there. Women, especially those who worked or had incomes of their own, would not want to take full responsibility for the household—laundry, marketing, cooking, and cleaning. Nor would they wait on a man as they had in a first marriage.

"If we both contribute financially, I expect equal contributions in household tasks," said a woman property manager. "Perhaps the dollars I bring in are less, but I wouldn't come home after a day's work to have him sit down with a martini before the television set while I prepare dinner."

"I would not marry without having the financial ability to hire outside household help," declared an executive secretary. "Being a homemaker is not the way I want to spend the rest of my life. I'm successful in my work and I could never be intrigued unless the man were a success."

Such views did not seem to bother the men. In fact, some wouldn't have it any other way, believing that a couple should either get outside help or do the housework cooperatively if both have jobs. If the man works and provides all the income, however, most men feel the household chores are the woman's responsibility. One pointed out that it's the attitude toward the work, rather than the job itself, that is important.

"If she's smart, she'll encourage her husband to cook dinner and praise him lavishly. If he's smart, he'll take her out to dinner more often."

275

Many men said they would like to relinquish their traditional role as chief—the sole decision-maker and provider. They want a woman who is intellectually alive, emotionally healthy, and financially independent, a woman who can think for herself, one who is willing to contribute to a good standard of living for both of them. As one man explained:

"I live very well on what I earn, but I don't make enough to support two people in this fashion." They also emphasized that they would want a woman who could cope competently with life's problems and tasks, even the ugly ones. "At this stage of life, I don't want a doormat or a gushing girl," one said. "A woman who has been too carefully taken care of would not attract me now."

A few men did not want this new wife to be *too* successful, have *too* brilliant a career, be *too* decisive.

"I want to be more significant in the business world than my wife," asserted one who was very significant by any standard. "The only exception would be if she had a special talent, like playing the violin. I would not want to hold that back."

Included in what singles did not want in a new spouse, stated very emphatically sometimes, were traits and habits to which everyone objects.

Women are not ready to put up with infidelity, lack of affection, excessive drinking. They do not want a man who is too demanding, a smart aleck, or who is not personally clean. They were not ready to take on nursing responsibilities for someone who might get sick. Above all, they did not want to be taken for granted.

Men are wary of women with delusions of grandeur, who want more than they can realistically get, who are careless of money. They don't want a woman who nags or bickers, who talks too much, or who is dull. They shun a domineering woman, but they don't want a subservient one, either. Above all, they would not tolerate a complainer.

Both sexes have reservations about children. While they could accept their spouses' children, they don't want to play second fiddle to an all-absorbing parent-child relationship. The same reservations extend to grandchildren.

"I refused his proposal because I would have been the wife of a small town's first citizen, babysitting his grandchildren while he watched TV at night," one woman said.

They would bring to remarriage skills they learned as a single. Both men and women flatter themselves that if they remarry—many called it "a big if"—they would be better equipped for success.

They have learned through practice to be better lovers—more skillful, more willing to experiment, more patient, more compassionate and understanding. Women, having learned to cope with financial responsibility, can now appreciate the load a man carries. With their children gone, they feel they would be more attentive to a husband, more loving, more able to give him generous praise and endearing appreciation.

"I am sure I would be a better companion," one said. "I am much more at ease with people, thanks to travel and meeting so many different types since my divorce. I would be able to talk to a husband and his friends as I never used to. I've knocked twelve strokes off my golf score, so he wouldn't have to be ashamed to play a round with me. I've also learned to manage myself as well as a household; I neither bemoan the past nor worry about the future all the time."

Men, not having to drive so hard to climb the ladder of business success, said they would take more time to show their wives they loved and needed them, understanding as they do now the importance of making a woman feel wanted and appreciated.

277

They would consider a written prenuptial agreement. Plain talk about money is another prerequisite for a good relationship in a second marriage at this age. Over half the men and women we interviewed said they would not marry again without a written prenuptial agreement on finances, particularly on how assets would be distributed in the event of death or divorce. Even those who are not sure exactly what it is and how it works report that they would investigate the subject carefully if they decided to remarry. A divorce lawyer of long and varied experience in his field gives his clients this advice:

"Prenuptial agreements are generally accepted in most states so long as three general tests are met:

"1. That there is full and accurate disclosure of assets on each side,

"2. That each partner has independent counsel, and

"3. That there is some consideration for the mutual promises in the prenuptial agreement.

"Generally, it can be said that prenuptial agreements are strongly supported by the court in the event of a death of either party, but are only moderately supported in the event of a dissolution of marriage."

These agreements need not always be legal documents or even deal primarily with property. Ann T. and Homer Q., both in their fifties, more casual than formal in lifestyle, have one they drafted themselves when they decided to share the same apartment after a year of exclusive dating. It is extremely personal, expressing what they expect of a permanent tie.

"Definitely have it in writing," says Ann, as Homer nods his agreement. "This specifies what you will give each other. In our case, it's thoughtfulness, attention, time, respect, and love. We go into detail, such as that we will answer a question honestly. We agree to review it every six months."

Tim W. has a minority opinion, which is that such

contracts are no good. Tim, a wealthy rancher, and his second wife entered into one and he is now disillusioned, complaining:

"They work against you because they outline who gets or doesn't get. My wife was a wonderful lover, but after the wedding bells stopped ringing it slowly became evident that she was interested in what she would get financially if we were divorced. She wanted what had been laid out for her in the contract, but she really did not want *me*."

Where substantial property was involved on both sides, unlike Tim's case, prenuptial agreements received wide support.

"It's terribly important at this time of life if there are estates involved that it be clearly enumerated what the disposition will be," remarked a woman who learned after some unpleasant experiences to manage the large property her husband had left.

But a well-to-do physician, cautious before remarriage and optimistic for the future, declared:

"I would want the contract to begin with, and I would *discard* it when trust and faith have been proved, in two or three years."

Even though most of the singles in our survey said that at this time they have no intention of remarrying, they often like to fantasize what the ceremony would be like when/if they did. They, like the traditional younger people, want to say "I do" in a ceremony that signifies happiness. Because remarriage among people in this age group is increasingly common, there is an entire section in *The New Emily Post's Book of Etiquette* entitled "An Older Couple's Wedding." Like the suggestions made in that etiquette guide, most felt the ceremony should be quite simple, low-key, and private out of respect for the previous marriage or marriages. But the singles, whether divorced in bitterness or widowed after years of loving companionship, insisted the nature of the ceremony was important because, as one said, "it signifies the person wants to try for or have again married happiness." Within that framework was room for diversity, as:

"I would want an intimate wedding with only our closest family and friends."

"We want nobody there except ourselves."

Women's next consideration was what they should wear. An informal gown of a soft pastel shade, either long or short but fairly conservative won the most votes, although a saleswoman in a fine dress shop opted for "something simple but smart, maybe even a bit sexy with a slit up the side."

Men were concerned with where the ceremony should take place and jotted down these suggestions:

"Aboard ship."

"In the county clerk's office in a small town in Mexico."

"In the judge's chambers in Las Vegas."

"Noon, a weekday. Coat for me, short but expensive dress for her, good flowers, best music, a really quick but gourmet pick-up lunch in the church social hall with live music, fast dancing, and lots of young people and guests."

"If it's a party, why not make it grand?"

Women were as explicit, and usually went into more detail:

"Marriage in a secluded romantic resort in a warm climate, just the two of us, where we would honeymoon sitting in the sun, golfing, swimming, and enjoying the fabulous sexy atmosphere."

"In front of a crackling fire in the fireplace of my home on a wintry (hopefully snowy) day with my children and his children and champagne in coolers."

"I would wear my jeans, invite everyone I know; we

would all drink champagne, eat my good food, and discuss what love is all about, and enjoy!"

One couple whose second marriage looks as if it will work are Abby and Carl T. Abby, a divorcée after twenty-one years of marriage, and Carl, a widower after twenty-eight, were both "in the same place emotionally" when they met at a church fellowship meeting. She had been single for a year, he for two, and while they were happy and comfortable with themselves, they had both made up their minds after a good deal of thought that they wanted to remarry. Each wanted a constancy of sharing and support with someone who was family-oriented and who enjoyed simple pleasures—a walk in the park, good talk, visits with family and friends.

Although both had dated, neither was a part of the world of interchangeable sexual relationships. Said Abby:

"For me, sex belongs in marriage. If you can't share your emotional and spiritual being, it's not worthwhile."

There was no question of their companionship, the "comfortable togetherness" that they felt for each other, nor of their attitudes toward money.

"If you are going to trust your emotional self to each other, you should be able to trust your money," Abby said, speaking for them both. Instead of moving into Carl's home, they bought a new house, each paying half, which would be free from memories of Carl's former wife, from the shadows of "kiddies growing up in corners."

Since Carl wanted a stay-at-home wife, Abby agreed to give up her job, even though she had just been promoted to supervisor of her department, a position she had worked long and hard to achieve; while Carl conceded that if she were dissatisfied in the homemaker role she should go back to work.

"From being a somebody—a supervisor who had to train seven people to fill my slot, a recognized leader in my political party, I moved to a smaller town than I had ever lived in before and became the second Mrs. Carl T.," she said. "I really had to hang in there for several months before it stopped bothering me."

Carl, for his part, agreed to step down as "head of house" and help Abby with the cooking and homemaking. He is also financing her college classes in social work as insurance for her future.

Abby's son Val, a well-adjusted fifteen-year-old, is no problem now, although "He had to come first for a while," Abby explained. "We couldn't go out on an adult date and shut him out, so we usually made it a threesome, even before we were married."

As for the family-oriented lifestyle they both wanted, they now have, between them, two mothers, a father, three daughters, a son, three sisters, two brothers-in-law, one son-in-law, and three drop-in-and-stay-a-few-days cousins.

There are also problems. For the first nine months of their marriage they were in rest homes in towns a hundred miles apart every single day visiting the mother or father of one or the other.

Another problem, one they both believe is crucial to marriage, is that of communication. Reserved and scientifically minded, Carl has trouble expressing his feelings.

"We knew we had things to work on before we married," Abby said, "but we both knew what they were."

They have also faced the chance that their marriage might not work out and, traditional in their attitudes though they both are, they have agreed to end it if it does not.

After a year, however, they are both optimistic. Their marriage is working, they believe, and will continue to do so because they love each other. The key is that somewhat antique word *love* which, Abby says, "is not something you feel, but something you do—like giving."

Most of the singles we interviewed, however, are not ready for this degree of commitment, this much giving, with all its attendant problems and complications. No one is rushing into remarriage and a few who did wished they hadn't. A twice-divorced woman, slowly readjusting to the singles scene, explained:

"I was so tired of handling everything myself and living in a house full of silence I married the first man who asked me. His children and grandchildern were a perpetual problem. I'm sorry I rushed into it. If it had been right, he would still be there, and I would still be there."

Singles who resisted the temptation of quick remarriage were glad they did. They see themselves as wiser, more mature, better adjusted to life and other people than when they were first thrown into the singles scene. They now will quit that scene only for something definitely better. They say with Dorothea L:

"I like my life. Remarriage is an alternate lifestyle. But it's not the whole pie."

Epilogue

In the course of writing this book, we interviewed one of the country's leading authorities on aging. At the end of the interview, she looked at us with motherly encouragement and said, from the vantage point of her forty years of marriage:

"I predict you will remarry. You both seem to have a *lot* going for you."

As we walked to our car in the watery autumn sunshine, leaves scudding along the walk in front of us, we allowed this thought to sink in, and then we suddenly burst out laughing, both for the same reason. It sounded as if she thought singleness was a condition to be recovered from, while we regarded it as a lifestyle to be enjoyed. It had taken us more than two years of single living, however, to realize its full potential.

ADELINE'S STORY

"I've always been amazed," an old-time married friend told me recently. "You seemed to have gone through the whole crisis of widowhood with no problems at all."

Anyone who has been through that crisis would have to wince at the comment, remembering as we all do the sense of amputation, thinking of the tears that still come coursing out when the right stimulus unplugs the valves.

When a divorced acquaintance introduced me to a friend one day as a woman who had lost her husband "the good way," I felt a hot surge of resentment. But after all the interviews and all the sharing we have done with others while writing this book, I believe now that death may be a better way to lose a mate—if there is any "good" way—than some of the other ways I've heard about.

Certainly life today is well worth living, happy and zestful, in fact, as any of our departed husbands or wives would want it to be for us. Why else would they carry insurance? Why else would Bob have said, over the years, "I would dance on your grave, and I'd want you to do the same for me"?

Keeping this thought in mind, knowing I would have wanted happiness for him had he been the survivor, helped me work my way from wreckage to renewal and remodel the inside of my head. My relationships today—with my children, my other relatives and friends—are better than they have ever been because they must fill in that gaping void. I try harder—to make and keep my friends, to look good, to feel good about myself, to be honest in my relationships, to eat better, and to create surroundings that satisfy me and prove an efficient springboard from which to lead my single life. Never have I felt so self-assured as I do today, so in control of my own destiny.

There are, of course, problems, apprehensions. Next year, the last of my three sons will leave for college, and then we'll see how good I'll feel about being totally alone. With the rest of America, I worry whether my finances will keep pace with inflation; and the focus of my teaching job has shifted from the simple self-fulfillment in a service profession that I experienced as a married woman to a serious financial necessity. On my next birthday I will be fifty-five, with sixty coming full tilt down the road. As the wrinkles deepen and the jawline sags, will I continue to feel this good about myself? Will there be anyone in my life, then, with whom to have that "sharing and caring relationship"? Will I still have energy for the rich, full, single life?

If anyone had told me, when I was in my forties and anxiously inspecting each new sign of age in my mirror, that I would be feeling this good about life in my fifties, I would not have believed him. As a result of the life I have today, however, it's easier to believe that the next twenty-five years an average woman can expect (twenty for a man) will continue to be enjoyable ones. Listening to the comments and life stories of the men and women in this book who are living those years competently and happily strengthens that belief.

People like to say that widows who have been happily married will do it again, that remarriage is a testimony to those years of happiness. Even though my marriage was a very happy one, I do not plan to do it again. There is a time to be married and a time to be single. Today, there are no children to be raised, no mortgage to be paid off, no struggles to be had, no dreams to be fulfilled. It's all been done. There is no necessity for a new partner. Perhaps someday it might be pleasant to have one, but not before exploring all the potentialities of a lifestyle that seems to offer everything I need at this stage of life.

Youth, they say, is wasted on the young, and so is the state of being single. My twenties were so preoccupied with finding "Mr. Right" that, like the sociologist we interviewed, I regarded my singleness as something to get over as fast as I could and missed all the benefits it had to offer. I don't have a second chance at youth, nor do I particularly want one. But single—well, this time I hope to do it right!

BEVERLY'S STORY

This is the book I so fervently wished for when I suddenly became single. Because writing it has meant so much for me,

I devotedly read and studied the questionnaires our interviewees filled out and digested intently the in-depth interviews I had with hundreds of people. As they relived and retold their stories of how they turned personal tragedy into victory, I felt I was again living through the anguish, anxiety, and confusions I had experienced in the early stages of my singleness. It was like a session of psychotherapy. In fact, many expressed that filling out the questionnaire was therapy that helped them understand their feelings and attitudes toward themselves and their circumstances. But more than that, I felt a surprising validation of my own progress. For the first time I felt authoritative about my state: being single and fifty as a member of a dignified, desirable, and capable group of people who knew where they were going and enjoying the trip. I, like them, am the navigator of my own life, following a new road instead of an old rut. I learned too that I am the happiest and feel the most worthwhile when I am contributing to the welfare of others and losing myself in a project that employs my brain, energy, heart, and experience.

It was the same feeling I had as the mother of growing children, a feeling I had intensely missed after my children left home. I had tried to compensate for that loss during the first year alone with a frenzy of uncharted activity as a worker raising money for charitable organizations and frequent dating, looking on every date as a potential husband in the belief that the only role I could capably fill in life was that of a wife. Now I see that those dating experiences were a growing period of great value and healing as they proved to me that I was still attractive.

My second period of recovery began on New Year's Day, 1976, a day I had always made resolutions and designed goals for the coming year. Until that morning I had been unwilling to let go of my past, a past when my identity was determined by my husband's position. It takes work to let go of the past, as those who've built a new life from scratch can verify, but the past is no platform on which to build a future. Instead, I promised myself, I would venture into areas where I would make my own identity. I went to night school at a talent agency, where I updated techniques of becoming a middle-aged model. I expanded my teaching activities at the University of Colorado to include more classes, including the psychology of divorce, a course I later presented at the University of California. I bought a condominium. I worked at improving my tennis game, my endurance at cross-country skiing, and my ability to relax through the practice of yoga.

All of these things were positive, forcing me to grow intellectually and emotionally. Being devoted to improving myself as a woman and my life as a single, the next step was to accept the fact that my circumstances would be the boundaries of my future. When my life became filled with work I began to feel a sense of exhilaration about myself, a worthwhileness I felt I was earning on my own.

Through my work, my life is better now. I feel less anxiety about the future. I recognize my strong dependency needs and take measures to cope with them. I believe I am healthier, more resilient, more tolerant, and more capable of coping with adversities that might have undone me five years ago. I am learning to adapt to my own abilities and strengths.

I entered marriage believing it was the panacea that would bring me everything forever. I entered singleness believing it would be empty and futureless. Paradoxically, my marriage left me with near nothing; singleness, through effort to be sure, is gradually bringing me many things I thought I would never be able to attain all by myself.

From uprooted, torn, and shattered beginnings, the people we have been writing about in this book have put together a lifestyle which is part of an influential new cultural pattern on the American scene. Instead of hovering around the periphery of the coupled culture, to babysit grand-children or to be charitably invited for Christmas dinner, they have become pioneers, blazing a trail—like all pioneers —in their own self-interest. With a longer lease on youth and vitality than people have ever enjoyed before, they are focusing the wisdom and experience acquired over half a century on the last two decades of life, to make them effective, creative, vigorous years. In so doing, they are making the world take another look at a double stereotype: the person who is older and who is single as well.

By their self-dependence, by their freedom, by their very happiness they are saying that it's okay to be single, it's okay to be older; that it is, in fact, a very good time and state in which to be alive.